Severe Gobbler Disorder

Reflections of a Grand Slam

**by
Brad Day**

Bloomington, IN   Milton Keynes, UK

AuthorHouse™
1663 Liberty Drive, Suite 200
Bloomington, IN 47403
www.authorhouse.com
Phone: 1-800-839-8640

AuthorHouse™ *UK Ltd.*
500 Avebury Boulevard
Central Milton Keynes, MK9 2BE
www.authorhouse.co.uk
Phone: 08001974150

© 2006 Brad Day. All rights reserved.

No part of this book may be reproduced, stored in a retrieval system, or transmitted by any means without the written permission of the author.

First published by AuthorHouse 12/14/2006

ISBN: 978-1-4259-6840-3 (sc)

Printed in the United States of America
Bloomington, Indiana

This book is printed on acid-free paper.

Table of Contents

Foreword	vii
Turkulese	1
Loverboy	37
The "Bus"	83
Hitman	117
Double Beard	163
Speed Racer	187
Puff Daddy	233
Double Trouble	259
Final Thoughts	289

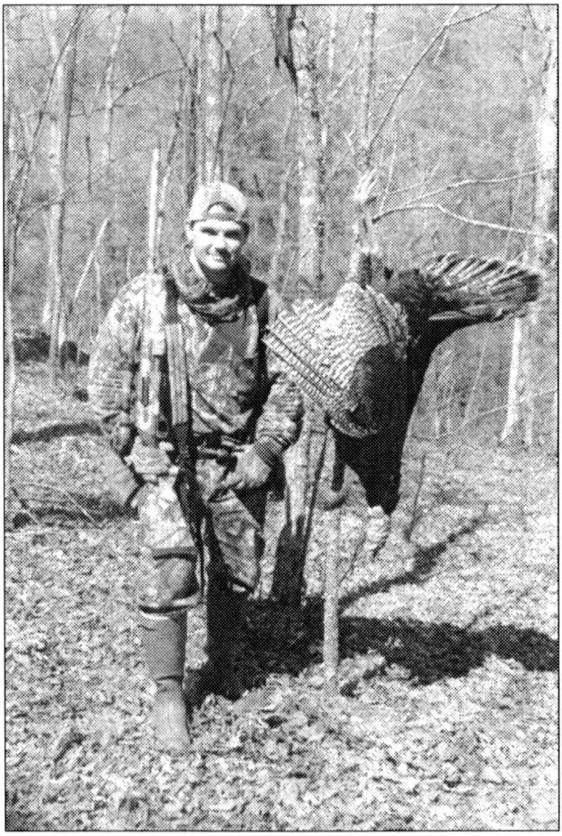

Foreword

"Severe Gobbler Disorder" is a collection of very personal short stories on the subject of spring gobbler hunting. The first story "Turkulese" (pronounced terk-you-leze – as in Hercules) was written to record my memories of that particularly special hunt for my family and me – it was never my intention to publish it. As my family members and close friends read the story, they passed it on to other friends of their own. Before long, over a hundred people had read the story, many of them strangers to me. I received a lot of favorable feedback and requests for more stories. Surprisingly to me, many of the folks who read and enjoyed the stories that I wrote were women who didn't hunt. (I guess they just like to read about a man that makes a complete fool of himself without much effort on his part!) Each new story that I wrote included a preface to bring the reader "up to speed" on the hunt that was to follow, and thus each story could "stand alone."

When I made the decision to publish these stories, which were written over a span of three turkey seasons, I wanted to include the preface that accompanied each story, even though it wouldn't be a necessity to the owner of a book that included all the hunts. As you read "Severe Gobbler Disorder" these prefaces may seem redundant, and, indeed, they are in several instances. However, the prefaces do provide some additional insight to each hunt, and so I ask for your patience as you read them. These are personal stories originally written for my family and friends and as such they contain some very intimate notes that may not be clear to a stranger who reads them. While tempted to revise and eliminate these parts of the stories, I was reluctant to do so as the stories would lose some of their truth and charm.

It will also be helpful to the reader to realize that these stories are absolutely true to the best of my ability and memory. These are accounts of real places, real people, and real turkeys. Some of the names of individuals and businesses have been changed at the owner's request to protect their privacy - other than that, it is all true. Please bare in mind that this collection of short stories was written by a turkey hunter primarily for other turkey hunters. Please accept my apology in advance for the use of redneck vernacular and turkey hunting terms that you may be unfamiliar with.

When I was boy, growing up in northern West Virginia, I became enamored with turkey hunting. It is a miracle, however, that I actually became a turkey hunter. I began to learn how to turkey hunt as a young teen with absolutely no help from anyone. I didn't know a single turkey hunter anywhere. At that time, my turkey-hunting arsenal consisted of a single-shot 20-gauge shotgun, a headnet, and one Quaker Boy diaphragm mouth call. (Boy, have things changed!) I became convinced (incorrectly) that the single most important skill that a turkey hunter needed to kill a gobbler was the ability to call well. So, in order to become a turkey hunter, I practiced with that one mouth call that I owned all the time.

When turkey season opened during those early years, each spring would find me in the woods of West Virginia or Pennsylvania setting up in the dark and trying to kill my first spring gobbler. I would hunt all morning and never even hear a gobbler. After each hunt I would return home disgusted with my inability to call well enough to make a turkey gobble. I worried that if I couldn't even get a turkey to gobble, I was never going to be able to convince a gobbler to actually come to my calls and present me with a shot. So, not to be deterred, back to the practice sessions I would go with my mouth call. What I didn't realize at the time was the problem wasn't necessarily with my calling ability: it was with the turkeys – or lack of them, I should say.

There were basically no turkeys in the woods near my home. Once in a great while I would discover a turkey track or find a feather. I would then be convinced there were turkeys about, and that I should be able to get one. Determined to succeed, I would hit the spring woods again, and I would call, and call, and call – never getting a response. It is truly a wonder that I didn't give up. At one point I began to think that killing a spring gobbler was nigh unto impossible. To me, the thought of killing a Grand Slam was ludicrous and was reserved for only the best of the turkey hunting elite. However, as fate would have it, I eventually went hunting in a different county that actually had huntable numbers of turkeys in it, and I killed my first spring gobbler.

I have learned a lot of lessons hunting turkeys. The first one was that no matter how well you can call, good scouting is more important than good calling. Ironically, there was a silver lining in all those years of practice with that mouth call – I learned how to call using a mouth diaphragm – and I learned well. Once I started hunting in the right locations, gobblers started dying.

Eventually, I started entering National Wild Turkey Federation (NWTF) sanctioned calling contests. I placed second in the first competition that I ever entered. During the winter each year, I traveled to numerous eastern states entering turkey-calling contests. Competing against some of the country's best turkey callers wasn't always good for my ego, but entering calling contests forced me to practice and perform under pressure. (If you can "Cluck and Purr" with a dry mouth, a pounding heart, and butterflies in your stomach on a stage in front of three hundred camo-clad turkey hunters when the Master of Ceremonies asks for it, you can probably do it when that gobbler you have been after for four straight weeks is drumming just on the other side of the ridge out of shotgun range, and you find your mouth, heart, and stomach in the exact same condition as previously described!)

My quest for a Grand Slam began when I decided to start practicing for a different kind of turkey-calling contest. Instead of traveling throughout Virginia, or to Maryland, West Virginia, or Pennsylvania in March to compete against men, I decided to travel to Florida and compete against Osceola turkeys in the swamps of public land. In the Florida contest you win by killing the judge.

This book wasn't written to be a "How To" guide on turkey hunting. In fact, if I were asked to write a "Dear Brad" hunting advice column, I would subtitle it "Turkey Hunting Advice No One Should Actually Take!" Thanks for taking the time to read my book. I can only hope you enjoy reading it half as much as I did doing the field research to write it.

Brad

Turkulese
—
The Osceola Gobbler

Preface

  Hunting is not a hobby or a pastime for me. It is a way of life. It is my way of life. It is a large part of who I am. Hunting is something that my family has done as far back as anyone can remember. However, spring gobbler hunting is different. No one in my family ever hunted turkeys, probably because there just weren't very many of them around in the area where we lived. No one ever took me turkey hunting or taught me how to hunt them. I learned to turkey hunt on my own. Over the years since then, I have taken dozens of people turkey hunting with me and have introduced numerous people to the sport. While I have killed a few turkeys during the fall season when I was younger, now I only hunt spring gobblers. I hunt them with a shotgun – up close and personal. I hunt them hard, and I hunt them with passion and respect. Every gobbler I have ever killed I have called in for myself with a mouth call.

  I taught myself how to call when I was about sixteen years old. I went to a sporting goods store in a small town located nearby in Pennsylvania with a friend of mine, Joey Nagy. Each of us bought a Quaker Boy diaphragm mouth call. Joey bought a cassette tape on how to use the call, and we wore that tape out listening to it while we practiced. We carried those dumb, diaphragm calls around in our mouths everywhere – to the woods – to ball games – on the bus to school – to the community swimming pool – riding our bikes…we took them everywhere we went. The only exception for not having our turkey calls with us was when we went out on a date with our girlfriends…I think! For all the practice I got with that call, it sure did sound bad! I started going spring gobbler hunting shortly thereafter. I hunted in my home state of West Virginia and even bought a non-resident Pennsylvania hunting license to hunt there too. (When a teenager spends a hundred dollars of his hard-earned money on a license to hunt a bird he has no clue how to kill, instead of spending it on his girlfriend or the latest trend in high-top Nike tennis shoes, it's a sure sign that he's not normal – which I'm not saying is a bad thing.) I can still remember some of those early, not-a-turkey-to-be-found-anywhere hunts. What I lacked in turkey hunting experience and know-how, I made up for with drive and desire.

It was several years before I killed my first spring gobbler. I struck the bird on the roost at daylight with an old Lynch World Champion box call. Before long the gobbler wouldn't answer the box, and I was forced to use a brand-new triple-reed Perfection mouth call. That mouth call squeaked, popped, and sputtered, but as bad as it sounded, it made the tones that the gobbler wanted to hear. Five long mountain-climbs and almost six hours after striking the roosted bird, I killed him in full strut using a Winchester Model 37A, single-shot 20 gauge at twenty-eight yards with a three-inch shotshell loaded with No. 4s. The gobbler was a jake with a 4-1/2 inch beard. A Legion member was born on that mountaintop near Hugh's Creek in West Virginia that April morning. (When I refer to Legion members, I'm referencing a term first penned by outdoor writer and dyed-in-the-wool turkey hunter Tom Kelly. Tom's book the "Tenth Legion" is a tribute to the wild turkey and to the small band of men who pursue them with a cult-like passion[1]. Tom likens these poor souls to the members of the Roman Army's famed Tenth Legion – a special detachment charged with guarding and fighting for Caesar. If you have studied history, you know the fame and fear this Tenth Legion commanded for their dedication to the tasks given them. Nothing would deter them from achieving their goal. Tom finds a striking parallel in the attitudes of some spring gobbler hunters, and I have all the symptoms.) By the way, Mom, please note that I just told a turkey story in five (5) short sentences!

When I graduated from college in 1987 with a bachelor's degree in Electrical Engineering, my family had made plans to attend the commencement exercises to see me receive my diploma. Commencement was to take place on a Saturday morning in early May. They were incredulous when I told them that they were more than welcome to attend commencement, but that I wouldn't be in attendance – my diploma was being mailed to me because it was spring gobbler season! I remember riding back into town after hunting that morning. Dressed in camouflage and spitting out the window of my F250 4x4, I could see the procession of my classmates, decked out in caps and gowns, making its way up the hill to the football stadium for commencement. None of my classmates were any happier than I was, and I didn't even kill a turkey that morning! My family is probably still mad at me. Case closed on the Legion member qualifications; they even waived my entry fee!

I hope you find the reading of this turkey hunt entertaining. However, it was not written to be such. I wanted to write about it in detail so I would never forget it, not that I think it will be easily forgotten.

When I was a kid, I used to write a story about each deer I killed. A few years ago I came across an old hunting book and those handwritten deer stories were folded up inside the cover. As I sat and read them, I laughed at what a total dork I was. The stories were so dramatic. The details I wrote were hilarious! As humorous as they were, it dawned on me as I read them how much I had forgotten about the little things that had happened on those hunts. Reading the written accounts twenty years later brought a lot of memories back. I was really glad I had taken the time and effort back then to record the accounts. That is why I wrote this hunt down in detail, not for the entertainment of others (although I hope you enjoy it thoroughly), but for my personal memories.

I'm sure that as you read this account you'll think, "What a dork!" too.

That's "OK"; I know it's true.

I had a saying after I came back from my trip to Florida when I was asked about my hunt.

I would say, "It took me two hours to kill the gobbler, and it takes me three hours to tell someone about it!"

After you have read my account of the events which took place on that magical morning, you will see what I mean. Heck, I could write a sequel about checking the turkey in. Forget about Disneyland – if you want some real entertainment in Florida, head to a backwoods, edge of the swamp, run-down country store, restaurant, and redneck, big-game check-station. Your redneck resume is incomplete if you haven't experienced something like it. Besides, how cool would it be to have to wait in your truck so an alligator can cross the road in front of you?

I wrote this account of my Osceola turkey hunt three months after killing the gobbler. In all honesty, when I was typing the paragraphs about the actual kill, I paused my writing and laughed, because my pulse had elevated and adrenalin was causing my stomach to feel funny – this is absolutely true and just goes to further prove my dementia! Enjoy!

Turkulese

The alarm sounded at 4:00 a.m. As I had done for the last four mornings, I rolled out of bed and started the coffeepot before reading my morning devotions. It was day five of my hunt for an Osceola gobbler. After dressing in Mossy Oak Trek-Lite treated with Duranon and filling my thermos, I gathered my vest and shotgun to head out to the truck. When I opened the hotel door, a torrential, south-central Florida rainstorm greeted me. I had to run to the 4-Runner, throw my gear in, and run back to the room. It was pouring! I undressed and put on my raingear. As I retied my snake boots, the thought of going back to bed entered my mind. I was dead tired from four days of hiking the swamps in the heat and humidity and then spending the afternoons and evenings hiking places like Disneyland with my wife, Lisa. Legion members don't quit though, and you can't kill 'em when you're laid up in the bed with mama. I grabbed my Primos deke-seat, a camo umbrella, a small blind, and an inflatable seat cushion and decided to give it my best shot, even though the rainstorm had now become a major thunderstorm.

My plan was to park in the same area where I had parked the day before and hunt a little opening in the palmettos along a swamp edge that I had found scouting after the prior day's hunt. The opening wasn't big, maybe thirty feet wide, but in the palmettos and swamps of Florida, any opening is a rarity. I would set up my small blind and umbrella, put out a couple decoys, and make the most of it. After all, I had used this method to kill Eastern gobblers in the rain.

The first three days of my trip were spent hunting the 50,000-acre Green Swamp Wildlife Management Area (an hour and fifteen minute drive from the hotel). Although I scouted and hunted three different places in Green Swamp, I didn't see or even hear a turkey while hunting there. The temperatures were reaching the mid-nineties during the day and only falling to seventy at night. The turkeys were shut-down. In the first five days of the season, only five gobblers were killed at Green Swamp, and only one in the three days I was there. To say that things were hot and frustrating would be an understatement. Green Swamp was one of the top three Wildlife Management Areas (WMAs) that a biologist from Florida's Wildlife Commission had recommended for taking an Osceola gobbler. While the turkeys were not cooperating, Green Swamp did provide me with plenty of entertainment. My first morning there found me twenty yards from a solid-black wild boar that I mistook for a bear initially. The boar's back was nearly as tall as my waist, and he probably weighed close to two hundred pounds. I managed to see my first armadillo in the swamp, and even got some pictures of him, after chasing him down. One final note about my time spent in Green Swamp – I made friends with a slew of barred owls. I'd turn loose one series of owl hoots before daylight and would get as many as seven responses, not from gobblers, but from owls. They were thick in the swamp. These jokers would fly in to my calling and join me trying to locate a tom!

Even though the hunts in Green Swamp weren't going as I had hoped, I hadn't lost my drive and enthusiasm for hunting Osceola gobblers. Back in November I had applied for, and drawn, a Four-Day hunting permit for the opening week of Florida's spring gobbler season in the Pipeline Unit of the Ocala National Forest, a place I had hunted in the spring of 2002. I was looking forward to hunting in an area I was somewhat familiar with, and that I knew had birds in it. An afternoon scouting trip on Wednesday, the day before my permit started, had left me optimistic about my chances. I saw a gobbler with two hens while scouting and found several droppings, tracks, and dusting sites. Things were looking up.

The first morning of my hunt in the Ocala National Forest found me three miles off the main road by four-wheel drive and another mile and a half back in the palmettos by foot. I was in the exact spot where a year earlier I had located three mature gobblers roosting within one hundred and fifty yards of each other. My inexperience at setting up on Osceolas in the palmettos and swamps had left me empty-handed that year, but I was hoping to change that in 2003. To my chagrin, however, sun up on Thursday morning was devoid of any gobbling. I couldn't believe it. I set-up for an hour anyway and blind called, but I got zero response from any turkey. Determined to find a gobbler willing to do business, I headed back to a dusting area I had found scouting the day before. On my way to the dusting area, I crossed paths with another hunter named Richard. He was heading to the area I had hunted at daylight. Richard was an older gentleman in his early sixties and was a local hunter. I had first met Richard the previous year in this same area when he was circling a gobbler that was answering my calls. In 2002 he couldn't believe that I had walked as far as I had from "the truck with Virginia license plates" and politely retreated. Upon bumping into each other again on this occasion, his response was nearly the same:

"I remember you from last year," he said. "Don't you drive that green truck from Virginia? I didn't think anyone was back here. I can't believe you walked all the way in here from where you parked!" Richard concluded emphatically.

I informed Richard that I had seen a gobbler with hens while scouting the day before and had parked farther away on purpose, so as not to spook them, because I had seen them from the road. (I mention this conversation for a reason!) I told him that I hadn't heard anything and the "pole bridge" (the local's term for the area I was in) was all his for the rest of the morning.

Fifteen minutes later I was set-up in a dusting area just off the trail that I had walked in on. A half-hour of intermittent calling yielded nothing, so I decided to move again. As I went to retrieve my decoys, I saw a hen standing twenty yards up the trail looking at me. We stared at each other for about a nanosecond, before she bolted into the palmettos. I decided to sit back down with a better view of the trail above the dusting site in case she had a gobbler in tow. Another half-hour of calling didn't raise a gobble, so I figured it was time to move again. Just as I prepared to leave, a shot rang out from two hundred yards in front of me, followed by a second shot from the same spot. I hadn't heard any gobbling, and I hadn't heard any hens or anyone else calling. I was really frustrated now.

"Who else was back in here?" I wondered.

I waited fifteen minutes before pulling my decoys. As I finished packing them up in my vest, I saw Richard coming down the trail with a gobbler over his shoulder.

I walked toward Richard and greeted him with a handshake and "congratulations." He was grinning from ear to ear and rightfully so. He had killed a two-year-old Osceola with a nine-inch beard. I asked him for permission to look at the gobbler closely since I had never laid hands on an Osceola turkey. He enthusiastically granted my request and questioned me as I examined his bird. I showed him how the dark primary wing feathers had very little white barring in them, and what white they did have was broken. This confirmed that the gobbler was a true Osceola, even though we were hunting well south of both the National Wild Turkey Federation (NWTF) and Florida Wildlife Commission (FWC) boundary lines for where the swamp turkey lives.

I mentioned to Richard that I didn't hear his turkey gobble before I heard him shoot.

"No, I wasn't even calling to him," he explained. "I decided to go get in an old deer stand of mine and just listen. This gobbler just came walking past my stand like he was headed somewhere else," he continued. "I shot him as he walked by, and he took off running. I wasn't sure what to do, so I decided to shoot him again, in case he wasn't going to die from the first shot," he furthered.

With a slight chuckle, I affirmed for him that he did the right thing by taking the second shot.

"Turkeys aren't like deer," I explained. "If they start running, you missed them."

Richard nodded in agreement, and to my surprise, told me that this was his first turkey.

"I have been hunting these things for the last several years," he said. "But I always end up messing up and not getting one."

I told him to get used to that when it comes to spring gobblers.

To be honest, at first, I wasn't real happy with Richard's tactic for killing a spring gobbler. I felt like he had short-standed me. However, when he told me it was his first gobbler, my attitude changed completely. I was genuinely happy for him and pumped him up with praise and encouragement. I told Richard he would never forget his first spring gobbler.

After all the excitement and camaraderie about his turkey, Richard told me something that would change the course of my hunt in Florida. As he had done earlier in the morning when we bumped into each other on the trail, he commented on where my truck was parked and how far I had walked to hunt.

He also apologized once again for intruding into the area I was hunting, saying,

"I thought that you were hunting across the road from where you are parked. There is a little, old trail that goes down into the swamp there. Someone has taken a machete in there and blazed a trail along the swamp's edge, flagging it with tape so you won't get lost. There's generally some pretty good hunting in there, and I just assumed you were hunting it."

Richard then asked me how many turkeys a person could kill on the permits that we had for this WMA. I told him that each permit was good for a quota of one gobbler. He thanked me and wished me luck as he shook my hand and departed for his truck.

I had one more spot I wanted to try before the morning's hunt was over. As I began the hike to my next spot, I thought about what Richard had said and decided that I would scout the trail where I had parked if unsuccessful the rest of the morning. Unfortunately, twelve-o'clock noon found me on my way back to the truck with no turkey. So, as planned, I took a walk down the trail across the road from where I had parked. (I use the term "road" loosely – very loosely!) The trail led through some live oaks and pines into extremely thick palmettos as one approached the swamp. Just before reaching the machete trail, which was flagged with yellow, industrial caution-tape, I noticed that the heavy undergrowth opened up into a small clearing, about thirty feet square. This was a major opening in the swamp. I decided that if worse came to worse, or if I had to hunt in the rain, this would be a place to try. What I didn't know at the time and would find out later is that this area of swamp is often unhunted by locals during the spring due to heavy concentrations of ticks – ticks so thick that you brush them off your pants leg like black pepper. When it comes to spring gobblers, ticks don't bother me.

The rain was falling as hard as it possibly could as I pulled out of the Mt. Dora Comfort Inn parking lot at 4:30 a.m. on Friday, March 17. Streaks of lightning lit the pre-dawn Florida sky and claps of thunder boomed in succession. Standing water in the road I was traveling splashed over the hood of my 4-Runner. A lovely day for a turkey hunt this was gonna be!

As I drove to my intended hunting area within the Ocala National Forest, I decided to park in the same spot I had the day before, walk the trail that led from my parking area, and set up in the small opening along the edge of the swamp. Fortunately, the rain was starting to let up as I turned off the pavement and onto the rutted-out, sand road that led to my intended hunting area. As was the case the prior morning, I didn't see a single vehicle parked anywhere as I crawled and bounced my way the three miles to my parking spot. I arrived at my destination around 5:30 a.m. and quickly began unloading essentials from my turkey vest into my deke-seat. I decided to take one friction call and striker, four mouth diaphragms, my license and Bible, three shells for the gun, gloves, headnet, pruners, and two decoys. Of course I would also carry my umbrella, portable blind, and seat cushion. (If you think that is a lot of stuff, you should see how much gear I normally tote around in my hunting vest!)

The rain had lightened up considerably by now, and the turkey hunting odds were looking better. I made my way to the end of the main trail where the opening I was looking for was located. I set out a hen and a jake decoy about eight yards from the tree where I would set up. I put my umbrella up, and was setting up my blind, when I saw something running right at me through the palmettos.

"It's an armadillo," I thought to myself.

However, the little critter that scampered nearly into my lap was an opossum. I literally had to chase him out of my set-up in the pre-dawn darkness. The little guy seemed confused at first, but finally scurried off along the edge of the swamp. I settled in to my dry, little nest, took off my raincoat (it was too hot and humid to keep it on), and pulled the hood up on my BugTamer jacket. It was 6:10 a.m.

I pulled out my MAD crystal call and rainy-day striker, put a Quaker Boy "Screamin' Green – World Champ" diaphragm in my mouth, and popped the scope covers on my Remington 870 Super Magnum. I made some tree clucks on the friction call at 6:15 a.m. My second series of tree clucks and yelps was answered by a distant gobble at 6:20 a.m. The gobbler sounded to be about four or five hundred yards straight in front of my set-up. In fact, the gobble was so far away that I didn't even consider the bird to be in calling range. I was happy to just finally hear one, and I encouraged myself that at least there was a bird in the general area.

I purposely refrained from using my mouth call and called sparingly on the friction call, just clucking and plain yelping about every three to five minutes. At 6:40 a.m., I scratched another set of calls on the crystal and the gobbler, which had been silent for the last twenty minutes, answered me. His gobble had changed, and I could tell he was on the ground. However, he was still a long, long way off. I was a bit perplexed with what to do. The bird was too far away to work from my present location, and the rain and thick swamp conditions weren't conducive to moving towards him. I decided to just keep calling sparingly on the friction call and stay put. Hopefully there would be another gobbler closer to my position that would be interested. After waiting several minutes before making another call, I resumed my friction calling. Almost immediately the gobbler responded. There was no doubt about it. This gobbler was answering me from over four hundred yards away in the rain. I picked up the frequency of my friction calling, and the turkey continued to respond to about every other series. I decided it was time to try the mouth call on him.

Sometimes gobblers will only answer a specific sound or tone, so I wasn't sure how, or if, he would react to the sound of a different hen. I clucked once on the World Champ and followed it immediately with about six plain yelps, then clucked again. The tom jumped all over it and hammered back with a thunderous gobble. That was a good sign. He loved the sound of the mouth call. Like a kid tasting potato chips, I decided to try once more just to be sure. A similar series on the mouth call brought an identical response from the tom. He definitely liked it, but he hadn't budged an inch since he flew down from the roost.

It was decision time. I ruled out moving to him for the same reasons stated before (rain and terrain). He knew where I was and seemed pretty interested, but how should I call to him? During the two seasons I had hunted Florida's swamp turkeys, I had yet to hear a hen calling. In fact this was the first turkey I had ever heard call while on the ground in the swamp. They would gobble hard on the roost, then fly down and shut up. Even the turkeys that did come to me on past hunts had all come in silent, so I was concerned that too much calling might not sound natural to him. I have heard all the manmade rules, which state that all subspecies of turkey call the same, but my personal experience with the swamp birds seemed to differ. Unsure how to proceed, I decided to bite the bullet and try calling to him like I would a gobbler back home. I would take his temperature and back off at whatever part of the scale he did. To be honest, I really didn't feel like I had a whole lot to lose with the bird being so far away and with there being so much jungle between us. Nevertheless, I had a few butterflies in my stomach as I centered the mouth call on my palate.

I clucked. He gobbled. I clucked and yelped. He gobbled. Holding my turkey hunting breath, I yelped and cut. He doubled gobbled. I yelped and cut again, louder and faster. He triple gobbled. This turkey was hot, but he still wasn't moving. Up to this point, I would pause briefly after each set of calls, but now I decided to let it all hang out. I began a tirade of cutting and yelping, to which the gobbler joined in with ferocious gobbling. Within a few minutes we were screaming at each other. This was one of the hottest gobblers I have ever been on (due to the extreme distance between us – usually I would have moved toward his position and set up closer and then called sparingly as the distance decreased). He gobbled at everything I did with the mouth call. This turkey was so hot that I began to play with him. I would cut to him with two or three notes to get his gobble started, and then when his gobble was almost finished, I would cut to him again. He would start another gobble to answer me, and when that gobble was almost finished, I would cut again, not giving him time to catch his breath. The poor, lovesick tom would then try to shove a third gobble out. I was nearly choking him to death! He would gobble so hard and so fast that he was just about suffocating himself, and I was enjoying every minute of it, except for one problem – he wasn't getting any closer. This gobblefest lasted for probably twenty solid minutes. The gobbler would move up to his left about one hundred yards and then come back to his original spot, but he was not a foot closer than four hundred yards.

All the cutting in the world wasn't convincing him to leave his lecht, so I decided to try another tactic – the silent treatment. Dr. Day has prescribed this treatment for numerous tough toms in the past much to the satisfaction of the doctor. (Of course I am not a doctor when it comes to turkeys. In fact, I am more like a dumb high school student that keeps failing biology and just wants to be a doctor when he grows up – but I did stay at a Comfort Inn last night!) So I began to tone down my calling and eventually just went silent. The gobbler followed suit…for about five minutes. I was hoping that this meant he was coming. Then from his four-hundred-yard strutting spot, he searched the swamp with a single gobble. He wasn't coming yet, but now he was calling and trying to locate me.

"How should I respond?" I wondered.

I decided to answer him, but to sound disinterested – you know like, "Hey big boy, you just missed your chance to go to the prom."

So I responded with some clucks, like a hen feeding and minding her own business. I wanted him to know that I was still around, but that I wasn't going to him either. Of course, he hammered back at my disinterested clucks with a booming gobble – you have got to love a turkey like that! More disinterested hen talk continued to produce excited gobbles. Try as I might to remain calm and sound disinterested, I just couldn't do it. That's one of the reasons I love spring turkey hunting so much. I am having a literal conversation with a wild turkey, and we are both expressing true emotion. The tom and I are each responding with all the feeling we can muster into our calls. It's not just what we are saying, but how we are saying it. If you have ever engaged in a calling sequence with a spring gobbler and experienced it for yourself, you understand exactly what I mean. So within a span of about five minutes, we are right back to screaming love notes to one another. No kidding, I heard this turkey gobble over one hundred times (probably more like two hundred times)! He was incredible. Another twenty minutes of this cutting / gobbling frenzy finally broke him – his gobble was getting closer and coming straight at my gun barrel! At first, I didn't believe it. I thought I was imagining it, but his steady advance left no doubt. After forty-five minutes of working him, the gobbler was coming!

My heart was pounding. I was out of breath – partly from calling too much and partly from excitement. Finally, he was coming! I was so shook-up that I think I took the safety off my gun when he was about two hundred yards away – something I would never normally do. I wanted this bird! However, my bliss was short lived. Only a few yelps were needed on my part to keep track of the gobbler's advance, as he continued to answer my every call. It was after one of these tracking yelps that the approaching tom's gobble was answered by another gobbler – behind me. My bird was at two hundred yards and coming straight on, while the new gobbler was about two hundred yards behind me. At first I didn't mind the imposter's challenge. I thought it might even help convince my tom that he had competition and had better step on it. I was pretty sure that the second gobbler was a subdominant bird because he never gobbled at my hen calls. He would only respond to the first turkey's gobbles. The routine went something like this: I would yelp and cut – then Gobbler No. 1 would gobble – then Gobbler No. 2 would gobble – then I would yelp and cut, and the cycle would repeat. Regrettably, things turned worse yet, for shortly after the second gobbler started chiming in on our conversation, a hen began yelping in the swamp to my left. No joke, I hadn't heard a turkey calling on the ground all week in the swamp, and now that I finally had a gobbler coming on a string, I was surrounded by the crazy things. I immediately put more urgency into my hen calls to convince my gobbler to hurry up. While he whole-heartedly complied with my urgent pleadings, so did the two other turkeys.

I just can't fully describe the situation in the swamp that morning. The rain drenched palms, pines, and palmettos were shrouded in misty fog in the morning's gray light. Spanish moss, drenched from the pre-dawn downpour, hung low, dripping from the tree branches. The mosquitoes were swarming me so heavily that, in addition to my headnet, I had my BugTamer hood pulled up and out in front of my face. The turkeys were going bonkers, absolutely filling the swamp with gobbles and yelping. It was surreal. (That's a turkey hunter's word for absolutely super!) I was calling frantically to the gobbler in front of me. He was answering me with each approaching step. The gobbler behind me was closing the distance too and responding to every gobble from the first turkey. Adding to the malay, "Miss Thing" down in the swamp was marching straight to me as well, yelping the whole time that she was coming!

I just kept calling and looking down my shotgun barrel for the gobbler I was working, all the while under my breath saying, "Hurry up and get here before these other two turkeys show up and complicate things!"

And then, like magic, there he was. I spotted his white skullcap and elongated snood bouncing around his beak, as he moved rapidly through the palmettos directly in front of me – maybe sixty yards out. I adjusted my gun's position to train the barrel on him, my heart beating at a frantic pace. He was at fifty-five yards, then fifty yards, then …

"Hey wait!" my mind shrieked. "He's starting to drift off – up to my right!"

Drift nothing! He was now heading at a forty-five-degree angle to my right and out of scattergun range!

"You have got to be kidding! He didn't come all this way to bypass the hen he was so intent on meeting – what's the matter with him?" I asked myself frantically.

I hadn't heard the gobbler behind my position for the last thirty seconds or so, and the hen was still yelping and approaching from my left, still maybe seventy-five yards away. The gobbler obviously hadn't seen my decoys yet.

"Maybe he's going to get on the trail that I walked in on and strut down to the decoys," I hoped.

While thoughts like these were racing through my head, I heard a strange, muffled sound off to my right. It was the sound of beating wings followed by a dull "thump." As I listened closely I could tell that the gobblers were fighting! Strangely, however, I didn't hear any fighting purrs. I listened intently and definitely could hear the two gobblers flying up, bumping chests in mid-air, and trying to gut hook each other with their spurs, but there were no characteristic fighting purrs, at least that I could hear. I have heard gobblers fighting during numerous other hunts in the past, and in every case I could always hear the gobbler's fighting purrs as they struggled, but I had never actually been able to see the gobblers in combat. They were always just over the edge of a ridge or in an area where there was heavy foliage. This fight started out that way. They were about sixty yards from me at the two-o'clock position from my set-up. The palmettos were so thick that I couldn't see a thing. However, as the battle progressed, they worked their way down the trail that I had walked in on and ended up in a spot where I could see them clearly through a tiny opening in the palmettos. The viewing lane I had wasn't much bigger than a large clothesbasket, but I think the Lord Jesus arranged it especially for me so I could see the drama unfold. The gobblers were now about fifty-five yards away, and I could see them flying up and trying to spur each other. My shotgun has a fixed, four-power scope on it, and I watched the fight through the magnified scope optics. It was unbelievable!

This went on for about five minutes and the hen was still making her way toward me. I began to consider belly-crawling into shotgun range of the two pugilists and whacking one of them while they were distracted, because once that hen got here, I was going to be in big trouble. As a side note, I should mention here that anyone who would even consider crawling anywhere in the swamps of Florida for any reason might not be exactly right-in-the-head (which my wife can attest to in my case!). But legion members don't think twice about minor inconveniences and inconsequential things like cottonmouths, diamondbacks, coral snakes, alligators, and wild boar. At least not until after the hunt is over.

I decided to stay put. With my track record of goof-ups performing unorthodox maneuvers on gobblers, staying put seemed a better idea. While I was making a mental assessment of the situation, the gobblers' fighting had actually intensified. The two gobblers were no longer flying up and spurring one another. They had now wrapped their heads and necks around each other in a serpentine fashion, and each one had bitten the other's cheek and was holding on to it. The fighting purrs that were missing earlier were now present and incessant. Locked together from the neck up and purring furiously, the two gobblers were still jumping up and trying to hook each other. This was a serious battle. One that lasted long enough for the yelping hen I feared so much to arrive on the scene.

This female Osceola had yelped all the way to my position and came to me like I had reeled her in with a fishing pole. When she stepped from the palmetto thicket, she stopped yelping and walked straight to my decoys. Now I should point out that my experience with hens and decoys, which has been extensive, has nearly always indicated a live hen's intolerance for the fakes. Hen turkeys just don't seem to like decoys and nearly always depart from them. But this wasn't your typical turkey hunt, and therefore, nothing went as normal (if there is such a thing in spring gobbler hunting). This hen began clucking and purring contentedly not five feet from the decoys and no more than ten feet from me, all the while preening herself from a wet night spent on the roost. I guess she understood that just a stone's throw away there were two big studs duking it out with each other for the right to win her hand, and she wanted to look her best.

I personally wasn't impressed with her and just wanted her gone. So much so, that I began to ponder the idea of spooking her intentionally. The two gobblers were so wrapped up in each other (literally) that I might be able to spook the old girl without the gobblers even knowing it. That way, when a winner was declared, he could march right down to my hen decoy to claim his prize. After considerable deliberation, I decided the risky move was worth a try. I knew that if the hen remained, my chance of getting the winning tom to come to me would be diminished by the natural tendency of the hen to go to the gobbler. However, spooking the hen had a lot of risks in itself, not the least of which would be spooking the gobblers. For the aforementioned reasons of past experiences with unusual tactics, I decided to try to spook her subtly. Hopefully she would get nervous enough to leave the area but not be sure about what spooked her. Now please understand that normally – there I go again using that word – even the slightest movement by a hunter within yards of a turkey, let alone within feet, will be promptly detected and rejected with a "Putt!" – followed immediately with the wild turkey's rendition of the Roadrunner escaping from Wiley Coyote. Usually, if a wild turkey sees you blink, they are gone, but not on this day.

I turned my head slowly to look at the hen hoping to spook her…nothing. I shifted my gun barrel…no response. I raised my gun barrel upward several inches…nada. I raised my elbow high enough for her to see…she just clucked and continued preening. She was happy where she was and wasn't moving. I gave up. It wasn't worth taking a chance to do something more obvious and risk spooking the toms. So I just resigned myself to accept the cards dealt to me and wait it out, which by now was nearing the fifteen-minute mark on the official fight clock. But then the purring stopped, and I couldn't see either of the two gobblers. As a matter of fact, for the first time in about an hour, there were no turkey sounds, just silence. I couldn't hear beating wings or the thumping of turkey breasts either.

"Finally, the fight must be over," I thought, and then it hit me; "He must be coming!"

The winning gobbler always marches right in to claim his hard won prize. It was just so thick in the swamp that I couldn't see him coming down the little trail. Better still, the hen that I had so wanted to spook was now my ally. As she purred near my decoys, all I had to do was wait. This was perfect! My heart was beating wildly again as I strained to pick up a glimpse of the gobbler's white head through the rain-slicked palmettos. And wait I did. So long that I knew something was wrong.

"He should have showed by now," I mused worriedly.

I began to call softly but got no response, except from the hen, which answered me from fifteen feet away. Apparently she knew something was up too. The hen began to leave my decoys and make her way up the trail to the spot where the gobblers had been fighting. That just wouldn't do. So I began to call to her, pleading with my yelps and clucks to return. She obliged my request and came back yelping all the way. Relieved by her return, I was at the same time alarmed by the fact that all of the calling between the hen and I had not brought a single response from either gobbler – especially for toms that had gobbled their heads off earlier.

After another few short minutes, the hen grew restless again with her boring, mannequin friends and resumed her plans to travel up the trail. This time, though, I was unable to convince her to return. I began to unravel.

"What was going on?" I wondered.

It appeared that my perfect "call him off the roost" turkey hunt was about to end as a dismal failure. The gobblers were gone, and now the hen was leaving to find them, and, try as I might, none of my calls were drawing any of them. I decided to try another tactic. I flipped the World Champ mouth call upside-down in my mouth and started kee-keeing to the departing hen.

The kee-kee is a sound that young turkeys make before they can yelp. They make this call to communicate with their mother and other turkeys in their flock, usually when they are lost or lonely. I had used this "kee-kee" tactic before to kill henned-up gobblers by preying upon the motherly instincts of the hens. The hens would come to find the lost juvenile and bring the big gobbler who was courting them along for the ride when no other call would work. Now we all know that there are no juvenile turkeys in the woods in the early spring of the year. All the jakes and jennies hatched last spring are capable of yelping clearly by now, and it's too soon for any new turkeys to have hatched this early in the season. However, the turkeys themselves don't appear to be able to put all this together. It is worth pointing out, for whatever it's worth, that adult turkeys, both male and female, have been observed kee-keeing. Regardless of the semantics, I have turned a bad situation for me into a bad situation for the bird by mixing kee-kees with jake yelps in the past. So, it merited a shot in the situation I presently found myself in.

The kee-kee tactic worked, and in more ways than one. The hen responded immediately and backtracked all the way to my decoys. However, I got a bonus from the upside-down mouth calling as well. A lone gobble rang out from the thick brush about one hundred and twenty-five yards from me at the one-o'clock position. Immediately, I flipped the mouth diaphragm right side up and called again to the gobbler. The yelps and cuts that had caused gobbles to explode from this turkey twenty-five minutes earlier, before his death duel, were now met with silence. I called again, and again. The gobbler wouldn't answer. He had gone back in the direction from which he had come, and I was afraid he was leaving the area altogether. With a flick of my tongue, I flipped the World Champ upside-down once again and whistled the kee-kee of a young turkey back in the gobbler's general direction. No response, so I tried again and again and again … "GAAAAROBBBBLE" finally rang out from the turkey's position a little more than a football field away. The hen turkey was still at my side apparently unfazed by the bush that sounded like a lost turkey.

I kept up the kee-keeing and jake yelping for five minutes. The boss tom's gobbles, which had come slowly after his fight, were now beginning to pick up speed and authority. Most importantly, as they were picking up intensity, they were getting closer. He was coming back! It became apparent that after the fight, the subdominant tom had gone back to the area of the swamp reserved for courageous, but whipped, gobblers. I never heard from him again. My turkey had retreated back in the direction he had come from, apparently to rest. These gobblers had fought so hard, for so long, that I believe the victor was too tired to breed a hen, strut, or even gobble! At one point, due to the silence, I thought maybe they had severely injured each other. Now, however, you could sense that with each passing moment the victorious gobbler was gaining strength as his gobbling increased, and he closed the distance. Once again I found my heart pounding and my breathing staggered as I strained to see the gobbler approaching. I heard the spitting and drumming of the strutting boss tom before I saw him. He appeared like a ghost strutting through the misty, gray palmettos into the very opening where I had watched him battle for fifteen minutes with his nemesis. I flipped the mouth call into its proper position and began laying the most seductive purrs I could on him.

This was a no brainer. The victorious gobbler was going to strut the remaining fifty yards down the trail to the waiting hens and jake, or so I thought. He held his ground in full strut and began a spit-and-drum calling seminar. He was moving no more than three feet in any one direction, and fortunately it was right smack dab in the middle of that basket-sized, palmetto opening that the Lord had made for me to see through. The rain had let up, but the heavy clouds and mist in the swamp gave everything a sort of grayish tone. The gobbler was strutting between me and where the sun would normally be. While the sun itself was not visible, it was causing a brightening of the gray, swamp sky directly behind the gobbler's tail fan. He had his tail feathers spread so far apart that there were spaces between the feathers. As far as I know, this is something that only an Osceola can do, I guess because they are a little smaller than the other three subspecies of wild turkey in North America and their tail feathers are a little narrower. I had seen Florida turkeys do this on hunting videos and on television, but now I was seeing it firsthand. It was so cool and beautiful that I will never forget it. As pretty as it was though, it would have been much more beautiful if I was seeing it at forty yards instead of fifty-five. I used every call a hen can make, and some they can't, to pull him into range, all to no avail.

No amount of cutting could convince the strutting swamp-boss to come to the hen. In reality, the hens normally go to the gobblers anyway and not vice-versa. Even if she couldn't see him through the palmettos, the longbeard knew he was close enough to the hen for her to hear him spitting and drumming, and for her to come running straight to him – something my hen decoy, or I for that matter, couldn't do. Unfortunately for me, there was a real, live hen at my side that could and, much to my disgust, did. I guess she finally decided that the time was right, and as the soft notes of the gobbler's "I'm in the mood for love" began to waft their way through the swamp, the hen left my decoys and nearly ran straight up the little trail to the strutting gobbler. Through the small window in the palmettos, I saw her reappear at the gobbler's side. My heart sank. The thing I had feared since I heard her first yelp earlier in the morning had come to pass.

As I found myself once again at an emotional low, the two turkeys were feeling something quite different. Apparently the hen was impressed by what she saw, because almost immediately after reaching the tom, she laid down in the trail directly in front of him. Likewise the gobbler wasted no time in reaping the rewards of his hard-won fight. He promptly mounted the hen's back, and, well, since this story is for the whole family, let's just say that he took care of business. Disappointed in this most recent turn of events (from the standpoint of being able to harvest the gobbler), I was at the same time grateful for being able to witness something I had never seen before, other than on video or TV – the breeding of a hen by a gobbler. I remember thinking about what an amazing morning this had turned out to be. What had started out as gully-washer rainstorm, snowball's-chance-in-a-hot-place of a turkey hunt had turned into one of the greatest turkey hunts I had ever been on – except for the killing part of it. I had never seen gobblers fight, and I had never seen the actual breeding of a hen. Now I had seen both, in the same morning, by the same gobbler. All I would have to show for it though would be a beautiful memory and a long story – a story that probably no one would believe anyway.

The whole breeding thing didn't take long. As quickly and quietly as it began, it ended. The gobbler dismounted the hen's back, and she stood and shook herself, none the worse for wear. The hen stretched her wings, preened a few ruffled feathers, and then began pecking around on the ground for something to eat. Meanwhile the gobbler, content with the realization that his genes would be passed on to the next generation of swamp turkeys, resumed strutting at the hen's side. I hoped once again that my chance to take the tom had come. I began the now tedious task of calling to him again. I gave him everything I could, hoping despairingly that he would venture down my way to breed the "other" hen, but he was having none of it. For nearly fifteen minutes I called to the gobbler using every trick I could. The only response the longbeard offered was the incessant drone of spitting and drumming that had brought his first hen to him. I didn't know what else to do. I was literally tired of calling.

"Just give up," entered my mind, "This wasn't meant to be."

No such thoughts ever usually occur to me, but what else could I do?

I prayed. Now, please understand, I pray before each and every hunt I undertake. However, I never ask my Lord and Savior to give me an animal or a bird. Instead, I thank Him for saving me and for the opportunity to be out in his beautiful creation hunting for his creatures. I then ask him to help me be a safe, wise, moral, and ethical hunter. I also always ask Him, if it be His will that I get an opportunity to shoot at an animal, that He would guide my shot in order to make a clean, one-shot-kill or a clean miss, so that no game would be caused to suffer at my hand. (I have caused enough suffering and pain in the lives of others during my life, most especially in the suffering of my Savior, Jesus Christ, who actually suffered, bled and died for my sins on the cross at Calvary.) So, that's the general extent of one of my prayers before I begin a hunt, although much of my time spent hunting finds me in prayer with my heavenly Father about many things and for many people. I had made just such a prayer before this hunt. Now, however, I did something that I usually don't do. I prayed and asked my

Heavenly Father, if it was His will, to allow me an opportunity to take this gobbler. It was just a short prayer, breathed in silence, in Jesus' precious name. I serve a God who hears those kinds of prayers though.

After my short prayer, I decided that there was one last thing to try – the silent treatment. All the turkey calling I could muster wasn't budging the tom, and the silent treatment had seemed to work on this bird earlier, so what did I have to lose? I slowly turned my head away from the gobbler until I was looking in the opposite direction from him. Then I raised my left hand to the side of my mouth with painstaking caution and began to yelp on the mouth call. I started out with low volume yelps and then began to make them softer and softer, while gradually covering my mouth with my hand, until the yelps were inaudible. Then I shut up and slowly resumed my normal body position. My intent was to sound like the hen had just grown weary of the game and had walked off, back into the swamp. I sat there silently for about five minutes, glancing at the strutting gobbler occasionally. In the depths of my depression, I considered the fact that if somehow I were able to kill this particular turkey, it would be one of the greatest hunts I could ever hope for, with any turkey, let alone my first Osceola. The hen that had been with the gobbler was no longer visible. I had no idea where she had gone in the palmettos after being bred. I tried to search for her by scanning with just my eyes, but I couldn't locate her visually, and she wasn't calling. Then the spitting and drumming of the gobbler stopped. I looked back through my little portal in the palmettos to his strutting spot, and he was gone! It is hard to describe the sinking feeling that landed in my gut and the sense of panic that gripped my heart. He was gone!

"No, it's just not fair; not after all I had to do to call him from the roost so far away. I can't believe it's not going to happen: not after driving seven hundred and fifty miles to hunt in Florida, traipse six to ten miles a day through the swamps, put up with the skeeters, ticks, snakes, boar, and alligators, get shortstanded by a local, force myself to hunt in a downpour when I hadn't heard a gobble all week, and then have a gobbler come over four hundred yards only to be sabotaged by other turkeys! No, No, No!"

Anyway, you might get a sense of the utter frustration I felt, as thoughts like these raced through my head, but that's spring gobbler hunting. If I didn't love it so much, sometimes I think it would just suck.

Suddenly, I caught movement in the palmettos. Something dark was making its way out of the area I had been watching and was headed to the swamp behind me. The dark form was moving about fifty yards to my right.

"Maybe it is the hen," I thought. "No, it's not the hen," I corrected myself, "it's the gobbler!"

I could hear the gobbler spitting and drumming again, but I could only get glimpses of something dark moving through the overcast, palmetto palms. This turkey had me so frustrated that I wasn't behaving as I normally would. I slowly turned to my right telling myself that if this old gobbler presented me with any kind of shot at all, even at fifty yards, I was going to try him. Even though I knew that a 2-1/4 ounce load of #6s fired from a 3-1/2 inch Super Magnum didn't possess the 3.5 ft-lbs. of torque required to break a mature gobbler's skeletal structure at that distance, I was going to try it if I had to. I figured he might die of a coronary infarction at the sound of the blast, or maybe some of the pellets would stun him and allow me to jump up and run closer for a lethal shot before he gathered his senses, or maybe the sound would disorient him, and he would turn and run in my direction, allowing for a closer second shot. (Obviously I hadn't learned a thing about luck from all my former experiences with wild turkeys. Other hunters might have such whimsical things occur to them while spring turkey hunting, but not me and my hunting partners. For us, anything that could go wrong usually did.) I really didn't care; at this point I was desperate. I couldn't bear the thought of missing out on this opportunity.

Although I wasn't able to see his white head, I was sure it was the gobbler because I could hear him drumming. What little I could make out visually as he slowly passed through the palmettos confirmed that he was still strutting as he moved. He was almost completely behind me now, so I decided to call to him again. I positioned the Quaker Boy mouth call a little farther back on my palate than I normally would to yelp, cluck, or cut. Then I did my best to make calling-contest-quality purrs. That was it, no other sounds, just the purring of a contented hen. "Periscope-up!" would be the best way to describe the gobbler's reaction to my offering, as he thrust his red, white, and blue head above the thick foliage and turned to look behind him. What happened next is the kind of thing turkey hunters dream of. Almost as quickly as he had stuck his white skullcap above the palmetto palms to peer toward the sound of my calls, he jerked it back down into his strutting position, and turned completely around to head in my direction! I didn't believe my own eyes at first.

"I must be seeing things," I thought hesitantly. "No, he is definitely coming!" I finally convinced myself after a few seconds.

The big gobbler was definitely coming at a 45-degree angle back to me and straight at my decoys! For the first time during this whole ordeal, I believe the tom was actually able to see my decoys when he stuck his head up to investigate my purrs. My jake decoy can either make, or break, a turkey hunt because it has been modified with a custom paint job by yours truly to make it look extremely aggressive. This aggressive, little decoy has sent numerous sub-dominant longbeards and almost all jakes that I call in to it packing on dead run for safety. However, that is a consequence and risk that I gladly take, because my jake decoy's beauty lies in its effect on dominant, boss gobblers – like the one that was now headed in my direction. I have killed numerous dominant birds "mean-walking" to my customized jake decoy, planning to teach it a lesson in pecking-order etiquette. I believe that is what turned the tide with this swamp gobbler. He was strutting in a straight line for the decoys, and he was "all out of bubble gum" (if you know Rowdy Roddy Piper's old line about butt whippin').

My heart rate was somewhere back around the two hundred beats-per-minute vicinity, as I strained to see the tom through my scope and track his progress to the decoys. Dark glimpses of black were barely visible in the gray-green palmettos as the gobbler slid through the thick, palmetto tangle. He was in shotgun range now, less than forty yards away, but I had absolutely no shot. I just couldn't see his head. As he strutted closer and closer, I was having trouble keeping it together. Thirty-five yards, thirty yards, and then twenty-five yards – the gap between us closed. I now had him where I wanted him and still couldn't get a clear shot at him through the palmettos. I took my eyes off the gobbler to survey the area in front of him. About five yards farther from his present location there looked to be a small break in the palms that would expose him. I pushed my gun barrel forward to cover the small opening, just to the left of a large palmetto. I drew ragged breaths as I stared through the scope waiting for the gobbler's head to appear. He was coming from my right to my left and should appear at any second. My finger rested nervously on the trigger, as time seemed to stand still. (Time can stand still on a spring gobbler hunt like no other – seconds seemingly turn into minutes and minutes into hours.) I waited and waited for him to appear in my scope.

"Where was he?" I wondered nervously.

I began to second-guess my estimation of his intended line of travel, and I worried that I was looking to the left of the wrong palmetto.

"What if he is already past where I am looking?" rang in my head, as I remembered similar mistakes on whitetail deer hunts with a scoped rifle.

I fought back the urge to look off the gun and pinpoint the gobbler.

"Keep your head down on the stock!" I told myself.

Just as another wave of panic began to swell up within me, his white head emerged from behind my targeted palmetto palm into the waiting cross hairs of my scope. I immediately squeezed the trigger after target acquisition.

At the sound of my Remington's blast, I immediately pumped another 3-1/2 inch round into the breech and jumped to my feet. (You turkey hunters know that's not as easy as it sounds after sitting tensely in one position for a long period of time!) As I arose, the first thing I saw was a turkey struggling in the palmettos to get airborne, which it accomplished in short order. As I looked up and watched the turkey sail through the moss-covered treetops into the heart of the swamp, I couldn't believe it.

"Don't tell me I missed him!" I wondered incredulously to myself. "How could I have missed him?"

A sound on the ground directly before me redirected my focus. There, seventeen yards in front of me, was the gobbler, beating his wings on the wet, sandy ground of the Ocala National Forest. I hadn't missed him at all! The turkey that had flown was the hen. The foliage was so dense that I never could see her until she flew. I'm not sure what kind of war whoop I let out, but let's just say the swamp had never heard anything like it before. I looked at my watch to mark the time. It was 8:30 a.m., one hour and fifty minutes since the gobbler had initially answered me from the ground.

As I walked to my fallen gobbler, I was overwhelmed with emotion. Now, it was all worth it. There is a feeling that I get at moments like this that is indescribable.

It is a mixture of adrenaline and emotion that is best likened to getting high. The difference between this high and the kind you get from drugs – besides being legal – is that this high never gets old. They say that one of the reasons for the widespread addiction to crack cocaine in our country is the tremendous high one gets the first time they use it. The feeling of being high is so wonderful that when they come down off the drug they can't wait, and will do anything, to get it back again. The problem is that the user can never achieve the same high again. Each time that they reuse the drug, the high that is induced falls somewhat short of their last high. This creates a greater urge for more of the drug, and leaves the user always struggling to get that initial high feeling back again. Hence, an addict is born – not so with turkey hunting.

Killing a spring gobbler never gets old, no matter how many times you experience it. I got just as excited and overwhelmed on this Florida gobbler (if not more so) as I did on the morning of my first spring gobbler seventeen years ago in West Virginia. Once I realized that I had killed my Osceola gobbler, I was so emotionally exhausted, and at the same time ecstatic, that I didn't know what to do with myself.

After I reached the fallen gobbler, I looked directly overhead toward heaven and just started saying "Thank You Jesus!" over and over.

The view of the trees and sky is etched in my memory as I stood there looking up, continually thanking God for this blessing. The rain had completely stopped, and the sun's rays were trying desperately to penetrate the clouds and gray mist of the swamp. Shafts of light streaked through the canopy of pines, palms, and moss covered branches. It was beautiful. I'm still thankful to the Lord for the blessing of that moment in my life. I briefly looked at the gobbler's beard and spurs, but not like I normally would. I just gave them a quick sort of glance, as I was kind of in a daze. I started to walk back to the tree where I had been sitting to get my Bible and license. I stopped, turned around, and walked back to look at the turkey closer. I stopped again, before reaching the bird, and headed back for my license and Bible. At this point, my brain, which has a history of lagging behind, caught up with the rest of me.

"Just unload your gun and calm down, Dummy!" I told myself.

I dropped to both knees and pumped the two remaining shells from the 870. I was nearly in tears from the flood of emotion and satisfaction. Still on both knees and leaning on the retracted forearm of the pump gun, I bowed in prayer and more formally thanked the Lord. A feeling this good doesn't come easily or often to a turkey hunter, but it is the reason that I continue to hunt them.

I'm not sure what Heaven is going to be like. Kneeling in the sand of the Ocala National Forest, I thought about it though. Yes, I know what the Bible says about heaven and how it is described physically, but I mean, what is it going to be like emotionally and personally for God's children?

The Bible says that "Eye hath not seen, nor ear heard, neither have entered into the heart of man, the things which God hath prepared for them that love Him" (1Cor. 2:9).

I believe that if you take the best feelings you've ever experienced in your life, that highest of highs, and somehow multiply that joy and sensation by ten, or a hundred, or a thousand, that is what it will be like to be in the presence of God Himself. No matter what it is like, I am convinced that no earthly experience will even come close to it, especially a turkey hunt. As ecstatic, thankful, and praiseful this turkey kill had made me, the emotions that I experienced will pale in comparison to the moment I am with my Savior, Jesus Christ. What an unbelievable state of happiness that will be! I'm not worthy of experiencing that blessing by my own merit. However, because I believed what the Bible says about Jesus' dying for my sins on the cross, his burial, and three days later his bodily resurrection from the grave, which proved He was God's own Son, and believing that in my heart, I repented of my sin and asked him for forgiveness and salvation, I was born again. Now I am assured of Heaven, not because I'm worthy of it, but because Jesus has paid my way in for me. Dear reader, I hope you will see your need for the Savior and will ask Him to save you, if you have never done so.

After praying to my heavenly Father, I found my spent shotgun hull and rounded-up all my gear. I was finally starting to get my emotional act together. Florida doesn't use field tags, so I didn't have to tag the bird. As is my custom, I read my Bible over the fallen bird and prayed once again. Then I began to really study the Osceola gobbler closely. He was all wet from the rain and had managed to get sand all over himself while flopping after the shot. The distance of the shot was seventeen yards, and it had completely severed the gobbler's spine just below the head. This was an answered prayer – no suffering for this bird.

The gobbler had a 10-1/4 inch beard and 1-inch spurs, which were both needle sharp. Probably a three-year-old tom, he had worn primary wingtips from strutting and a nice full fan. His wings were very dark, the characteristic mark of a true swamp turkey. The undersides of both his wings were bare at the joints. The feathers were missing from fighting and breeding, and they had been replaced by ticks – hundreds of them. The ticks were packed tight next to each other like scales on a fish, row after row of them. The gobbler had several fresh battle wounds on both legs from his fight with the other tom. One of his "drumsticks" had a gash in it about two inches long. I stood back up from examining him closely and from a standing position admired him. Actually he looked more like a sandy, drowned rat than the monarch of the spring swamp that he was. The gobbler's ratty appearance not withstanding, it was then and there that I decided to have him mounted. He was wet and sandy and ruffled. He wasn't the biggest turkey I had ever killed by far, or even the toughest, but what more could a person ask for in a turkey hunt? I had seen this bird do everything a gobbler is created to do in the spring and then was able to take him. I doubted if I would ever have such an opportunity again. Beside all that, he was my first Osceola, killed on public land with no guide or help. That made him special regardless of the other details of the hunt. (During a discussion with the gun shop manager / assistant store manager of Bass Pro Shops in Orlando, I told him I was from Virginia and was on vacation to hunt Osceola turkeys. An avid turkey hunter himself, he told me I was crazy for hunting the swamps of public land in Florida for a gobbler without a guide! He said it was something even he wouldn't do. Also, before leaving for Florida, I had spoken to a taxidermist in Richmond, Virginia who wanted to kill an Osceola himself, but he wouldn't consider it without having a guide.) Those kinds of statements can discourage a hunter, but after a successful hunt, they make it all the sweeter.

As I carried the gobbler up the trail to my truck, I arrived at the spot where all the fighting and breeding had taken place. I couldn't believe it. The spot where all this had happened was right at the edge of the opening that I had found while scouting the day before – the area that I thought I had set up in. As it turns out, I had set up in the wrong spot! In the pre-dawn darkness and heavy rain, I had gone too far and missed my intended set-up area. The area that I actually set up in was smaller and didn't offer the same good view as the area I wanted to hunt. Man, did I feel dumb! If I had just set up in the right spot, I wouldn't have had to go through all this! I would have had a shot at the boss gobbler as soon as he showed up to fight the other turkey!

"Boy, that mistake almost cost me a trophy turkey," I told myself.

"Not so fast," I replied my inner self, as I began to think things through.

If I had set up in the "right" spot, it could be that the second gobbler – the one that came from behind me – would have seen me, spooking both gobblers, because he would have had to walk right up my back to get to the fighting spot. It is also possible that I might have gotten so preoccupied with Gobbler No. 2 behind me (I get very nervous when a gobbler comes from behind me – it's bothersome!) that I might have spooked Gobbler No. 1 by not paying close enough attention to his whereabouts, allowing him to see me moving slightly as I looked for the bird behind me. Actually, I began to believe that my missing the intended opening was providential; in fact, I'm convinced of it now. It has occurred to me that even if nothing would have gone wrong and everything went as planned, I would have killed my gobbler as soon as his head appeared within forty or so yards, and that would have been it. Not only would I have missed the fighting and the breeding, but I wouldn't have had to work so hard to get him either. No, in retrospect, I'm glad I missed the first spot, and I thank the Lord for that little window in the palmettos to watch the drama through.

To help you get a feel for the remoteness of the area I was in, let me tell you about my cell phone. Now I am in Florida, right? The state is basically what I would call flat. (I'm from West Virginia; I'd call Pennsylvania flat!) I'm something like an hour and a half from Orlando, one of the biggest cities in the country. My cell phone got no reception at all where I was hunting – not one bar – except for about five minutes the morning I killed my gobbler. Back at the truck, I checked the phone and it showed two bars of reception. It was 9:00 a.m., so I called my brother, Kevin, at his job in Virginia. The cellular reception lasted just long enough for me to let him hear the sound of an Osceola gobbler's wing beating the ground and to tell him that I had gotten one, and then I lost service. That short phone call was a special moment, I know made possible by my heavenly Father.

I'm going to skip all the details about my adventure in finding a checking station and having my bird properly checked. I will say this, though, as confusing as I think Florida's game laws are, Florida does a thorough job at the check station. They measure and record the length of the bird's beard and spurs, and they also weigh the turkey and put that on record. I figured the woman who checked my bird wouldn't know how to properly measure the turkey, but I was wrong – I mean mistaken – I have never been wrong. (That's a joke, in case you were wondering!) I asked her what the beard measured; guessing it would be a good ten inches.

"No," she responded as she taped the beard, "he'll go a little better than that…ten and a quarter," she remarked, writing the dimension down on her clipboard.

It really looked to me like he had an eleven-inch beard, because it was wet and the fibers were stuck together. When I finally taped it for myself back at the hotel, I discovered that she was dead-nuts-on…10-1/4 inches. Ditto for the 1-inch spurs that she measured. The turkey weighed in officially at seventeen pounds and eight ounces. That's not the biggest gobbler in Florida, but it is a fine bird for the Florida swamps. As a matter of fact, the NWTF will not even accept the submission of an Osceola with a weight of twenty pounds or greater for the turkey record books unless there is certified proof of it. So while he isn't the biggest turkey weight-wise of my hunting career, he is indeed a trophy for his subspecies, and he is as heavy as many of the Eastern gobblers I have killed in the mountains. Anyway it don't matter to me, he is bound for a wall of my home in Virginia. I hope to show him to you – in half-strut and gobbling on a limb that has been draped with Spanish moss, which I brought back from the swamp where I killed him. I will treasure the memories of this hunt every time I look at "Turkulese" in my rec room.

Before I can bring myself to write "The End," I have to mention something about my dear wife, Lisa. Next to being saved, meeting and falling in love with her is the best thing that has ever happened to me. How she puts up with me and my hardcore, outdoor lifestyle I'll never know. She is the greatest. She not only puts up with me, but she actually helps and encourages me. I will never be able to share all the crazy things that have occurred in our lives because of my outdoor pursuits. Some of them are unbelievable, a few of them are sad, but many of them are downright hilarious. An example of the latter, depending upon your sense of humor, follows.

Every day, after my hunt in the swamp would end, I would return to the hotel around 1:00 p.m. I would get a shower, and we would then drive to Orlando – about an hour away. We would spend the afternoon and evenings at different attractions in the city. Now Lisa and I have been married for fourteen years, and she has figured out that when I kill something, I usually return from hunting earlier than when I am unsuccessful. During this week in Florida, Monday through Thursday I had showed up at the one-o'clock hour without a gobbler to show for my efforts. Lisa would be showered and all dressed up to go to town each day when I arrived. Now, on Friday, I killed my turkey at 8:30 a.m. and should have been back to the hotel early. However, it took me until 11:00 a.m. to get the turkey checked in. That's right, it took me longer to get the gobbler checked in than it did to kill him, and that was two hours in itself! (I'm telling ya, I'm going to do a sequel on the Florida Checking Station Ordeal!) Therefore, I didn't arrive back to the hotel until after twelve noon. Lisa greeted me when I entered the room with a kiss at the door and then turned away to resume getting ready for town. She almost always asks how I did on my hunt, but this particular day she didn't. She began asking me something inconsequential about whether I was hungry or something like that. I just stood at the entrance of the hotel room smiling, not answering her. Eventually she figured something was up. Lisa turned to look at me, and the light finally came on in her pretty little head.

"Did you get one?" she asked excitedly.

Trying to remain calm, I just nodded in the affirmative. She ran back to me and hugged and kissed me. Now you know why I hunt so hard for turkeys. It's not for hunting's sake, but for the hugs and kisses that I know

Lisa will lavish upon me when successful! Now if you believe that, I've got some swampland you might be interested in buying! A successful turkey hunt back in Virginia usually goes something like this: I go to the bedroom and jump on the bed to wake her up.

She will open her eyes and mutter, "Did you get one?"

After I respond with a "Yes," she will say something like, "I'm happy for you, Babe," as she rolls back over to sleep!

But this Florida hunt was different. Lisa knew how hard I had been hunting, what little sleep I was getting, and how much effort I had put into getting this gobbler, and she was really happy for me. Her delight quickly turned to disappointment though, as she loosened the grip her arms had around my neck and slid back down to the floor.

"Does that mean that we're not coming back to Florida anymore?" she asked with a sullen expression.

Before I could answer, she followed with, "Where do we have to go to kill a Rio?"

(A "Rio" is short for "Rio Grande" which is another one of the four subspecies of wild turkeys found in the United States.) Now you can see why I married this good lookin' woman!

After a phone call to my brother on a landline to tell him about the hunt, I called my taxidermist friend, Mike Gray, in Richmond. Mike had told me previously that if I ever wanted to have a turkey mounted, the most important factor in achieving a quality mount was not to get its feathers wet. As you can imagine, I had a little problem with my gobbler being a tad moist, since I had killed him in the rain. Mike couldn't believe I had actually done it (kill a public-land Osceola), and was really happy for me. When I told him that I wanted to have the "Tominator" mounted and that the bird was ringing wet, he asked me if I had a hair dryer. I told him that I did, as he explained how he had hand-dried his son's first gobbler for two hours with a hair dryer. Needless to say, it wasn't long before the dead turkey was flopped up on the bathroom counter, and Lisa's hair dryer was blowing hot air. (You know, it's kind of cool to see the looks that well-dressed people give you at a hotel as you carry a big, dead, wild turkey from the parking lot and disappear with it into your room!) In the room, I meticulously worked the gobbler's feathers with one hand, while I used the hair dryer with the other.

It didn't take too much of this until something moving on the vanity top caught my eye. Remember what I said was attached to the underside of the turkey's wings where feathers had once been? They were detaching themselves – in droves! Ticks! The little, nasty buggers were crawling everywhere – in our hotel room! Now how would most women react to this most unfortunate turn of events? Not Lisa. The next thing I know, she is taking pictures of me using the hair dryer on the turkey. She just takes it all in stride – life with a redneck Legionnaire. Besides ticks, there is one other advantage to drying off a dead, wet, swamp-chicken in your hotel room – the aroma! Man, that is one good smell. I thought about charging the hotel extra for leaving it behind. That's not something just every hotel can offer its guests!

The maid we had probably quit after we left. I mean I didn't even mention the 4-1/2 foot snakeskin that I brought back to the room after a morning's hunt on the Withlacoochie River in Green Swamp. (Yeah, that's right, Withlacoochie – I think it's Native American for "Ain't got no turkeys here.") I found the shed snakeskin forty yards from where I had been sitting one morning and within a few feet of where I saw my first, and hopefully last, cottonmouth. Lisa wanted to know what I was going to do with the skin. I told her I was thinking about leaving it in one of the dresser drawers when we checked out, so the maids would stay alert when they cleaned the room. Just so you know, I didn't do it – I'm not that bad! I brought it home to Virginia with me. Anyway where was I, oh yeah, the ticks…If you think popping those plastic bubbles in bubble wrap is fun, you should try tick popping – it's fun for the whole family, just ask Lisa! On second thought, I suggest that you wait about a year, say sometime around March 2004, before you bring the subject up with her. Three days after the tick-fest, when we were back home in Virginia, she found a tick on her – talk about being ticked-off! (Pun intended). If it helps you feel any better, I pulled one off of my waist the day after that. I hope that you can forgive me for adding to the length of this turkey hunt narrative, but for all Lisa puts up with, I felt I would be remiss for not mentioning it.

I hope you enjoyed reading about my Osceola turkey hunt. I hope that you have a personal relationship with the Lord Jesus Christ – the One who owns everything and made my hunt possible. If you're a turkey hunter, I hope that this story brought memories back to you of your own hunts, while giving you a glimpse of what swamp hunting can be like, and the desire to try it for yourself. If you are not a turkey hunter, I hope that this story transported you into a turkey hunter's world for just a few minutes of your life. If you think you can stand it, I'd encourage you to give turkey hunting a try, but I'm not responsible if you get hooked. The Spring Gobbler will be responsible for that.

Date: March 21, 2003
Time: 8:30 a.m.
Location: Ocala National Forest
Weight: 17-1/2 lbs.
Beard: 10-1/4 inches
Spurs: 1.0 inches

Turkulese' Spurs

Turkulese' Wing

"Limbhanger"

Turkulese mount in my home

Loverboy
–
The Rio Grande Gobbler

Preface

An unbelievable turkey hunting experience in the swamps of Florida during March of 2003 was the catalyst for me to take the time to write about spring gobbler hunting in general, and that hunt in particular. Many of my family members, friends, and acquaintances took the time to read my account of "Turkulese" and the details that surrounded my pursuit of the Osceola gobbler.

During the late winter months of early 2004, I began making plans to pursue a third subspecies of Melleagris Gallapavo. My vacation schedule would permit me to hunt the Rio Grande subspecies during the first week of Oklahoma's spring gobbler season, or the Merriam's subspecies during the last week of South Dakota's turkey season. (This vacation schedule, by the way, excludes any interference with Virginia's spring turkey season. The prerequisite for my Grand Slam quest is that I hunt before, or after, my home state's season, and that Lisa wants to travel with me.) The thought of traveling 1700 miles to hunt the last week of South Dakota's spring gobbler season didn't exactly thrill me, so I asked Lisa if she would like to go to the Sooner State. Her "yes" may have been somewhat hesitant, but I hit the ground running. Phone calls to biologists, state wildlife employees, chambers of commerce, hotels, and ranchers in Oklahoma ensued. It wasn't long before I had a nonresident hunting license with a spring turkey tag, and a game plan to hunt in northwest Oklahoma.

Strangely though, as word began to spread throughout my circle of family and friends that Lisa and I were planning to travel to Oklahoma on vacation, the first question that everyone seemed to ask me was, "So, are you going to write a story about it?"

My immediate response was "No, that was a one time deal."

Since you are now actively engaged in reading this, you can accurately assess me as a liar.

The truth is that writing one of these narratives takes a lot of time and effort. I just didn't think that I would be willing to do it again, but something happened during this past turkey season that would change my mind. To determine what that would be, you will have to read on.

Enjoy.

Loverboy

Dust flew as his cowboy boots hit the ground, and he shut the door to his pickup truck. With a firm grip, he took my right hand and gave it a hearty shake. With a clear, glassy-eyed stare, he looked me directly in the face and watched for any sign of doubt. Then with a steely, hollow voice he interrogated me.

"So, how was your turkey hunt in Oklahoma?" my brother asked.

"Well, I picked a great week to go spring gobbler hunting," I replied. Then with just a moment's hesitation, I continued, "But I picked a lousy week to kill a longbeard in Oklahoma!"

Okay, enough of the B.S. My response to Kevin's question was accurate, however. It was indeed a great week to hunt turkeys, with the notable exceptions of four days of rain, the turkey-chasing cattle, a landowner who spooked two longbeards on a suicide mission sixty yards from me, and the warm front which embraced the Midwest at the end of March – a warm front that, according to a wildlife biologist, had caused the gobblers to gather their hens about two weeks early. This "henning-up" of the gobblers just happened to coincide perfectly with my vacation in Oklahoma.

Upon our arrival in Cheyenne, Oklahoma, I should have known this was going to be a vacation to be remembered. Lisa and I pulled into a quick-stop at about 4:00 p.m. Central time, on Sunday, April 4. After filling the truck with gas, I paid the clerk, who was an attractive lady about thirty years old. She asked me where I was from, and when I said, "Virginia," her expression brightened.

"Are you here to hunt turkeys?" she queried.

Up to this point, I was in a hurry to get to our motel and check-in. Now, however, I began to see the benefits of the slower pace of life in western Oklahoma. It isn't often that an attractive woman asks a legion member about turkey huntin' you know!

When I affirmed for her that was in fact the reason I had traveled sixteen hundred miles in the last two days, she said, "We just love to have you hunters in town!"

I just about fell over. Most places where I have traveled to hunt treat "tourists" with contempt. I wasn't sure if it was the Mossy Oak shirt I was wearing, or that handsome look I develop after twenty-one hours spent in a four-wheel drive vehicle, but something was different here. (Lisa says that the lady just felt sorry for me!) Normally, I'm not much on small talk with strangers. In this case though, I felt that I had an obligation to all Virginians to represent our state with friendliness, and I know my father-in-law would have been disappointed in me if I weren't talkative. So after several minutes of conversation, it struck me as odd when the clerk chuckled as I asked her for directions to the Washita Motel.

"You can't miss it," she mused, "It's on your left about a block from here."

(A block in rural Oklahoma can be anywhere from one hundred feet to one mile in distance). As I skipped back to the 4-Runner, Lisa was wondering what the Sam Hill had happened to me.

"Boy, the people out here are so friendly!" I said to her as I climbed back into the driver's seat.

The closest thing that I saw to a traffic jam in Oklahoma occurred a block from the quick-stop as we turned into the motel parking lot. Besides our own vehicle, a truck from North Carolina and a truck from Louisiana were entering the motel at the same time. All three vehicles had some sort of National Wild Turkey Federation (NWTF) sticker or designation on them, and all three contained turkey hunters. The truck from the Tar Heel State was driven by a kind, older gentleman who made my acquaintance as soon as we had both parked outside the motel office. As we discussed our plans to hunt Rio Grande toms during the week, our conversation was interrupted by one of the four men in the truck from Louisiana. The boisterous leader of the bunch was shouting to us across the parking lot, while his companions were dragging duffle bags, gun cases, and shooting boxes from the truck bed. He wanted to know how many turkeys we had killed so far. He then informed us that Oklahoma was the fourth state for them to hunt this spring as they had already hunted in Florida, Mississippi, and Alabama.

"It must be nice!" was all I could say about that, as I turned to the gentleman from North Carolina and muttered something about the benefits of being independently wealthy.

In the motel office, we checked in alongside our new friend from North Carolina.

He commented to me that he sure was glad he had reserved a room. I started to question the guy's sanity, because this motel looked to have about sixty rooms to rent and there was a grand total of three vehicles (the three previously described) in the parking lot. I shrugged his comment off and attributed it to the long, lonely drive he had just completed. As one of the two elderly ladies behind the desk handed Lisa our room key, I picked up one of the motel business cards from off the counter. The business card had a full color picture of a gobbler in full strut on it.

I showed it to Lisa and exclaimed, "Man, this is the best looking business card I have ever seen!"

Lisa's contacts must have been blurred because she didn't seem to appreciate the card in the same manner as I. Anyway, things in Oklahoma just kept getting better and better, until we arrived at Room 119.

The motel we had chosen to stay at was basically located in the middle of nowhere – which is a good place to be if you're a turkey, or a turkey hunter for that matter. I had asked Lisa if she would mind staying at a "not so nice" motel for a couple of days that would put me closer to the areas I wanted to hunt. The area we were in was so remote, that even the little town of Cheyenne (population 700) was still a thirty- to sixty-minute drive from the Wildlife Management Areas (WMAs) open to public hunting. (Cheyenne is located near the spot where General George Custer defeated Chief Black Kettle and the Cheyenne Indians at the Battle of the Washita in 1868.) The plan would be for me to hunt in the mornings, and then we would drive an hour or more to a larger town in the afternoon to shop and eat dinner. Hopefully, I could tag a tom early in the week, and we could check out of Cheyenne and relocate to one of the nicer hotels in a larger town. After relocating to a larger town, I would make the two-hour drive in order to hunt the remainder of the week. At least that was the plan. The motel in Cheyenne was an old, two-story affair. It wasn't totally rundown on the outside, but let's just say it had seen its better days. The motel advertised having sixty-three rooms, which seemed pretty big to me for such a small town with only two restaurants, two gas stations and no stoplights. So everything looked to be Okay in OK until Lisa turned the key and opened the door to our vacation suite.

At first glance, Room 119 looked like a heavy-metal rock band had spent the night there – with their groupies. The beds were unmade with the covers and pillows lying strewn about on the floor. The trashcan was knocked over with beer cans spilling out all over the place, and there were several large holes in the wall. Whatever else may have been wrong with the room wasn't immediately visible due to the dim, yellow lighting controlled by the wall switch and the closing motel door controlled by my hand.

"It looks like they gave us the wrong room," I said, frantically trying to shut the door, which had decided that it had been shut long enough and was not about to cooperate.

I would try to describe the look on Lisa's face at this particular moment, but I believe my subconscious has deleted the file from my memory bank!

I was still banging the Room 119 door against the aluminum jamb trying to get it shut, as Lisa returned from the motel office with a key for Room 121. I gave up on the stubborn door and tried not to let Lisa see my crossed fingers as I took the new key from her and opened the door to Room 121. Well, the same lighting designer had apparently done all the rooms with the same vision in mind, as I flipped the switch and peered through the dim, yellow light straining to see what was behind "Door Number Two."

Even I will have to admit it's pretty bad when you look around and say, "Well at least the beds are made and there's no trash on the floor!"

The carpet in our cozy, love nest was probably installed in the early '60s, judging from the color and amount of pile left in it. The carpet had numerous burn marks in it and some of them were quite large. The bed linens were purchased at about the same time as the carpet, the walls had been damaged, the toilet (which appeared to be fairly new) was loose on the floor and rocked from side-to-side when you sat on it. All of the floor and wall trim in the bathroom was rotten and falling from the wall, and the bathtub, faded tan from its original white, was covered with caramel colored stains of all shapes and sizes made by who-knows-what. The spigot for the tub was covered with a hard, white, calcium deposit, except for the bottom of it, where it had corroded through – letting water run continually into the tub. I think I have covered the highlights for you without boring you about the five channels available on the small TV, the curtains, mirrors, and HVAC unit. I do still remember the look on Lisa's face after perusing Room 121. My subconscious hasn't quite figured out how to repress it just yet – it is a sort of "burned-in" memory. I will not describe the look she bore for fear of you requiring therapy afterwards and having me billed for it. I did turn to her and do what any loving husband in my shoes would have done.

I said, "Well this ain't so bad now, is it?"

Oh, please, you have got to know that I'm kidding. I wouldn't be alive to type this if I wasn't. Actually I told her we would leave right then if she wanted to and drive back to a bigger town.

Lisa, the trooper that she is, said (with a sigh I might add) "No, I think I can handle it…but you had better get a turkey…Quick!"

I told her that we would make a list of things we needed to make our stay more palatable and drive sixty miles to Elk City immediately to find a Wal-Mart. Our list of items to be purchased included (not necessarily in any order of importance) 1) Lysol, 2) a bath mat, 3) sheets, 4) pillows and cases, 5) a plastic box to be used as a seat in the tub, and 6) flip-flops to wear in the bath.

So after driving about eight hours from Springfield, Missouri to Cheyenne, Oklahoma, we climbed back into the 4-Runner and headed for Elk City, a little over an hour away. As we drove, I remembered that chuckle from the lady at the quick-stop when I asked for directions to the motel. I had an idea now of what that was all about. We stopped at a Western Sizzlin while in Elk City for supper, and they were out of baked potatoes. While this was not a big deal in itself, things weren't looking quite as promising for our Oklahoma vacation after the motel incident. So much for things getting "better and better"!

Spring Gobbler season opens in Oklahoma every year on April 6. In 2004, that was a Tuesday, which meant that I had all day Monday to scout. I had secured maps of three different WMAs open to public hunting from an Oklahoma wildlife biologist. Two of the areas were located in Roger Mills County, and the other was in adjoining Ellis County. All three areas were known to have huntable numbers of Rios, and all three were close enough together that I could hunt them from a central location. My plan for Monday, April 5, was to scout as much of each one as I could, in addition to meeting two private landowners with whom I had made contact and secured trespass fee hunting privileges for their private farms – excuse me, I mean ranches. I had decided to try and secure these private-land hunting opportunities at the adamant request of the wildlife biologist who had provided me with the WMA maps I needed.

A brief note about Rio Grande turkey hunting is in order here. Rios can be found predominantly in eleven states of our great nation. Of these eleven states, Texas, Oklahoma, and Kansas generally hold the majority of birds classified as Melleagris gallopavo intermedia. Texas is probably the most famous state for Rio Grande turkeys as it has the largest population of the birds, and most hunters wanting to bag one end up hunting there. The drawback with hunting Texas, for me anyway, is that they have little to no public hunting. Most all Texas turkey hunting is done on private ranches with lodging and guides provided – not what I was looking for. That is why I decided on Oklahoma. However, no matter what state you hunt them in, the Rio's terrain is one of mostly open and flat grasslands. The arid, brushy terrain of the Rio Grande turkey is basically treeless, except along the streams and rivers of their domain. The key to hunting these Great Plains birds is understanding that turkeys don't sleep on the ground – they roost (sleep) in trees. Now a tree with branches large enough to support a twenty-pound bird can be a rare thing in the home range of Mr. Rio. This lack of trees is not a problem during the daylight hours for a bird that loves to strut in the open and be seen for miles around. A treeless landscape is also not a problem when the sun is high in the sky for a bird with a keen eye and the ability to see any sign of danger approaching from a long way off. However, at the end of the day when the shadows grow long, and the coyotes begin to howl, a tree is not just a turkey's best friend, it is imperative to his survival.

So now you know what a turkey hunter who wants to call in a Rio Grande longbeard needs to find – trees. Typically if you can find a stand of cottonwood trees or large hackberry trees in a creek bottom or on a riverbank, you can find turkeeez. That's right "turkeeez," because there will be lots of them – all concentrated together. If I haven't lost you so far, read on. Now any turkey hunter may or may not be smart, and I mean that in the classical sense, because we all know in the redneck sense that if you hunt turkeys and eat them, you're brilliant. But no matter how "dumm" a turkey hunter may be (and there are a few, believe me), he knows that to hunt a Rio, he has to find trees. The problem this creates is that everyone who is trying to kill a Rio tom is looking for trees, just like the turkeys. Like the turkeys, hunters find the trees too, and according to the biologists in Oklahoma, they then proceed to spook the turkeys off the roost. Unfortunately this usually occurs when they are scouting before the season even comes in. Some of these hunters have perfected the spooking of turkeys into an art form. They arrive a week before the season opens, camp on the public land, and then methodically travel to each roosting area the WMA has to offer – scaring off everything wearing feathers with four-reed mouth calls, video cameras, and truck doors. Oh, did I mention that a Rio that has been spooked from a roosting site is gone for good? Yep, sadly, a majority of the time they will not return to that stand of trees for the remainder of the hunting season. So where do the birds go to find a new roosting area? – the nearest ranch that has trees and nobody messing with the birds, which are sleeping in them. Obviously, I am referring to private land. The outfitters and guides that I spoke to in Oklahoma and in Texas told me that they treat the roosting areas on their properties as sacred. In other words, they don't allow any hunting near the roost trees. Protecting the roost site insures that the birds will always come back home each night and be there again the next morning. Many of these Rio Grande outfitters hunt turkeys like a deer hunter pursues whitetails. They set up a blind in an area where they think the birds will be going to feed, and then they put their clients in the blind to just sit and wait. If the morning hunt is unsuccessful, in the afternoon the outfitter will set up a blind between where the turkeys spent the day and the roosting area trying to catch the turkeys going back to the roost, but they never hunt the roost. (Oklahoma and Texas allow all day hunting for spring gobblers.) One outfitter in Texas told me that they kill ninety-six percent of their gobblers in the evening. Scott Parry, an Oklahoma wildlife biologist, told me that if I was fortunate enough to find birds and a roosting area on a WMA, I wouldn't be alone, and I should be prepared for company. That prospect really bothered me from a safety standpoint. So my biologist contact exhorted me whole-heartedly to seek a private ranch to hunt on, since I was traveling so far.

I was able to secure the right to hunt on two different ranches in Oklahoma before I left home in Virginia. Danny Pierce of Rush Creek Guide Service had a hunting lease near his home in Reydon, Oklahoma on his cousin's farm. I was fortunate enough to get permission to hunt this farm during the opening week of the season. Danny and his guides do nearly all of their guided hunting in Texas. Rush Creek is a very reputable outfitter that I had seen showcased on outdoor television shows and had read about in hunting magazines. Danny wanted me to hunt in Texas with them, but I told him "No," I was planning to hunt in Oklahoma – on my own. Danny had leased his cousin's farm for the quail hunting it provided, but he told me that turkeys used it as well, at least for a while. This farm was surrounded by public hunting land, and Danny told me that the public hunters would eventually run the turkeys off his cousin's farm as the season progressed (because the farm was so small). I planned to hunt this farm first. Danny said he wouldn't charge me to hunt on his lease by the day, which was a lot different from any other landowner. He said that I could hunt as many days as I needed to take a gobbler, and if I killed one, he would charge me for the bird.

The other ranch that I was able to get permission to hunt belonged to a blue-collar rancher named Max Montgomery. Max's ranch was located outside of Durham, Oklahoma. (Durham, by the way, consisted of two buildings and one stop sign.) By the Lord's providence, Max called me early one morning in February. He said that he had heard I was looking for a place to hunt in his neck of the woods. He explained that while he did not allow anyone to hunt on his ranch, he did have a remodeled farm house on his property that he would gladly let me rent for thirty dollars a day, if I needed a place to stay. I graciously thanked him for his offer but declined his invitation. I told him I was looking to pay a trespass fee to hunt private land for a mature gobbler. He told me that he had turkeys on his ranch, but he enjoyed watching them too much to let anyone shoot them. I certainly respected his position and told him so. After about another half hour of "good ol' boy" conversation concerning everything from cattle farming to turkey hunting, Max had a change of heart.

He said, "Heck, you sound like my kind of hunter. If you are coming all the way out here to kill a turkey, you won't hurt the turkey population on my property by killing one. Come on out and hunt my place for free."

I nearly dropped the phone into my coffee cup.

"Thank you sir," I replied, "but I told you I would pay to hunt and I will, fifty dollars a day."

Max responded by telling me to just bring him a ball cap from Virginia. What a deal! (I did both, in case you were wondering. I took him a Virginia ball hat and paid him fifty dollars for each of the two days I hunted his ranch.)

Before leaving for the Sooner State, I felt pretty good about my arrangements. I had five places lined up to hunt in two different counties. The area where I would be hunting allowed a hunter to harvest one gobbler per day, two per county, and a maximum of three per year. Also, the biologists informed me to only buy one turkey tag with my hunting license. Oklahoma hunting regulations allow you to purchase an additional tag after you have already killed a bird. So it looked to me like I had set myself up for a decent chance to get a gobbler, and if things worked out right, possibly two or even three.

Having the entire day Monday to scout for gobblers, I couldn't wait to get started. I left the dingy motel room early in the morning and headed for the public land areas I was planning to hunt. I could spend several hours determining where to access the wildlife management areas and, hopefully, glass for birds from the roads. I would have a tight schedule though, as I had previously made plans to meet both Danny Pierce and Max Montgomery later in the day to scout their respective properties as well. As I was driving to the first WMA that I planned to scout, I saw my first Rio Grande gobbler. The large gobbler was in full strut in the back corner of a private-land wheat field. The mature tom had four hens feeding near him. All the turkeys were approximately three hundred yards from the county road I was traveling and were staying in close proximity to a large tree line as they fed. I pulled the 4-Runner off the road and retrieved my 35mm camera from the back seat. I took several pictures of the strutting bird with a 400mm zoom lens, using the hood of my SUV as a rest to steady the camera. During the course of my trip to the Sooner State, this would be the only group of turkeys that would not run from my vehicle when I pulled off the road to watch or photograph them. (These birds were so far away that they must have felt safe.) After shooting several frames of film, I pulled out my cell phone and called my brother, Kevin, at work back home in Virginia. He was out of the office, so I left him a message informing him that I was on the side of the road watching the first Rio Grande gobbler I had ever seen strutting with his hens. Little did I know that before the week was over it would be a sight that I would see numerous times. It would be a sight that would spell trouble for a hunter from Virginia trying to kill a mature gobbler.

As I continued on my way to scout the public WMAs, I passed an Oklahoma Division of Wildlife (ODW) truck headed in the opposite direction. I figured there was a good chance that it was the biologist, Scott Parry, who I had been speaking with by phone during the months leading up to my trip out west. So I turned the SUV around and headed back in the direction the ODW truck was traveling. I found the truck parked along the side of the road at the entrance to one of the WMAs I was planning to hunt. I parked my vehicle next to the truck and made my way to the driver's side door. I introduced myself and asked the uniformed gentleman occupying the driver's seat if he would happen to be Scott Parry.

"No, I'm just an assistant," the man replied warmly. "Scott is my boss," he continued. "I'll get him on the radio. He's supposed to be meeting me here in a few minutes."

I told the gentleman, whose name was Lewis, that I would stick around and wait to meet Scott. As we waited, we began to talk about spring turkey hunting. In just a few minutes, we were engrossed in an excited discussion. He told me that he loved to hunt turkeys but wasn't very good at calling them. I spent a few minutes encouraging him that calling was very overrated in turkey hunting. I gave him some sound advice about turkey calling that I have offered in the past to others who felt like their calling ability was inadequate. I had seen my advice put a longbeard over the shoulder of a novice caller in previous years, and knew it was effective. I basically just encouraged him not to put too much emphasis on calling, but to rely on the more important skills of woodsmanship and scouting. I told him to become comfortable with one call that he could yelp and cluck with and to use the call sparingly – giving the gobbler whatever sound he would gobble at – nothing more. A hunter who does this, while remaining patient and still, has as good a chance as anyone for busting a nice gobbler, even if they aren't confident in their calling ability.

Via the truck's radio, Scott called back to inform us that he had been detained by some out-of-state campers and was going to be a while before meeting us. I couldn't afford to wait any longer, so I politely excused myself to depart for a meeting with Danny Pierce. Before leaving, I pulled a Gideon New Testament and Gospel tract from my truck and offered it to Lewis. He looked at the Bible, as I explained that it was the best thing that I had ever been given. Lewis lifted his eyes from the small New Testament to look directly at me, as he smiled and grabbed my right hand, shaking it.

"Brother," he said, "I really appreciate this, but I already have one. I'm a Christian, too. Give this one to someone else who needs it."

I accepted his return of the Book, and we began to talk about spiritual things. As we concluded our conversation, before I could get back into my 4-Runner, Lewis beckoned me back to his state truck. He pulled his map of the WMAs he was responsible for from the dash of his pickup. Lewis then proceeded to take a pen and personally mark the map for me. He marked every area where he had observed turkeys roosting and strutting. He even went so far as to put distances and directions to places I could park to access the birds. I was floored by his act of kindness, and extremely grateful. In a spiritually dark world where a born-again Christian typically expects to be put down for his witnessing, it is a blessing when it is received with appreciation. Who could have guessed that witnessing to a man beside the road would lead to more beneficial turkey hunting information than a week of scouting could secure?

I was to meet Danny Pierce at a small cafe in Reydon, Oklahoma at 11:00 a.m. for lunch. Danny would then take me to his cousin's farm and show me a few different access points. I was hoping to see some gobblers at the farm as well – to give me an idea where to hunt the next morning. I arrived at the little gas station / store / café precisely at 11:00 a.m. I should mention here that Oklahoma has a lot of good points in my humble opinion. All of the people that I met in person while hunting there and every person that I spoke to by phone while planning my trip were exceptionally nice and gracious, but other things make Oklahoma special too. One such example of the things that make Oklahoma a unique and special place met my eyes at the small restaurant. The door to the greasy-spoon café had a printed flyer attached to it at eye level.

The flyer read, "ATTENTION: Team Roping Championships to be held Saturday ..." and then went on to detail location and entry times.

Man, you gotta like that! The whole area was nothing but cowboys, cattle, and pickup trucks. We were in the Cheyenne area for two days before we passed a car on the road. I mean it was all trucks – pickups and eighteen-wheelers.

When I finally did see a car it was at night returning from Elk City, and I yelled, "Car!" to Lisa.

Several miles later we saw a second one, and I repeated my previous blurtation. I then made mention to my wife that it was ironic that the two cars we had seen were both at night.

To which she replied, "They're scared."

I laughed and agreed. They are just ashamed to drive them in the daylight, I reckon.

Anyway, back to the café. When I told her I was looking for Danny Pierce, a young waitress directed me to a large, round table in the corner. Three men in camouflage were seated at the table enjoying their lunch. I introduced myself and met Danny, one of his guides named Mike, and one of his clients from a Texas turkey hunt. I ate lunch with them and pretty much kept silent. The Texas client was one of those independently wealthy types who flew around the world with nothing better to do but hunt and fish. This man had already killed two or three turkeys in Texas during the first three days of the Texas season hunting with Rush Creek. He pretty much talked enough for all of us, with only Danny getting a word in edgewise. During his monologue, he asked Danny if he had ever seen a hen strut.

"Yes, at another hen," Danny replied.

The hunter then informed the group that he thought he had seen a hen with a beard while hunting the day before. When there finally was a break in the solo chatter, I told Danny that my brother and I had shot video of both a "strutting" hen and a bearded hen. Until now Danny was nursing his soft drink with a sort of bored and disinterested look on his face. (Working with the public has to really suck sometimes.) At my comment, however, he sat forward, and I could see his expression change. We discussed turkeys for a minute or two, and Danny was ready to get out of there and take me to my hunting destination so I could scout.

We arrived at Danny's house after a ten-minute drive from Reydon. His home was located in close proximity to Rush Creek, hence the name of his outfitting business. We left my vehicle at Danny's house and took his truck to his cousin's farm about a mile away. We four-wheeled down a rutted-out, red clay road along a cottonwood tree line to reach his cousin's trailer and cattle lot. Almost immediately I saw turkeys feeding along the edge of the cattle lot. We sat parked in Danny's truck glassing the birds from about one hundred and fifty yards away. Six hens were feeding in some silage strewn beside two large round-bale feeders. Fifteen yards off to their right stood an old longbeard pecking the ground. The gobbler was absolutely beautiful in every possible respect. His iridescent feathers looked fake as he moved in the midday sun. He had a long, heavy beard at least ten inches in length and large spurs – spurs so long that I had no trouble seeing them through my eight-power Nikon binoculars at over a hundred yards. The feature that struck me the most, though, was the light-cream color at the tips of the gobbler's tail feathers. The cream color was very striking and beautiful. It was a shade I wasn't expecting, and when I saw it, I knew immediately that I wanted to kill a gobbler with a tail fan just like it. In fact, this gobbler was a perfect specimen of a Rio in every way but one – he was badly injured. The tom we were glassing could barely walk. He had been severely hurt in a battle with another gobbler. I wasn't sure from the look of him if he would be able to fly up to roost in the evening. Injured or not though, this tom still had his share of the local ladies, as his six hens stayed near him. Danny and I also saw a couple of jakes while glassing before Danny decided to show me some other access points to the small farm. I made up my mind right then that I wanted to kill this wounded gobbler. "Gimp" is what I would call him. Gimp was a big, beautiful bird and with his injury, he was a prime candidate for a coyote's main course. Killing him would be good for the both of us, or at least that's how I saw it.

Leaving Gimp and his small harem of hens, Danny drove me over to the National Forest in order to access the backside of his cousin's place. Bouncing down the dirt road, I noticed a coyote in the high grass on the left-hand side of the road.

"Coyote!" I shouted at Danny, who slid the pickup to a stop in the middle of the road. "One hundred yards straight out your window! He's running to the top of the hill!" I blared.

"I doubt if he'll give me a shot" Danny replied, as he grabbed his .22/250 from beside his bucket seat.

"I'll watch him while you load," I told him as I followed the varmint with my binoculars.

Danny had a box of shells on the dash of his truck, which he accessed, and fed, into the chamber of his rifle. When I saw him get the barrel of the gun out the window, I directed him to the dog.

"Big cottonwood at the top of the hill…He's twenty yards below it standing in the grass broadside," I said.

Two seconds later I heard Danny say, "I got him," as he pushed the safety off his gun.

When I heard that safety go off, my fingers immediately let go of my binos and went directly into my ears. (I am from West Virginia ya' know, and let's just say I know a little somethin' about hearing loss due to muzzle blast in the cab of a pickup truck!) KABOOM! Danny's shot was true at one hundred and fifty yards as verified by both the "thuwhump" of the bullet striking its target and the ringing of the coyote's tail straight up in the air.

"That's one less we have to worry about," Danny said as he retracted his rifle back into the truck.

Now this is the first time in my life that I have ever been anywhere with a hunting guide, and after a grand total of fifteen minutes in the field together, I had "guided" him to a coyote kill! I don't know who was more impressed – him or me – but it was probably me. Truthfully though, I don't think I was like most people Danny encountered in his profession. I won't bore you with all of our conversations or other details, but suffice it to say, after making my acquaintance, Danny was sold on some of my gear and tactics. He did laugh at me though when he saw me in my knee-high rubber boots when we went scouting.

"You guys from the East," he said, "and your rubber boots! We get so little rain out here, we can hunt in tennis shoes it is so dry," he concluded.

For that comment, I give full credit to Danny for the rain which set in and continued for the next four days of my Oklahoma hunt – more on that later!

Danny wanted me to be at his house the next morning at 5:30. He volunteered to drive me to his cousin's farm and help me decide where to set up since he didn't have any clients hunting in Texas with him on that day. It sounded like a good idea to me, as I left Danny's house and headed for the area around Durham, Oklahoma.

I was to meet Max Montgomery at his barn in the early afternoon, and I needed to step on it. I found Max's place with very little trouble thanks to the driving directions he had provided me with. I wish now I had taken a picture of his ranch overlooking the Canadian river on the Texas border in Northwest Oklahoma. His place was awesome. He had three large barns. The main barn, if I can call it that, was much larger than the other two. There was a billboard-sized sign at the entrance that read "Trespassers Will Be Shot"! After you got to the barn and looked back at the billboard, it also had a message on the back, "Survivors Will Be Shot Again"! I liked this guy already! There were four large, four-wheel drive pickups parked in front of the barn. All of them had OU license plates on the front (that's OU as in Oklahoma University). There was a large stainless-steel flagpole in front of the barn as well. The pole had a white, four-foot by six-foot OU flag flying at the top of it. These guys were serious about their Sooners. To complete the picture of Max's barn scene insert four John Deere tractors, you know, the hundred-horsepower-and-up types with dual wheels on the back. Throw in a handful of German Shorthair bird dogs by the door on the porch, and you've got a pretty good idea of the place. My repeated knockings at his door went unanswered, so I walked down to the other barns.

Shortly, I heard someone yell, "Hey, Brad!"

Max was standing on the back porch of his big barn waving at me. I walked back up to the barn, and he invited me in the front door. You might be getting the idea that this wasn't your everyday kind of barn. You are getting the right idea. It was unreal. As I entered, the first thing I saw was a large-screen TV hanging from the right side of the barn rafters. The barn had its own Direct TV satellite and the news was currently airing. The second thing I saw was the antler chandeliers hanging from the ceiling. I'm going to stop right here, otherwise I'll never get around to writing about turkey hunting. Max shook my hand and took me into the back of the barn where he and three of his friends were eating barbecued ribs and drinking longneck beers for lunch. The back of the barn had a full size kitchen in it with a tiled bar and barstools made from tractor discs and tractor seats. It was bad (I mean that in a good way)! Two of Max's friends were ranchers and the other gentleman having lunch was the local veterinarian. They were discussing cattle – go figure. I heard the one cattleman say he was going to Texas to get a new cattle chute because he had worn his old one out. He said that it had been a good one, because he had run at least 30,000 head through the thing. These guys were serious about cattle, too.

Eventually, Max and one of his buds got around to taking me out to see the property I could hunt.

Max first explained that the area around his barns was loaded with turkeys every morning, "But," he said, "You don't want to kill one of them, because that would be too easy."

While Max may have had extensive knowledge with regard to cattle, it appeared that he didn't know squat about hunting spring gobblers with a shotgun. When it comes to the latter, I have this general rule that easier is better. So instead of scouting anywhere near the areas that gobblers frequented on a daily basis near his barns, Max took me on a long drive that eventually led to a gate, which we entered. Shortly past the gate, Max stopped his truck, and he and his buddy got out. I followed suit behind them. Max pointed to the desolate looking Canadian River bottom below.

"Down there," he said, "is where you need to go if you want a real challenge at killing a wild turkey."

He then turned to me and asked if I had any bug spray.

"At the motel, but not with me in the truck," I said.

To which he replied, "Well good luck, these bugs are eating me up, and I'm getting out of here."

At which point he and his pal got back in their truck and headed back to the ranch, leaving me standing there wondering how early they had started drinking.

I proceeded to scout the river bottom all by my lonesome, and I have to say, turkey sign was scarce. As I left Max's ranch to head back to Cheyenne, I saw him working in a field, and I pulled off the road. I climbed the barbed-wire fence and made my way to where he was working. I asked Max if the river bottom was the only area I was permitted to hunt.

He replied, "No, but if you want a real challenge, that is where you need to hunt."

I just shrugged my shoulders and said, "OK."

Despite the lack of turkey sign along the river at Max's place, I was pretty upbeat about my chances for having a successful hunt, as I perused the day's events while driving back to Cheyenne. I was hoping Lisa had enjoyed herself during the day, and I was looking forward to spending the evening with her. I was planning to drive back to Elk City and find a nice restaurant where we could eat dinner.

However, when I finally arrived back at the motel around 5:00 p.m., I was totally unprepared for what I saw. There was no place for me to park! The deserted ghost town of a motel was now a buzzing hive of activity. Four-wheel drive trucks and SUVs from all over the country were in the parking lot. I counted license plates from at least fourteen different states. Some had trailers loaded with four-wheelers, one had a camouflage boat trailered behind it, one was completely camouflaged in Mossy Oak, and a couple bore the graphics of professional hunters and outdoor TV shows. People were scurrying about, in and out of their rooms. Some of the folks were unloading their luggage and gear, while others were standing outside their rooms in huddles of three and four talking. They were all men, and every single one of them was wearing camouflage. You could have knocked me over with a feather. There had to be well over a hundred people now staying at this dive. What happened while I was gone? That dude from North Carolina was right. I, too, was glad I had a reservation now!

As I entered the motel room, I asked Lisa if she had seen all the people and vehicles. She gave me one of those looks that I'm not quite sure how to describe and asked me how I thought she could have missed them. Lisa told me that there had been noise outside the room all day, starting shortly after I had left. I asked her how it felt to be the only woman at the motel. That was a bad question. It is probably the reason that she has elected not to join me on my trip to try and harvest a Merriam's turkey in 2005.

Something else strange happened after I returned from scouting. It began to rain. According to the locals, rain was something they got very little of, hence all the windmills and water tanks. All they needed was Brad Day to drive twenty-one hours to hunt there and "whah lah"…Rain! After dinner in Elk City, we stopped at a store and purchased a can of Scotch Gard. Back at the motel, I readied all my gear for the next morning's hunt. A portion of that readying included me setting up my Double Bull hunting blind in the motel room. (This blind is large, about the size of a big tent and has four sides and a roof.) The blind took up about half the room space, but I wanted to spray it with the Scotch Gard to waterproof it. The smell of the Scotch Gard was so stifling, that within five minutes of treating the blind with it, I had to open the motel door to get some fresh air. Lisa was thrilled. There she is lying on the bed trying to read a book, and the door is open, the rain is pouring outside, and hunters are continually walking past our room and pausing to look in and check out the idiot with a blind set up in the middle of his room! This story just keeps getting better, huh?

I was awake the next morning before the alarm sounded. I opened our motel door to check on the weather. As I feared, it was still raining. After morning devotions and making coffee, I loaded my hunting gear, including the Double Bull blind, into the Toyota. I figured if it was going to rain all day, the blind would offer me protection from both the precipitation and the wary eyes of approaching turkeys. I had purchased this blind mainly for the purpose of taking children hunting with me. I had used the blind previously to take my nephew and niece hunting, and it was instrumental in videotaping my seven-year-old nephew Caleb's hunt for his first squirrel. However, I had never hunted from the blind myself. This particular blind is probably the best that money can buy and has a hefty $350 price tag to prove it. One of the great advantages to this type of blind is that wild turkeys, for some reason, do not pay any attention to it. The blind could be stationed at the edge of a field without spooking the birds that were feeding in the pasture. On this rainy, Tuesday morning in Oklahoma, I was about to use the blind for turkey hunting, and I was going to find out just how effective it could be.

As I drove to Danny Pierce's house as previously arranged, I learned something about the roads in rural Oklahoma. During the normally hot and dry conditions that persist in the area, the secondary roads, which are made up of a combination of red sand and clay, are hard-packed and dusty. When it rains, however, they turn into something much more nasty. The normally decent roadways turn into a mess of red mud ranging from three to six inches deep.

I had to put my 4-Runner, which is equipped with oversized, all-terrain, off-road tires, into four-wheel drive just to travel the county road. I would later discover that the sloppy, red clay/sand mixture, which covered the outside of my vehicle, would once again become as hard as concrete after it had dried. Despite the slow going of four-wheeling for several miles to reach Danny's house, I arrived there fifteen minutes early at 5:15 a.m.

As I loaded my blind and gear into Danny's truck, he questioned me about the blind. He told me that his son had a few old blinds built around the perimeter of his cousin's farm, and I was welcome to use one of them. I thanked him, but declined his invitation, pointing out the advantages I hoped to gain from using the Double Bull. Danny drove me to his cousin's farm and walked with me to the area where I was going to set up. A strip of cottonwood trees about sixty yards wide lined a small creek bed and separated the farm I was hunting from the National Forest grasslands. An old, cottonwood tree was located inside the pasture field along the fence line. It had some low hanging branches and I figured I could set my blind up under them. This set-up would put me in the field that the turkeys were using. Danny told me that the location looked good to him too, as he pointed out where he thought the turkeys would be roosting. He indicated their preferable roosting area would be behind me, to my left, in the sixty-yard wide stand of cottonwoods. The area of the field I would be hunting was within one hundred and fifty yards of the cattle lot where I had seen the injured gobbler, Gimp, the day before. Danny wished me luck and headed back to his truck, as I pulled the blind from its carry-bag and set up.

I placed two hen decoys and a jake decoy fifteen yards from the blind, out in the field where they would be visible to any turkey that entered it. The rain began to slack up as dawn was breaking. I commenced calling with some soft, tree yelps on a mouth call and debated whether I should do a flydown cackle. I had a hard time getting used to calling from inside the blind. Something about it just seemed weird to a turkey hunter who was used to calling with his back against a tree. I elected to skip the cackle and continued doing some very soft yelping. It had just barely started getting light when movement to the left of the blind caught my eye. Even though I hadn't heard a gobble, I could see the dark silhouette of a turkey emerging from the cottonwoods and entering the field about a hundred yards from my position. I immediately did some clucking and plain yelping with my mouth call and then reached for my shotgun. I figured I would get it pointed out the blind and use the 4X scope to get a better look at the bird. As I looked out the small window of the blind to make sure it was safe to ease the barrel of the shotgun out, I began to panic.

The lone turkey I had seen emerge had been joined by four others; that wasn't so bad, but the fact that all five of them were running as fast as they could straight at my blind was. I literally freaked out. I shoved my gun barrel out of the blind and unsuccessfully swung it all over the place trying to find the birds in the scope. Eventually, I got the gun trained on them when they were almost within gun range. They were all hens. They ran all the way to me in single file. The hens looked like roadrunners, they were coming so fast, and they had come from the exact spot where Danny had said they would be roosting. The five hens joined my decoys and began feeding in the field and calling to one another. They were only thirty yards from the blind and didn't pay any attention to it. I had it made! I didn't even have to call! I was pumped, because I knew that the old gobbler was about to emerge any minute and strut right down to them. I hoped it would be "Gimp." This Rio hunt was going to be over before the sun was up, or so I thought.

After a few minutes another turkey finally emerged from the wooded area the hens had come from, and this time it was a gobbler. He ran all the way to the blind just like the hens. I had the gun on him when he was a mere ten yards from me, but I wouldn't shoot him. He was a jake…a jake with a double beard. I have never killed a turkey with more than one beard, and the thought to shoot did enter my mind, but I dismissed it immediately. He just stood there looking at the hens, with both of his four-inch beards sticking straight out from his breast. Man, he would be a beautiful trophy in another year or two.

Ten minutes passed before I saw a mature gobbler enter the field at 7:40 a.m. Only he didn't enter like the other turkeys I had seen. This big tom entered under a barbed-wire fence near the two large, round-bale feeders where I had observed "Gimp" and his hens the previous afternoon. The problem with that? He was located a hundred and fifty yards from me. The gobbler had about eight hens with him, which also crossed under the fence to enter the field and feed. Of course I began calling to him, but it was a total waste of time. My calling had no noticeable affect on him, his hens, or the harem of hens I had around my blind. None of them paid any attention to me. Before long I could see the tail fan of another mature gobbler coming to the fence from behind the tom that was strutting in the field. This gobbler also had seven or eight hens with him. As soon as he crossed under the lowest strand of barbed-wire, both he and the other strutting gobbler "slicked-up" and ran straight at each other. I was watching them through my scope at one hundred and fifty yards and was ready to see them rumble. As soon as they were face to face, they jumped up and started to fight. This brawl lasted for all of about two seconds. Then they both just stopped and began strutting.

"What is up with that?" I thought.

The two goofs just stood there side-by-side strutting like two twins. All the hens were in the field together feeding. I didn't know what to think. I didn't have long to ponder it either, because shortly thereafter, I could see another full tail fan coming through the brush on a dune above the field behind the twin strutters. (I'm tellin' ya at the end of the week I was seeing full tail fans in my sleep. Oh wait – no, I do that all the time anyway!)

This third tom had a slew of hens stringing along with him. (Slew is the bio-techno-logically correct term for too many to count!) My best guess is that he had somewhere close to twenty lady friends. It was unreal. Talk about who's on first? There were turkeys everywhere…one hundred and fifty yards from me. There were still only six hanging out at the Double Bull.

The third gobbler hung back as his hens began to enter the field to join the others. It appeared that he was strutting in circles around one of the round-bale feeders. He kept this up for at least fifteen minutes before he finally decided to join the birds across the fence. All was well until he crossed that fence. The instant he stepped foot in that field the two twinseys went after him. It was something to see. It kinda' reminded me of the "Three Stooges." The three gobblers were up there running around in circles, and the hens weren't paying any attention to them. You know, "BOYS!" they must have been thinking. I figured I should at least call or something, so I started cutting on the mouth call like some kind of nut. As soon as I started that aggressive cutting, the gobbler that was being double-teamed turned and started running straight to me. Even more bizarre, the two gobblers chasing him fell in single-file behind him. All three were bearing down on me…fast! I panicked all over again. I was trying to get my shotgun barrel out the blind's window and get the birds in the scope. It's one of those "You had to be there" kind of things. I was in shock and awe. As the gobblers hurriedly closed the distance, I was thinking to myself that if I killed one of these longbeards, no one, and I repeat no one, would believe this story – including me! Everyone knows that it is impossible to call three, mature gobblers away from some thirty hens, and each other, to a blind located over a hundred yards away!

When the toms were about fifty-five yards away from the blind, the two gobblers in the rear finally caught up with the lead bird. The big tom in front made a sharp turn to his right and then turned back towards his harem, and his pursuers immediately followed suit. I cut to the gobblers as soon as they turned. The two stooges stopped instantly and went back into strut. These two "twin" gobblers just stood there strutting side-by-side again at fifty yards, while the other made his way back safely to his hens. Fifty yards was as close as I would get to these birds as they slowly strutted their way back across the field to their lady friends. The third gobbler crossed the fence out of the pasture and was content to strut on the brushy dune above that side of the field. All of his hens joined him on the dune and only a handful remained in the field with the two "Bullies." I watched these birds for three straight hours until they all eventually left the pasture at the opposite end. What a morning!

All the hens and the jake that had been keeping me company eventually left the field as well, drifting into the wooded creek bottom behind me. I was actually glad that I could take a break from the intense pressure of trying to keep an eye on so many birds at one time. My relaxing break was short lived. First a single hen came out of the creek bottom and began feeding just outside my blind. Then at the bottom corner of the field to my right, I could see a full tail fan coming through the brush. This big gobbler entered the field with about fifteen hens and one large jake in tow. I couldn't tell if he was a new bird or one of the three from earlier. This big, beautiful Rio Grande tom strutted right out to the middle of the pasture ninety-six yards from my blind (trust me on this – I used a laser range finder to check the distance). From my vantage point the hens were just to the left of the gobbler, and the jake was on his right. The big gobbler was strutting, the hens were feeding and preening, and the jake was feeling it. The year-old gobbler kept raising his feathers to display but then would chicken out and go all slick. I could just barely hear the mature gobbler spitting and drumming, as he turned in slow circles, like a ballerina in a little girl's wind-up jewelry box. After several minutes of the gobbler's pirouetting in the middle of the field, one of his hens split from the group of female birds. She made a beeline to the gobbler and approached his left side. What took place at this point surprised me.

The hen, which had approached the longbeard, began to run in a clockwise circle around him. Keeping the hen about twelve inches away from his left wing, the strutting gobbler spun clockwise with the hen. It was an amazing thing to watch, and something I had never witnessed before. I figured this breeding ritual would last about a turn or two, but I was way wrong (a familiar position for me to be in with turkeys). These two, crazy birds continued to do this spin-a-rama for about twenty revolutions! (I started counting how many times they completed a full circle, but when I got to fifteen, I quit counting.) I got dizzy just watching them. For some reason known only to the hen, she finally quit doing laps around her "main man" and proceeded to lie down on the ground, directly in front of him. The gobbler followed her move by strutting over to where she lay, facing away from him. Just as he attempted to step on her back, the hen jumped up and ran away to rejoin the group of female birds.

"You gotta be kidding me!" I thought, "That just ain't right!"

For the first time in my turkey-hunting career I decided to name a hen. I'll let you use your imagination to determine what I decided to call her! I was totally bummed at not being able to witness the gobbler breed the hen. However, I must admit my frustration with the hen's antics ranked nowhere near the gobbler's frustration with the same. He was so worked-up that he just...er'...um'...relieved himself...on the ground. His wings just shivered as his whole body shook. He then composed himself and resumed strutting. In just a matter of minutes, a second hen approached the tom. (This was a different hen than #$@&#*%, who had approached the gobbler originally.) When this second hen reached the gobbler's side, an instant replay of the spin-a-rama turkey-dance occurred. This new twosome did the exact same thing, spinning in a clockwise rotation for twenty-plus revolutions. The female bird then lay down in front of the gobbler and as soon as he reached her back – up she jumped! She was gone! This may be the first time that I ever felt sorry for a mature, longbearded gobbler. He dealt with the frustration that this hen inflicted upon him in the exact same way he did with the first nasty girl. He relieved himself on the ground. By now the jake that was observing all this had become so excited that he relieved himself on the ground too. This was fast turning into an X-rated turkey hunt. Of course, during all this, I had tried in vain to sound like the hottest, sexiest hen in the Midwest, but it was useless. My calling had little to no effect on the circus taking place in the middle of the pasture. I typically never hunt turkeys in the fall when hens can be legally harvested. However, after this particular morning's events near Reydon, Oklahoma, I began to reconsider the option of fall hunting for hens!

The gobbler and his hens eventually left the field, re-entering the brushy area they had come from. One, lone hen remained in the field and she was less than twenty yards from my blind. I began calling to her just to pass time more than anything else. She was a very vocal hen, and we yelped back and forth to each other for about ten minutes. Growing weary of the game, I fell silent as she continued yelping. After five minutes with no response from me, she eased out of the field and into the cottonwoods behind me. I was glad she was gone. I looked at my watch: it was 1:00 p.m. I had been sitting in my Double Bull blind for seven and a half hours! Even more amazing, I had been watching turkeys for nearly the entire time! I decided to get out of the blind to use the restroom and pack it in for lunch back at the motel with Lisa.

Normally on these trips with my wife, I only hunt in the morning. At noon I return to our motel, and we spend the afternoon doing something she enjoys. Considering the fact that Oklahoma permitted all day turkey hunting and the motel accommodations we were enjoying were less than favorable, Lisa and I had agreed that I should hunt all day for at least the first day. We hoped I would be fortunate and get my Rio early in the week, so we could move to more favorable accommodations in a larger town. With the first morning yielding no gobbler over my shoulder, I was mentally exhausted and was looking forward to taking a break with Lisa over lunch. As I began to take my blind down though, I had second thoughts. I had been seeing turkeys entering this field all morning from four different directions.

"Maybe I should hang out for just a little while longer," I convinced myself.

I reset the blind and got back in. I wasn't a moment too soon. A hen started calling from the cottonwoods behind me. I figured it was the same one from earlier, but I called to her anyway. We started out yelping and ended up cutting to each other. It didn't take much of this until a timber shaking GARROBBLE thundered from the wooded creek bottom behind my blind. It was a good thing I had just used the restroom! I got turned around in the blind and opened the windows on the blind's back side. I called again, cutting on the mouth call. This time two gobbles thundered back in response. There were two gobblers headed down the creek toward me and the lone hen was just inside the woods. I didn't have to wait long to see them. The lone hen I had been calling to took off running up the creek bottom to unite with the approaching birds. I first began seeing hens making their way toward me, and then I saw the full tail fans of the two strutting toms. I could hear them both spitting and drumming as they advanced. It was perfect, even if they didn't turn and come straight to me, they would pass by the blind in easy shotgun range, no more than thirty-five yards away. The only thing I was worried about was missing the farmer's barbed-wire fence that was between the gobblers and me. When the birds were about sixty yards away, I saw the hens start running away from my position toward the National Forest grasslands. In short order, the two gobblers followed suit and disappeared running straight away from me as well. Two lagging hens ran right past my blind in their haste to vacate the wooded strip. What the heck happened? I was dumbfounded as I pulled my gun back into the blind. I didn't have to wonder long, as I saw a man in camouflage walking along the creek bottom toward me; it was Danny.

"Hey, we're headed into town. Want some lunch?" he asked innocently.

I exited the blind and tried real hard not to say something I shouldn't.

"You just spooked two big gobblers that were coming to me," I said as politely as I could.

"No, I saw those two birds," he replied, "They were hens."

Now I really had to bite my tongue.

"I know the difference between hens and gobblers," I said, "And hens don't strut and gobble!"

I explained to Danny that the gobblers had been gobbling and strutting through the wooded strip approaching me and the two turkeys he had seen were the two hens lagging behind which ran past my blind. Danny was embarrassed and very sorry, and he apologized for his error. He was concerned that I had hunted so long without a break for anything to eat and just wanted to check on me. (See I told you he wasn't used to being around hunters like me.) I told him I would take a rain check on lunch, but that I would be back to hunt the afternoon.

When I arrived at the motel, Lisa was waiting with lunch. She had walked in the rain down to the quick-stop and picked up some sandwiches for us. Due to the inclement weather outside and with no vehicle to drive, my poor wife was stranded in the motel room – a room she wasn't particularly crazy about. The day before when I had scouted, the weather had been beautiful. She had walked to the park and spent some time in the small town, but not on this day though. She had spent the entire morning studying for a professional test she was planning to take. We were both glad to spend some time together and take a break, as I relayed the morning's events to her. I was pretty optimistic about my plans for the afternoon. The rain had let up almost completely, and I had a better feel for how the turkeys were using the pasture field. I was going to hunt without the blind, up near the two round-bale feeders where I had seen the three gobblers strutting at first light. I was at the room for a total of twenty minutes before I headed back to Danny's house.

During the drive back to Reydon, I kept remembering the route the turkeys had taken to access the field after they had flown down. My plan for the afternoon was to position myself so that any turkey returning to the roost from the field along this same route would be in shotgun range. This was a new type of turkey hunting for me, but when in Rome…you know the rest. Unfortunately for me though, turkeys were already in the field when I returned to the farm. This condition ruined my plans for setting up at the round-bale feeders in the small cattle lot. I couldn't take a chance on spooking the birds by letting them see me. So I crawled on my hands and knees through the sand to get to another vantage point that would permit me to get in shotgun range of the birds if they returned to the roost as I expected. I got sand spurs in both my hands and one of my knees as I eased toward a small cedar tree that I hoped would break up my outline. I crawled right up to a jackrabbit that jumped from its hiding spot and then stopped just ten yards away. The large rabbit just sat there looking at me, twitching his nose. I began to wonder how many Indians had crawled through this same terrain and got sand spurs, like I had, trying to get a shot at a wild turkey.

I eventually got to the small cedar without spooking anything. I decided not to put out any decoys for this set-up. I didn't want to risk being seen, as I was now positioned on a sandy dune located above the small cattle lot. This was the same brushy dune where gobbler number three had strutted for most of the morning, after the two bullies ran him out of the pasture. The pasture was now holding about twenty-five turkeys, as best as I could see. The majority of them were nearly two hundred yards from my location. I began to call and nothing gobbled in response. The turkeys were busy with their daily routine and seemed disinterested in anything I had to offer. Eventually though, I noticed two mature gobblers working their way toward me along the fence line that led to the cattle lot. I began to concentrate on them as I called, letting their body language and reactions dictate my calling. At first it seemed like wishful thinking that they would come to my calls, but as the gap between us shrank to seventy yards, I started getting excited. I began to examine both gobblers through my scope to judge which one I should shoot. One had a beautiful, long, thick beard, but his spurs were short, probably a two year old. His associate, on the other hand, had really good spurs, better than an inch in length, but his beard was short, like it had beard rot. It would be a tough decision, which bird to take if given the opportunity. The two gobblers finally reached the fence that sectioned off the cattle lot holding the round-bale feeders. I needed them to cross the fence and advance another fifteen yards to be in range. As I waited for one of them to make the move under the lowest strand of barbed-wire, a large, brown cow approached the gobblers. When the cow had approached to within ten yards of the birds, the bovine bellowed and charged the birds at the same time. I thought I was seeing things as the cow chased the two gobblers for fifty yards down the fence away from me. Even as I type this, I can't believe it. It was so unlike anything I had ever had happen to me on a turkey hunt. So far this day I had gobblers that were coming straight to me run off by: 1) other gobblers, 2) my host, and now 3) a cow. This was starting to suck.

After my unpleasant experience with the cow, I decided to relocate to a small water hole Danny had told me about. The cedar tree set-up was uncomfortable anyway, and the small pond was located fifty yards further along the same dune I was currently on.

Just moving fifty yards can help a hunter feel better when things aren't going his way. It felt like I had a fresh start as I decided how to set up for the rest of the evening. I was now nowhere near where I really wanted to be to intercept a large gobbler heading for the roost, but I was convinced that the best thing I could do was not spook the birds. I could always come back in the morning and try again. At the water hole, I hoped that I would catch a longbeard stopping off for a drink before calling it a day. If that didn't work, I hoped to sound like a lonesome hen that had done the same and wanted some company. Of course there wasn't a decent tree to set up on that offered the view or comfort I wanted. So I settled for neither at the base of a small, twisted cottonwood above the pond but below the top of the dune. I put a single hen decoy at the edge of the small pond and began calling. I called in seven birds during the late afternoon. All of them came in alone and none of them were mature gobblers – three were jakes and four were hens.

Shortly before dark, I heard something running at me from my right. If you can hear something running at you in the sand it has to be either big or close. What I heard was both. As I turned my head to the right, I spooked a hen that was about to run me over. When she "putted" and turned away from me, she was merely a few feet from me. Another hen was running with her, but the second bird wasn't nearly as close. Before I could ask myself what was going on, a small, solid-white calf came barreling through the sand behind the turkeys chasing them. What in the _ _ _ _ was wrong with these Oklahoma cattle? I sat there and just chuckled to myself, because it seemed a better option than crying. Little did I know that my escapades with the cattle were just beginning. As sundown approached, cattle started filtering in to the water hole, as I had hoped the turkeys would do. About fifteen of the heifers had assembled themselves in the pond's vicinity, when I noticed a small calf making its way to the water hole – a small, solid-white calf. It was my buddy from earlier. I watched him make his way to the water and then freeze in position. He froze when he saw my hen decoy at the back edge of the water hole. Instantly, the little bugger took off running straight to the decoy. Unlike the real thing, my hen wasn't intimidated by the calf. Instead of running for her life, my hen just stared defiantly at the juvenile steer. The calf didn't know what to make of this. He tried to bluff the decoy by turning around to walk away, and then he would swap ends and charge the fake bird. Much to his displeasure, the decoy just laughed at him. This upset the little beef so much that he ran off, scared by the rubber demon. This outcome didn't sit well with the rest of the herd. That stubborn turkey might scare off a baby, but let's see how brave she is with a twelve hundred pound cow in her face. That must have been their thinking, because a large, brown cow charged the decoy next. She skidded to a stop in the muddy sand when she reached the statuesque hen, bewildered at the audacity of the feathered creature, which again remained motionless. Big Brown was no match for this bird, as the frightened cow ran in retreat from the decoy. By the way, all of this is absolutely true. I have taken poetic license in the description of the events, but the rest is accurate. I sat there laughing at the stupid cows and was quite pleased with the revenge my decoy was reaping for me. That was until Big Mama decided to take matters into her own hands, or…uh…I mean hooves.

A big black cow with a white face had had just about enough of this belligerent hen, which apparently was hogging the best spot at the water hole. She literally stomped her way down to the water's edge and faced the decoy. The big cow started stomping and bawling at the decoy. Slobber was running from the cow's mouth and nose, and the mucus was hanging and dripping on my hen decoy. I was laughing out loud now, forget turkey hunting. Besides there was no way a gobbler was going to come anywhere near this turkey-hating herd of cattle. I started wondering if, perhaps, it wasn't a cow instead of another longbeard that had injured Gimp! Appalled at the decoy's lack of respect for her intimidation tactics, the big white-faced cow began to head butt my decoy as she bawled at it. After the second head butt, my decoy fell backwards on its stake until its tail stopped it. When the decoy fell, the movement scared the big cow and she retreated about six steps. The decoy was now facing upward at a forty-five-degree angle. Realizing that she had just been humiliated in front of fifteen of her closest friends and family, the big cow returned with a vengeance, bawling and slobbering and stomping at the decoy. My amusement now had worn thin and for fear of having my decoy and stake damaged, I stood to lend a hand to my fearless partner.

I scared the "you-know-what" out of those cows when I stood from the base of the tree completely camouflaged and started down the dune towards them. The dumb things were all worked up and were running everywhere. I wiped the slobbers off my decoy and put it in my vest. It was time to call it a day. What a day it had been. I climbed to the top of the dune and used my binoculars to watch the turkeys leave the field and go to roost. There were still three gobblers strutting in the field. Take a wild guess where they were. Would you believe they were standing in the exact spot where my blind had been sitting for eight hours that morning? Of course you would. There they were strutting under the branches of the lone cottonwood tree in the pasture. Talk about adding insult to injury, I was beginning to dislike these gobblers. It was about time someone gave them a good killin'. They went to roost in the wooded creek bottom where they were supposed to have been that morning. Predictably, nothing went to roost up near the dune, where I had spent the afternoon.

I made the drive back to Cheyenne in the rain, which had started again with a vengeance. I pulled into the parking lot at 8:30 p.m. When I arrived at the motel, I wasn't as tired as I would normally have been after a day of hunting spring gobblers, but then again I wasn't climbing mountains all day either. Heck all I had really done was sit around all day. Even so, I was starving. As I opened the door to our dimly lit accommodations, Lisa was sitting on the bed watching "Star Trek – The Next Generation". Although the hunting had been somewhat frustrating, overall it had been an enjoyable day for me. The day had just been frustrating for Lisa. I had never – and I stress <u>never</u> – seen Lisa watch anything on TV remotely like Star Trek, old or new generation. Sometimes a husband should just observe his wife's behavior and refrain from asking questions. And sometimes I should take my own advice, because when I questioned this anomaly, I was immediately informed, with a stern voice, that the TV only had five channels on it, and that was all there was to watch. Of all the days for there to be a Star Trek marathon on TV, this had to be the day. I was impressed.

Most people take several years to become a "Trekkie," but that wife of mine became one in only a twelve-hour time period – a new world record. To this very day she is hooked on it. (Actually, she hasn't watched it since that day. As a matter of fact, she's so emotionally scarred, that now she won't watch anything involving a spaceship of any kind, not even the Jetsons!)

It was so late that we couldn't drive to a larger town to eat, so we hoped that the small restaurant across the street was open. It didn't appear to have any lights on, but we could see hunters moving around outside the entrance. We were both hungry, and my marriage depended on me finding someplace for us to eat. The rain was pouring down as we entered the small Mom & Pop eatery. Fortunately, they were open due to the influx of hunters. Lisa and I both had a decent meal, as groups of hunters, still clad in camo, entered the restaurant at the late hour.

When we returned to the room, Lisa told me that she couldn't hack it any longer. She asked if we could check out in the morning. I agreed to check out after my morning hunt and thanked her for her patience. She was packed before I got in bed that night. All in all, it wasn't that bad. At least we were warm and dry. The reason the bathroom was falling apart was the shower. There was so much water pressure that it went everywhere, hence the baseboard and trim coming loose. I told Lisa that I didn't think the small hole in the wall at the back of the bath stall was a peep hole, either, and once you got used to the rocking toilet, it was kind of fun. Did I mention she was packed before I got in bed that night?

I have had pressure put on me before to kill a turkey, but nothing like this. My plan for the next morning's hunt was going to be critical. I was musing over two options: set up in the blind in the same spot as the day before, or take an umbrella and hunt from the ground near the cattle lot where Loverboy had strutted around the cattle feeders. Option one had merit, because I saw the birds go to roost in the woods right behind that position. Option two had merit because even though the birds weren't roosting there, I had seen "Gimp" and five other mature birds use that area with their hens during the day and a half I had been in Oklahoma. What to do, what to do? I would sleep on it.

I made up my mind after morning devotions to hunt the cattle lot. The two round-bale feeders within it were empty, but old silage was strewn about their perimeter. I figured the hens feeding there were scratching up some loose grain that remained or were picking up spent grain from the cattle droppings (gross, but true). Either way, they liked feeding in that area, and their gobblers were sure to follow them. Calling gobblers was basically out of the question unless you wanted a jake, which I did not. I also came to the conclusion that the use of a jake decoy was futile at this point in Oklahoma. Jakes seemed to be everywhere, and the gobblers basically ignored them. I planned to use only one hen decoy positioned in the strewn silage. Hopefully, with the decoy and hen calling, I could convince other hens that there was still some food available there in the feedlot. At least that would be my plan.

When it rains hard during turkey season, I refrain from wearing my turkey vest. Once my vest gets wet, it takes forever to dry out. So for several years during heavy rains, I have been using a neat, little backpack made by Will Primos called a "Deke-Seat." This little jewel is nothing more than a camouflage bag sewn to a camo seat cushion. The bag will hold two decoys, my camo umbrella, license, Bible, calls, shells, pruners, gloves, and headnet. I can sit on it, after I take my gear out of the bag, and it doesn't take too long to dry out when it gets soaked. I employed the use of my Deke-Seat before I left my Toyota on the morning of Wednesday, April 7, 2004. I loaded the bag with all my necessary gear, or so I thought, and grabbed my Remington 870. I also slung a small, portable camouflage blind over my shoulder. Danny drove me to his cousin's farm from his house and wished me luck as he dropped me off. It was raining steadily.

There were so few trees in Oklahoma that setting up without a blind was tough. The only cottonwood I could find, that was decent enough to use, was farther away from the area around the cattle feeders than I wanted in order to be able to cover it with my shotgun. Another drawback this lone cottonwood had was some kind of sticker bush was growing at its base, right where I needed to sit. It was the best chance I had though, so I started pruning branches from the bush at its base. Once I had my umbrella and small blind in place, I crossed the five-strand fence and set up my hen decoy. I positioned her to my left – past the area I wanted the turkeys to come to. Decoy in place, I returned to my nest and settled in. It would be another fifteen minutes before dawn began to break, and I used the time to ready myself with clothing and calls. Shortly into my preparations I was shocked to discover that something was missing from my Deke-Seat. I had forgotten my headnet. For all the hundreds of turkey hunts I had been on in my life, I had never forgotten my headnet, until now. Somehow, I had missed it when transferring gear from my vest into my rainy-day pack, and now I would have to hunt without one. I sat there so mad at myself. How could I make such a rookie mistake? – of all times too, as Lisa was really counting on me this morning.

I pulled the hood up on my rain jacket and fastened the beard guard. "That ought to do it," I tried to reassure myself.

My mind raced for an option to use something else as a headnet. The only thing I could think of was the small blind I had set up around the tree. It was made of die-cut Cerex and was camouflage. The blind was actually brand new. I have two others that are veterans of many rainy day hunts, but I had picked this new one up on clearance at a retail store because it was a great buy. I pulled out my pocketknife and cut a swatch of the material from the bottom of the blind. I wedged the camo material between my face and hood. It worked "ok" – it worked "ok" as long as I didn't move my head or try to breathe! It would fall down if I moved, and one of the die-cut flaps would plug my right nostril every time I tried to inhale. But hey this is turkey hunting, it is supposed to be hard.

I began calling at daybreak. I was using an H.S. Strut "Alumistrut" 3.5 reed cutter and a MAD crystal friction call. I started with tree yelps as most early morning hunts require, but I skipped any flydown calls due to the heavy rain. I put the friction call aside and began yelping and clucking loudly on the mouth call. I could hear three different gobblers answering from the roost as the sky lightened, even though the rain was still steadily falling. Two of the gobblers were answering from the lower end of the pasture's woodline. The third bird was gobbling from the wooded creek bottom at my end of the field, where I had seen the birds go to roost. I could also hear two hens calling in the wooded bottom. I didn't let up on the 3.5 reed cutter. When it's raining I like to call loud and often. (Some of my hunting partners would accuse me of that when it's not raining too.) I didn't see the birds fly down, but at 7:30 a.m. I could see what looked like seven hens working the fence line toward me. They were a hundred yards away, and they had a big gobbler in tow. I cranked up on the mouth call again. I refrained from doing any cutting. I kept the calls to plain yelps and clucks. I wanted to sound like a hen that was interested in food and friends, not gobblers. Whether my calling had anything to do with it or not, those hens were heading right for me, and so was the stud bringing up the rear. It took them about ten minutes to reach the barbed-wire fence, which segregated the feedlot from the pasture. I needed those birds to cross the fence and come another ten or fifteen yards for a comfortable shot. There was a small dip at the edge of the field before the birds reached the fence, and as they entered the dip I lost sight of them. I had my gun pointed right where they disappeared, and I quit calling except for some contented purrs, like those of a feeding hen.

When the birds reappeared, the big gobbler was no longer at the back of the pack. Two hens crossed under the fence into the feedlot. The next bird up was the tom. Instead of crossing though, he just stood there, head up, looking around. The two hens got nervous and started back toward the tom, but fortunately, he crossed under the fence and pushed the two females back into the lot. The three of them eased their way toward the hay feeders with the gobbler at the rear. I eased my shotgun's safety off. I wanted him to come another five yards at least, and hopefully ten. All three birds stopped and looked uneasy. The rest of the hens, all five of them, were standing at the fence and wouldn't cross it. The two at the round-bale feeders got nervous again and turned around to leave, walking back to the gobbler. The gobbler followed their lead and turned to go as well. The shot being presented was farther than I really wanted, but I was going to take it. I made certain none of the barbed-wire fence strands were in the path of my intended shot. I put the crosshairs on his neck and hesitated as a hen walked quickly past him through my scope. With the hen clear, I squeezed the trigger. Turkeys went everywhere at the sound of the muzzle blast – all but one. He lay in the cattle lot beating the ground with his wings. I did it! I bellowed out a "BULLLLYAHHHH!" and a loud owl hoot before crossing the fence to see my gobbler. He was gorgeous. I knelt in prayer thanking the Lord Jesus and God my Father for His special blessing bestowed upon me. I know this is wrong, but I have to say that of all the places and situations I have prayed in, I really enjoy doing it with the sound of a flapping gobbler by my side.

When all is said and done, a turkey is a turkey. However, I wish I could convey to you the euphoria that comes from harvesting a mature spring gobbler that you have driven twenty-one hours to hunt. It is a very special feeling to actually kneel down beside the bird, and put your hands on your first Rio Grande gobbler. In many ways he is physically no different than any other turkey I have taken. Yet, he is different and I know it. After months of research, phone conversations, and planning, followed by a long trip and scouting, it is extremely satisfying to accomplish the goal. It is especially satisfying when you know the little woman back at the motel is counting on you to get it done as well. But it is even more rewarding when the gobbler you put your hands on is a real trophy. This was such a bird. He had the light-cream tips on all of his primary and secondary tail feathers, the feature that struck me as the most desirable in all the different color phases a Rio might possess. He was a mature gobbler, four years old, with 1-1/8 inch spurs. He had a broad, heavy beard, 10-1/4 inches in length. The beard was so wide; it looked like two beards, as it had a split down the center. The gobbler weighed nineteen and one-half pounds. The big tom's incessant strutting had worn his primary wing tips flat and the white barring in them was stained red from the clay, for about the first four inches of the feather. I had never seen feathers stained from a gobbler dragging them before. He also had the absolutely prettiest head of any gobbler I have ever seen. (Be sure to pay attention to it in the photos at the end of this story.) A taxidermist had told me that, in his opinion, the Rio was the most beautiful of all the wild turkey subspecies. I had doubted his opinion, until my trip to Oklahoma. The Rios I had watched had the most iridescent feathers of any I have ever seen. Even in the rain, they would turn from black, to purple, to blue, and then to green as the turkey moved though the pasture, or strutted for his hens. I had now killed such a bird; it was 7:40 a.m.

I gathered all my gear and stowed it in the Deke-Seat, before returning to the bird to read my Bible and tag him. I used my laser range finder to determine the distance of my shot; it had been forty-two yards. This was my second gobbler using Remington's new Hevishot shotgun shells, but it was my first at long distance. The load of number six shot had done its job. All the patterning and tweaking of my turkey gun had just paid off – in spades, as they say. As I slung the large, wet turkey over my shoulder, it occurred to me that both my Osceola, and now my Rio, had been killed in the rain. Killing mature gobblers is always a challenge, period. Introduce hens and the task becomes even greater. Add rain to the mix, and you've got a recipe for about as tough a turkey hunt as one could ask for. On both of my first two legs for a Grand Slam, all I had planned for was a mature gobbler. Both hunts, however, ended up with hens and rain in the mix, factors that I had no control over. If I was to successfully complete a slam, it appeared that I was destined to do it the hard way.

I had a picture taken with Danny Pierce at his house before returning to Cheyenne to check in my gobbler and check out of the motel. Before leaving Danny's place, I gave him and one of his guides, who happened to be deaf, New Testaments to take hunting with them. Danny also had me set up my Double Bull blind for him. He couldn't believe that it only took me ten seconds to do so.

He informed me that he was going to order one from Cabela's that day. As I began the rainy drive back to our motel, I couldn't wait to see Lisa. I checked my turkey at the quick-stop in Cheyenne, before arriving at the motel.

When I opened the door to our room, Lisa said, "You had better have killed one!"

It was quite possibly the most romantic thing she has ever said to me. She needs to work on her delivery, though; it sounded somewhat harsh! No answer on my part was necessary; Lisa already knew I had busted one. It was only 9:00 a.m., and I never quit early. For the first time in my life, Lisa was happier than I was about me killing a gobbler. She already had a hotel in Elk City picked out to spend the rest of the week at, and she had all of our stuff packed and stacked by the door. Before loading the truck with all our gear and luggage, I got her hair dryer out and started drying the turkey off in the room. (Those who have read the story of my Florida gobbler will recognize this as Déjà vu. Although the Oklahoma bird wasn't infested with ticks.) The neat thing here was that nobody would notice if I got feathers, sand, mud, and straw all over the room. The aroma was noticeable, but that was a good thing. Dang, I'm starting to get hooked on it! Once dried, the bird looked spectacular. Before we even arrived in Oklahoma, Lisa had been trying to convince me to have the gobbler mounted, if I killed one. I really didn't want to, until now. She would get no further argument from me. I told her we would take pictures of him after we checked out.

With everything all packed up, I drove the truck over to the motel office so we could check out. Three hours had passed since I had experienced one of the greatest thrills of my life. Lisa was now on the verge of experiencing one of hers, as I let her return the key to Room 121 and sever our relationship with the Washita Motel. While she went to the office, I walked across the parking lot to converse with an elderly gentleman from Missouri. He was in the process of cleaning a wild turkey on the tailgate of his truck. I laughed as I walked toward the man, because there were turkey feathers blowing across the parking lot – everywhere! The feathers weren't from the two-year-old gobbler being cleaned by the gentleman from Missouri. They were from other hunters' birds that had been harvested and, I suppose, cleaned previously. After an enjoyable, but short, conversation with the Show-Me-State hunter, I saw Lisa returning to the 4-Runner. When I met her at the vehicle, I pointed out the turkey-feather storm blowing around the parking lot.

"That is so cool!" I said. "You know this place wasn't really all that bad, now was it?"

Lisa rolled her eyes at me and said, "Start driving!"

We took numerous pictures of the gobbler before heading to Elk City. Once there, we checked in to a Ramada Inn. It was sort of like entering into an alternate universe. Our room was immaculate and well lit, the TV had cable with thirty channels, and the toilet was securely fastened to the floor. The hotel also had an indoor swimming pool, a restaurant, and a hot tub. Lisa was happy, I was happy, and the maid was nervous – the maid who saw me, wearing knee-high boots covered in red mud, unpack the 4-Runner and carry a dead turkey into the room. As I continued unpacking the Toyota, I was the one becoming nervous. Back in Cheyenne, I was the "Bomb." Dressed to the nines in Mossy Oak camo and Rocky snake boots, while driving around in a 4X4 covered with red clay from bumper to bumper, I was the envy of the town. In Elk City, however, I began to doubt my fashion sense. The maids called an emergency Union meeting. Whole families would stop what they were doing and stare when they saw me.

"What?" I thought to myself, "Did I forget to shave?"

Although Lisa was much more comfortable in Elk City, I was more comfortable in Cheyenne.

We had a good time in Oklahoma. Lisa and I went to the Black Kettle Museum, drove to Amarillo, Texas to shop for boots and eat a steak, visited the Battle of the Washita historic site, shopped at an authentic Native American (I mean Indian) store (twice), relaxed in the hotel's hot tub, and went out to eat every night. We got to hear George Strait on the radio while in Amarillo, Texas and Toby Keith on the radio while in Oklahoma. We also marked Wal-Marts both in Texas and Oklahoma off of our national to-do list. From an outdoorsman's perspective, I saw my first pronghorn antelope, my first jackrabbit, and my first prairie dog while in Oklahoma. I also saw whitetail deer, a coyote, a bobcat, bison, quail, ducks, skunks, armadillos, and, of course, Rio Grande turkeys. I killed two, Rio Grande gobblers during our stay.

It took me nearly two hours to make the drive from Elk City to Max's ranch outside of Durham. I had to be on the road by 4:00 a.m. to get there in time to hunt at first light. On Thursday morning, I parked my truck under the same cottonwood tree where Max had parked his truck to show me the river bottom where "the really challenging turkeys would be." It was still dark as I unloaded my gear from the back of the Toyota. Once I had everything I needed, I closed the rear door of the 4-Runner. A turkey shock gobbled at the sound of the slamming door. The turkey was close, really close – he was roosted above the truck – in the tree I had parked under!

If I were you, I would quit reading this story right here, and say something like, "He's full of ____!"

If you have decided to read on, believe me, there is no way you are experiencing, even remotely, the amount of disbelief about this that I was when it happened. I literally did not know what to do. I just stood there, half in disbelief, half in frustration. I was laughing to myself to keep from crying. These kinds of things only happen to me I thought. I couldn't set up on the bird where I was, because I would have to shoot my truck to shoot the turkey. I thought about getting in the vehicle and driving back down the road to get it out of the way, but I was afraid the bird would spook, as it was starting to get light. An immoral, unethical murderer would have just shot him off the roost, but fortunately the gobbler didn't have to worry about that being one of my ideas. I decided, if you can believe this, to leave him alone and head off to the river bottom. (That's where all the really challenging birds were anyway, right?) I just hoped he didn't poop on my truck while I was gone. As I walked away from the truck and a gobbler on the roost, I kept reminding myself what an idiot I was. I would probably spend the rest of the morning trying to locate a gobbling turkey, and here I was leaving one before daylight. When I had gone a hundred yards from my parking spot, I stopped and owl-hooted. Three turkeys gobbled at the barred owl imitation. You already know where one of them was located. The other two gobbles came from the cottonwoods dotting the banks of the Canadian River, three hundred yards below me. I now had a legitimate reason for leaving the gobbler at my truck, and down to the river I went.

I didn't kill a gobbler on this morning, but I had a wonderful time. (That sounds kind of like "She wasn't real pretty, but she had a good personality.") Some of the morning highlights are as follows: I saw a gorgeous sunrise on the Canadian River. I had turkeys gobbling in front of me while mallards and pintails called behind me (some of my favoritist sounds). I saw a longbeard with eight hens. I saw a gobbler still on the roost at 9:15 a.m., and he would gobble every time I called. (He was on another ranch, which I couldn't hunt, but I took his picture while he strutted on the roost.) After repositioning to my Double Bull blind back near my truck, I called two jakes to within ten yards of the blind and photographed them, letting them pass by. To make the day even more enjoyable, it was the only morning that I had hunted with no rain.

Back in Elk City, we were getting things ready for the long drive home. Checkout time was 11:00 a.m. at the Ramada Inn. Lisa and I hoped to check out early Friday morning, in order to arrive in Springfield, Missouri at a decent hour in the evening. Springfield was an eight-hour drive. We would eat dinner and spend the night there, before rising early on Saturday morning to make the thirteen-hour drive home. Since it had finally stopped raining, I took the 4-Runner to a spray-n-wash and spent ten bucks in quarters trying to blast all the concrete-like red sand/clay mixture from the vehicle's exterior and undercarriage. I washed the windows and cleaned the inside, too. (I learned the hard way that you don't go scouting in Oklahoma and leave a window down on your vehicle. When the wind conjures up a dust storm, your interior gets a nice, red, sandy film applied to it.) I then filled the truck up with gas and drove back to the hotel. There is a turkey hunting reason for my mentioning of all these details.

Lisa asked me if I planned to hunt in the morning, before we left for home. I told her I was planning to, but I wasn't positive. We were planning on leaving the hotel around 10:00 a.m., 11:00 a.m. at the latest, to start the drive to Springfield. It took me two hours to get to Max's ranch. So in order to hunt, I would have to leave the hotel at 4:00 a.m., hunt two hours from 6:30 a.m. to 8:30 a.m., drive two hours back to the hotel, arriving at 10:30 a.m., pack the truck and check out by 11:00 a.m., and then drive another eight hours to Springfield, Missouri. Oh yeah, I almost forgot, I'd also have to part with fifty bucks to pay the trespass fee for the privilege of this turkey rally. Would you do it? Those of you Legion Members who read this will have answered, "Yes."

When my alarm sounded at 3:30 a.m., again, I didn't feel like getting out of bed. I was beat. I should just rest up for the twenty-one-hour drive back to Virginia, my turkey-hunting alter ego whispered in my sleepy little ear. I got up and looked outside – it was pouring rain. Not again! I didn't want to hunt in the rain again. If I did, I was going to get the shiny-clean 4-Runner covered with red clay again. I had just spent an hour and ten dollars at the spray-n-wash yesterday.

"It's not like you haven't killed a gobbler already, plus, you could save fifty dollars," Turkey Hunting Alter Ego continued. "Why drive for four hours, so you can hunt for two, only to come back and drive for eight more?" My little alter ego nemesis reasoned.

Any guesses as to what I did? That's right. I punched alter ego in the mouth and got dressed – in Mossy Oak. I kissed Lisa good-bye and hit the road. An hour later, as I drove back through the town of Cheyenne during the pre-dawn darkness, the motel we had stayed at looked nearly deserted once again. I don't know if that was because of the weather, the accommodations, or the turkey hunting success of those who had stayed there. I would suppose a little of all three. I saw one of the hunters at the gas station. He was wearing street clothes and gassing-up his truck to head home. The rain and henned-up gobblers were just too much. Alter Ego started to say something like "That's what you should be doing right now, too," but his mouth was still smarting from his last run-in with me, and he thought better of it.

The gobbler I had intended to hunt was already on the ground with two hens when I finally got past Max's cattle and shooed one of his bird dogs back to the barn it had come from. The big Rio had flown down into a small pasture, before it was light enough to see. I spooked his hens while trying to get set up against a tree that didn't have enough lumber in it to make a ball bat from. I sat and called to the longbeard, but he just strutted and gobbled, going away from me following his hens. As it started getting light enough for traditional fly down time, hens started landing in the pasture before me. It was awesome to hear them cackle and watch them sail down right in front of my poor set-up. After landing and stretching, they would each make their way to the gobbler strutting a hundred yards from me. I didn't have much time to hunt, so I decided to try and get in front of their intended travel route and cut them off. It was a nice plan – it just didn't work. There was no cover or terrain to hide behind, as I tried in vain to get in front of the birds. I tried running through a muddy creek bottom, crawling, and even using the cattle to walk behind as a screen. The gobbler never saw me, but one of his growing number of hens always did. The hen would putt, and they would all run, leaving me to come up with a new plan. Finally, my new plan became "sit down and call." I had about thirty minutes left to hunt at this point. So I sat down at the end of some stumps that had been dozed up to enlarge a cattle pasture. I put a lone, hen decoy to my left, and a Woodhaven "V3" diaphragm call in my mouth. Then I started studder calling.

There is no magic call for turkeys, but studder calling is one of my favorite tactics to fire up an otherwise disinterested bird. I'm not going to describe my studder calling technique for you. If I did I would have to kill you, as the saying goes. After fifteen minutes of this calling technique, I saw a gobbler approaching me from the right. He was jet black with a bleached-white head and blood-red waddles. I looked for a beard but didn't see one. He was a jake. Two more jakes emerged behind him as I loosened the grip on my shotgun and eased the butt down off my shoulder. Maybe a longbeard will come behind them I told myself, as the first jake began displaying after spying my hen decoy. I let the three birds walk right past me at fifteen yards. The jakes surrounded my decoy with the first bird still displaying only a few feet behind the fake hen. It occurred to me that I had to leave in fifteen minutes, in order to get back to Elk City by 10:30 a.m. I prayed for wisdom about whether to kill a jake, or wait out a longbeard to the bitter end. I got peace about shooting the jake. I shot the dominant jake at fifteen yards. He dropped straight to the ground and never so much as twitched. If you ever visit my home, and you don't have a queasy stomach, ask to see the picture I took of the bird, immediately after shooting him. Hevishot from a 3 ½ inch magnum 12 gauge, shot out of an extra full choke, directed by a four-power shotgun scope, at the head of a gobbler fifteen yards distant, is, in a word, devastating. It may sound bad, but trust me, that turkey never knew what hit him. One moment he was in love, and the next, his worries were over.

As I drove back to Elk City, my turkey-hunting cup was full. Even though as a rule I pass on shots at jakes, I was glad to have shot this one. Overcoming all the obstacles that the morning had presented is what made the event so rewarding, not the size of the gobbler. I had passed up easy shots at some nine jakes during the week, but during the last fifteen minutes of an out-of-state hunt with a gobbler tag and trespass fee paid for, it's "In The Pot You Go." Passing through Cheyenne for the last time, as I drove by the gas station, I remembered the hunter who was packing it in earlier in the morning.

Tugging at the lucky feather stuck in my cap, I thought, "He must not be a member of the Tenth Legion."

I then started looking for Turkey-Hunting Alter Ego, so I could rub his nose in it, but he was nowhere to be found.

"Skeered," I told myself.

Back in Elk City, Lisa had reverted to her old self. Her actions upon seeing the second gobbler were nothing even remotely as romantic as with the first Rio. Just a peck on the cheek and an, "I'm happy for you Babe."

"That's it?" I thought. "Why this wasn't much different than a normal hunt back in Virginia!"

Unlike my first Oklahoma Rio there was no jumping up and down, no dancing around the room, no hugs and kisses while saying, "Thank You, Thank You, Thank You." No, she just wasn't that excited about this bird.

"Well, after all, it was only a jake," I reminded myself. "Dang, she must only like big gobblers!" I concluded, which, in a way, seemed kind of romantic to me.

I mean, hey, you gotta love a woman like that!

I took the truck to the spray-n-wash one more time because I had another five dollars in quarters I needed to get rid of. Then we loaded all the gear and two Rio Grande gobblers in the 4-Runner. We checked out on schedule and made it to Springfield, Missouri late that evening. There was only one room available at the hotel where we planned to spend the night, which we gladly took. It was a handicapped room. You know, the kind that has huge bathrooms with oversized sinks and countertops? It was just what the doctor ordered for cleaning a full-grown wild turkey! I cleaned the jake in the motel room that night. The jake would provide two meals for Lisa and me, but he would eventually do much more than that. Little did I know, that five weeks later, in my home state of Virginia, I would kill the biggest gobbler of my life – because I decided to kill this Oklahoma jake, but that's another story.

Rio Grande

Date: April 7, 2004
Time: 7:40 a.m.
Location: Reydon, OK
Weight: 19-½ lbs.
10-¼ inch Beard
1-1/8 inch Spurs

Beautiful Rio

Rio Spurs

The "Bus"
–
The Eastern Gobbler

Preface

In 2004 my wife, Lisa, and I traveled to Cheyenne, Oklahoma where I hunted for four days trying to harvest a Rio Grande gobbler. The "Rio" is one of the four subspecies of wild turkey which inhabit the United States. I killed a big, beautiful, mature gobbler on the second day of my hunt and then killed a jake on the last day with less than fifteen minutes of hunting time remaining. Lisa insisted that I have the mature Rio mounted, as we felt it was the most beautiful turkey I had ever killed. Upon our return from Oklahoma, many people asked me if I was going to write a story about the hunt, like I had done when I killed my Osceola turkey in Florida. My initial response was "No!" However, after the conclusion of Virginia's spring gobbler season that year, I had a slightly different answer.

My response went something like this, "If I'm going to write another story about a turkey hunt, it won't be about the Rio I killed; it will be about The Bus!"

That story can be found on the pages that follow, because on May 15, 2004, a boy graduated from an obscure school located in the mountains of western Virginia. This wasn't your ordinary school. This school had only one professor and one student. The student's major? – Advanced Turkey Hunting Tactics. The curriculum took the student five long years to complete. Even though he did his homework, the student flunked numerous exams, and he nearly dropped out due to his frustration. This school was tough because its professor was a wise, old master, which cut his understudies no slack. This was Turkey School. The professor was known to his student as "The Bus," and the student was me.

Graduation from Turkey School is completely different from that of any other institution of higher learning. You graduate from Turkey School when the professor dies.

SCHOOL'S OUT!

The "Bus"

The alarm sounded at 4:15 a.m. just as it had every morning for the last fifteen days (with the exception of Sundays). There was something different about this morning though. This was the last day of Virginia's 2004 Spring Gobbler season – a season that had been my personal worst ever in the Old Dominion State.

While hunting in Virginia, I had not called a single gobbler into shotgun range the entire season. This phenomenon had not occurred due to any lack of effort on my part, as many of my acquaintances would assume.

"Hey, Brad, have you got that turkey yet?" they would query.

When I responded with, "No, I haven't even called one in yet," they would ask something like, "What's the Matter? Have you not hunted much this year?"

(Asking me if I hadn't hunted much during the spring gobbler season would earn a spot in my top-ten list of stupid questions.) That is why I call these kind, sincere folks acquaintances. If they really knew me, and saw that I was breathing and healthy, they would have disposed of their inquiry subconsciously.

In polite response to this absurd, but sincere, question I would dogmatically and earnestly reply, "I have hunted harder and longer this year than any other season, and the truth is, I can't even spell Turkey!"

My fellow legion members who read this will already understand the mathematical relationship that exists between the number of turkeys he kills in a season and the number of times he will be asked about it. It is a proportional relationship – an "e" to the power of "x" relationship to be exact. The number of times one is questioned about his success in the spring woods increases exponentially as the birdless season progresses. However, this doesn't really bother me personally – basically because I would rather talk about turkey hunting than eat. (I'm not lying. I skipped lunch at work on multiple occasions during the spring to talk with other hunters about spring gobbler hunting.) I'm not alone with this disease either. I had a little over a dozen legion members at my home prior to the opening of turkey season to talk about hunting. A sizeable spread of food, snacks and soft drinks were on hand for the event. Now, fifteen grown men can normally put away the chow in large quantities, but on this occasion, after everyone had left, I noticed that the food was barely touched. Maybe three-quarters of a can of mixed nuts and a dozen donuts were missing, along with maybe two cans of soda pop, but that was it. Hey, who has time to eat when you just have to tell that old gobbler story one more time? As a side note, just to be clear, I purposefully haven't mentioned coffee. It is the exception to a turkey hunter's apparent disdain for culinary delights. Coffee was consumed in large quantities at the get-together. According to my brother, Kevin, it was just a test to see if my Bunn coffee pot could actually produce four gallons of coffee per hour as advertised. However, I digress.

The tough hunting in western Virginia during 2004 was due to a variety of reasons in my opinion. Too many to discuss in detail, so I'll leave out the lesser factors – food supply, predators, and an abundance of hens. However, I will mention that the tough conditions I experienced were a direct result of poor turkey hatches the two previous years. The majority of toms harvested each spring are two-year-old or one-year-old birds (jakes). Therefore, with a lack of one-and two-year-old gobblers in the woods, hunters are faced with the task of outwitting three-year-old and older gobblers. This poses problems other than the obvious ones of age and experience. The bigger problem posed by a majority of three-year or older toms in the woods is, in a word, something that has caused grown men to stomp, shout, cry, cuss, throw their hats, and shake uncontrollably. The problem? – Hens! Older toms will have hens, and if all the toms are long-in-the-spur, they will all have hens. Gobblers with hens are an extremely tough sell for a human who is trying to sound like a hen. You know the old saying, "A hen-in-hand is better than a hen that looks like a bush," or something like that.

While "henned-up" gobblers can be killed for sure, the task is much more difficult than it is for taking a lonely, lovesick tom out looking for a date. Heck, even the latter scenario has its share of problems. All the gobblers I hunted from the opening week of turkey season to the last day of turkey season in 2004 were with hens – all of them. Even the henned-up gobblers that I could get excited and coming in my direction would be diverted at the last moment by the boss hen in their harem. "Old Bossie" would put up with his love talk to another lady until he was about one hundred yards away. Then she would join in the conversation and drag a previously northbound gobbler in a southeasterly direction. Any experienced turkey hunter knows what I mean. I tried every trick I could think of to call the boss hen to me, but not once was I successful in 2004. The turkeys would just move away from me with the tom still gobbling at my calls, as if to say, "If only I wasn't married."

Another unique problem associated with henned-up gobblers is that they tend to gobble very little, if at all. As you can imagine, this doesn't bode well for the hunter trying to locate and set up on a longbeard before dawn. One gobble from his roost in the morning is all that's needed for a boss tom to advise his court of suitors as to his exact location. The hens will fly down and head straight for his majesty's tree. When the boss tom can look down and see all his lovely ladies assembled below, he just jumps, or flies, down into the midst of them. A pretty foolproof plan isn't it? Once he's on the ground with his harem, the boss tom has no need to gobble and is usually occupied with other things that don't require but may inspire gobbling, if you catch my drift.

I'm not complaining about all of this. It is the way God Almighty made them, and it is perfect. Every spring season has a dreaded lull in gobbling activity, which usually lasts about two weeks and coincides with the peak of breeding and the gobblers being "henned up." However, for me the lull in 2004 lasted for six weeks – the entire season. Not once did I hear a longbeard gobble from the roost before dawn the whole season. So every hunt I was on during this particular year started without the valuable information that lets me get close to a gobbler before daylight. I would only hear turkeys gobble sparingly, usually fifteen minutes or so after first light. Many other turkey hunters I know weren't hearing turkeys gobble at all. At least I was hearing them. My problem was that the turkeys were always on the wrong mountain! (Yes, I said they were on the wrong mountain and not me.) I have been hunting these hardheaded birds long enough to know what mountain to be on – they're the ones that just don't get it!

Imagine there were five adjacent mountain ridges and let's be creative and name them One through Five. If I went to Ridge No. 2, the turkey(s) I would hear would be on Ridge No. 3. He or they would gobble at every call I made for thirty to forty minutes. Since I could hear their hens calling with them, I would pack up my gear and hike for an hour to get to their location. Upon arrival I would sneakily set out my decoys and begin calling to them, and I would get no response – none. So the next day I would start the day on Ridge No. 3, and where do you think the turkeys would answer me from? Yep, they would be on Ridge No. 2, or perhaps even Ridge No. 4: i.e., the wrong mountain. So I would climb over to Ridge No. 2, and the turkey would lose his voice again. This is how my whole season went.

It got so bad that even though I didn't have any more vacation time to take, I hunted before work – every morning – for the last two weeks of the season. My job requires me to be at work by 7:00 a.m. That doesn't leave much time for turkey hunting. However, I had called a large tom off the roost a few years earlier and killed him at 6:10 a.m. On that hunt, I had time to thank the Lord, pray, read my Bible, check the turkey in, and arrive at work at 6:59 a.m. So I knew it could be done, but it just wasn't meant to be in 2004. In the final two weeks, I had only heard turkeys on three mornings, and only one of these birds was close enough to be a candidate for an off-the-roost hunt, and he apparently had other plans. So that is how things stood for me on the eve of the last day of Virginia's 2004 Turkey Season.

When the alarm sounded at 4:15 a.m. on Saturday, May 15, I awoke in one of those stupors where you don't know where you are. This may have been the result of my habitual lack of sleep, or the splitting headache that was dominating the entire right side of my head. Fortunately, I am blessed with good health and do not get headaches regularly. When I do get one, it is usually the result of a sinus infection or prolonged sleep deprivation. I would get them due to the latter when I was a kid after a week at Boy Scout camp. We Scouts would stay up at night, sitting by the campfire until 2:00 a.m., then turn in to the tent and tell stories, only to rise at dawn and go fishing – that is, if we didn't spend the entire night catfishing. When I returned home after a week of this, I would develop a headache behind one of my eyes. The only thing that would cure the headache was eight to ten hours of uninterrupted sleep. Nowadays, I have a history of acquiring these sleep-deprivation headaches at the end of duck season, turkey season, and deer season.

Morning devotions, extra-strength Tylenol, and hot coffee provided no relief for the pounding condition in the right side of my head. I knew what the cure for my condition was, and it would have been so easy to crawl back into bed, but you can't kill a turkey there. As I trudged down the stairs to get dressed, I kept telling myself that this was the last day, and after today, I could sleep the rest of the summer. My prospects for this final hunt weren't helping me feel any better either. After much mental wrangling about where to hunt, I decided to hunt for an old nemesis of mine. For the eighth time during the 2004 season, I was going to hunt for The "Bus."

I first met The Bus in the spring of 2000. I was tagged out and calling for a close friend of mine, David Oliver, on the last day of spring gobbler season. At about 10:30 a.m. on that fateful day, I called in a big throaty gobbler who still had a hen with him for David. David elected to let the gobbler pass in full strut at forty yards, fearing the shot was too far for his 3-inch magnum 12 gauge. After the two turkeys were well out of sight, David and I relocated to the ridge where they were traveling to. We set up and called aggressively until 11:30 a.m. with no audible response from the longbeard. With only thirty minutes left in the season, we picked up again and decided to make one more move farther out the ridge. We were hoping that the hen would leave the gobbler, and he would eagerly return to my calls.

David and I had gone about ten steps from our previous set-up, when he grabbed my right arm and whispered through clenched teeth, "There he is!"

Motionlessly, I asked David what the gobbler was doing.

"He was strutting about sixty yards away and coming to us," David replied.

"Was?" I asked worriedly.

Still standing like two, department-store mannequins, David informed me that the gobbler had quit strutting and "just disappeared" after he saw him.

"Game over," I said disgustedly, as we finally relaxed from our "turkey-freeze" positions.

As we left the woods that day, I told David I was going to make a date with that gobbler the following spring, and, "Next year he won't be so lucky!"

The following year rolled around and spring gobbler season found me haunting the ridges where David and I had encountered this "lucky" turkey. These ridges, however, were not easy to access. Typically, it would take me an hour, to an hour and a half, to get into this gobbler's lecht. This journey consisted of a fifteen-minute ride on my 4-wheeler followed by an hour's hump on foot. This was a nice gobbler though, and he was worth the effort. At the beginning of the season, I figured I would concentrate on killing this particular tom to settle the score from the previous year, and then I would move on to other birds I had scouted. I presumed this turkey would waltz right in to my calls, just as he had done the previous spring. Hunting alone, he would be much easier for me to take by myself – or at least that's how I figured it. However, my plans for a slam-dunk on this bird quickly evaporated, much to my dismay. What had started out as a sort of light-hearted and fun, one-day turkey hunt, turned into a season long, down and dirty, no-holds-barred war. A war waged between man and bird – a war which the bird won. This gobbler was either the luckiest or smartest bird I had ever hunted, or both. This longbearded tom got every break possible, and some that were impossible.

 I called him up to within seventeen yards of David one morning. The gobbler had circled us (as was his predictable custom) and periscoped his head up over a fallen tree on the crest of the ridge. David wouldn't shoot him because he couldn't see the turkey's beard, as the law requires. The gobbler "periscoped down" and snuck to a point about thirty-five yards behind me and reappeared, looking intently at our position. David again refused to shoot the gobbler fearing he was too far away, despite my repeated urgings of "Shoot!"…"Shoot!" The gobbler proceeded to drop out of sight again into the adjoining hollow and apparently left the area. Thirty minutes later, as David and I stood to pick up the decoys and go after another gobbler that had been answering my calls, I heard something walking in the leaves to my left. It sounded like a turkey's gait, and it was coming from the same hollow the elusive gobbler had disappeared into. I quickly told David to sit back down and put his headnet on. With my gun pointed toward the sound of the approaching footsteps, I heard a sharp "Putt," followed by the sickening sound of a turkey's retreating footsteps. As I turned to look at David, he was still standing with his hand on his headnet about halfway up. For the third time in one hour, the gobbler had gotten away from us. That was the way hunts went for this bird.

 I won't even begin to retell other accounts of my encounters with this gobbler. They are either too painful, or embarrassing, or both to relate. I will say that this turkey became an obsession to me in 2001, and I should have killed him on each of the last two days of that season. On one of those days, another longbeard snuck in about ten feet from me and spoiled the old gobbler's demise, and then on the last day I spooked him from the roost, because I just had to get six feet closer to him…ugh! The disappointment was so great after trying for an entire season to take this tom that I was ready to cry, literally. I was so frustrated with this bird, that for the first time ever, I was actually glad when the clock struck twelve-noon ending the season. I was glad the season was over, and I wouldn't have to hike for an hour every morning to be humiliated by a bird with a brain the size of a pea.

When I arrived back at my truck that day, David met me. I told David that while walking out of the woods in the ninety-degree heat and thinking about all the encounters I had with this cantankerous old gobbler, that I had decided to name the despicable bird.

"I have decided to name him The Bus," I said to my friend.

"The Bus?" David said puzzled, "Why The Bus?"

I turned to David after putting my shotgun in the truck's gun rack and replied,

"Because he has taken me to school every morning for the last three weeks!"

We both chuckled, although my chuckling undoubtedly disguised a few mournful whimpers.

I hunted for The "Bus" in 2002 and in 2003, but not with the same "I'm gonna get you or else" kind of mentality that had driven me in 2001. One of the many lessons I had been taught by The Bus was that there were other turkeys out there for a man to hunt, and a hunter shouldn't blow a whole season chasing any one particular bird. So I hunted other less accomplished gobblers and killed them to regain my self-esteem. Once I got to feeling cocky again, I would return to hunt The Bus. My old buddy would unfailingly knock me back down, usually without much effort on his part. All of my friends and close family members had heard about The Bus for so long that he became a sort of legend within our circle. After I returned from a hunt, my poor friends were either bored or entertained at length with each new chapter in The Bus' autobiography, as I relived how he outsmarted me and got away again.

I am sometimes asked if I believe that there are turkeys that cannot be killed. My answer is always, "No, but I do believe that there are turkeys that I cannot kill!"

We don't give names to very many turkeys, but, occasionally, we run across a special bird that merits a moniker. A large portion of the time, if we do decide to name a particular gobbler, we never kill him (and not for lack of trying I might add). For example, there was "Tantaka." Tantaka lived on Griffith Knob and was the biggest, baddest turkey in the woods. My brother, Kevin, and I called him in more than once and shot some video of him gobbling, but we never killed him. Then there was "Gravelhead." Gravelhead didn't gobble much, and when he did it sounded terrible, like his mouth was full of gravel. This old bird always had all the hens in his domain and would walk straight away from anyone running a turkey call. As far as I know, Gravelhead was never killed by a hunter. I began to resign myself to the fact that The Bus would probably die of old age as well. If not old age, he would eventually succumb to the sharp spur of a younger, quicker tom, or to the fang and claw of a coyote or bobcat after being wounded in a pecking-order battle with another longbeard. To be honest, I wasn't sure The Bus would still be alive in the spring of 2004. He would have to be at least six-years old.

Nevertheless, when asked if I was going to hunt for The "Bus" in 2004, I would say, "If not for him, then for his son, because there is still a gobbler roosting in his home turf."

May 15th was a busy day for me. Not only was it the last day of turkey season, but as luck would have it, it was also "tire amnesty" day.

"What the sam-hill is tire amnesty day?" you might ask.

Tire amnesty day occurs at the local trash-transfer station once every five years and runs one day from 8 a.m. until 2 p.m. It allows residents to bring used tires to the dump with the usual two-dollar disposal fee per tire waived. I had picked up forty tires off of our farm, which had been left by the previous owner, and twenty of them were loaded in the bed of my pickup truck. My father-in-law, Earl, had the other twenty tires on his truck. Taking advantage of tire amnesty day would clean up my farm and save me about eighty bucks in disposal fees. Also on my schedule for this Saturday afternoon in mid-May, was a trip to the Natural Bridge Safari Park. I was planning to drive our church van with twelve children, ages two to six, from our Wednesday evening "Pee Wee" club at the church to the park. The absolute latest I would be able to hunt would be 10:00 a.m., in order to get to the transfer station and unload the tires, drive home to shower and change clothes, and then arrive at the church in time to pick up the kids at noon. Common sense tried real hard to convince me to just call it quits for the season and sleep in so I would feel better. A normal man would have listened to common sense. True, die-hard turkey hunters aren't like normal people, and they seldom, if ever, listen to common sense. They don't stay home when they are sick, and they certainly don't stay home because their schedule is crowded. They don't stay home for any reason, no matter how compelling the excuse or inconvenience, even if staying home makes the most sense. So, with a truck bed full of tires and a splitting headache, I pulled my red Ford F250 out of the drive and headed out one more time for a rendezvous with The Bus. Forty-five minutes later I parked the truck and eased the door shut; it was still dark. A twenty-minute hike put me in my favorite place to try and set up on this tom. (I no longer had to hike for an hour to access the gobbler's home territory thanks to a land purchase by my friend David. I now had easier access to the gobbler, which in previous years was prohibited.)

I didn't use a light as I wound my way through the now heavily foliaged woods to the hardwood ridge that The Bus called home. I didn't try to raise a shock gobble during my hike to his lecht either. I'm not sure if it was due to my headache or to my frustration with all earlier attempts to kill this turkey, but I just decided to slip into the old gobbler's bedroom quietly. I made another key decision after reaching the swag in the ridge that was as close to the turkey's normal roosting area as I had ever dared to go in the pre-dawn hour. I decided to push my luck and travel another one hundred and fifty yards to a spot at the top of the ridge where two finger-ridges came together. The Bus would probably be roosting about a quarter of the way down on one of the two fingers. I had spooked The Bus in the past by trying to get closer than this. I was really taking a chance on knocking him off the roost by advancing the extra distance, but, to be honest, I really didn't care. Heck, nothing else had worked, and it was a gamble I was ready to take.

I reached my intended spot without incident. The woods were beginning to gray-up, and crows had started calling especially early for some reason. I would pause and listen intently for a gobble when the crows would sound off, but no such response would come. I carefully studied the layout of the ridge-top before deciding on a plan for my set-up and decoy placement. It is worth pointing out that determining how and where to set up on a gobbler is extremely critical to being successful as a spring turkey hunter. I concluded that the best approach would be to set up on the very crest of the ridge against an old oak tree that was leaning away from the area I wanted to watch. This tree was what we call a snake tree, because of the holes located under the tree's roots at its base. I have seen several copperheads emerging from holes under trees like this in the mountains during the spring. (My brother and I have videotaped such copperhead activity while spring turkey hunting.) Needless to say, we never sit down to call a turkey from such a tree, but on this morning I didn't care. It was the only tree that gave me the view that I needed to track the gobbler's approach if he was roosting where I suspected, and, due to its angular growth, it would allow me to lean back, recliner style, and close my eyes in an effort to subdue my throbbing headache. The tree offered other advantages as well. The ridge-top I was on dropped straight off to my right, and I mean straight off. The leaning tree was at the very edge of the drop-off, and would prevent The Bus from circling behind me to the right, if he was in the neighborhood and decided to play ball this morning. Being right-handed, I could set up looking straight down the crest of the ridge and shoot from the crest all the way back around to my left, where finger-ridge number one came up. In addition to its location on the drop-off, the tree's position provided a clear view of the small, brushy "bowl" that was formed where the two finger-ridges came together. This bowl was located in front of me and slightly to my left. It provided a natural travel corridor for a love-struck tom to strut into and look for the hen of his dreams. I placed two decoys, a hen and my aggressive hand-painted jake, twelve yards from the snake tree at a forty-five-degree angle to my left. I then took up shop at the base of the snake tree and closed my eyes in prayer.

After praying, I just sat there with my eyes closed. I didn't even want to call. My head was pounding behind my right eye, and I found it most tolerable just to half doze and listen as God's creation began to awake and join the crows in their morning serenade. As good as just resting my eyes felt, I reminded myself what I was there for, and that if I wanted to sleep, I had a perfectly good bed at home made for the purpose. I pulled a rosewood striker from a leg strap and pressed a Woodhaven "V2" diaphragm call to the roof of my mouth. I tree yelped first on a Primos "Freak" friction call strapped to my right leg and then again with the V2 mouth call. Nothing gobbled at my first offering, and I was content to just close my eyes and do nothing else for several minutes. I debated about whether to skip my traditional flydown cackle and wing-beating scenario. I almost opted for excluding it, but after another couple of rounds of soft tree yelps went unanswered, a flydown cackle was executed to perfection. This evaluation of the flydown cackle that I rendered reflects my own personal opinion only, because no gobbler found it worthy of a response. Normally this would have aggravated me but not on this day. It was just a minor inconvenience and validated my desire to close my eyes and do nothing.

It was probably about 6:15 a.m., or fifteen minutes after sunup, before I decided to start calling again. I began plain yelping and clucking on the friction call and then would join in, like a second hen, with the mouth call. Almost immediately after this dual hen series was concluded, a throaty gobble boomed in my direction…from a location behind me…on the next mountain to the north. This day was probably going to be the same as every other day this year. In fact, I believe I heard this particular gobbler every time I hunted The Bus in 2004. The problem? The boisterous gobbler lived on private land that I didn't have permission to hunt, and I was on public land with a great gulf of private land fixed between the bird and me. So I just went back to resting my eyes. Normally I would have called a little more often, but on this last morning, I paused between yelping sequences for at least five minutes. The big tom on the mountain to my north would gobble each time I decided to call again. After three or four of these scenarios, a second gobbler began to chime in. This second tom was also located on the private land mountain to my north, but he would gobble from the point of the ridge, approximately a quarter mile from the other gobbler.

Sometime after 6:30 a.m., I thought I heard the faint sound of a gobbler drumming. Every muscle in my body locked itself in place, with the notable exception of those which control my eyelids, which proceeded to jerk both eyes wide open. The light which greeted my pupils revealed a drab, gray forest, punctuated with dappled shades of green – the greens of late spring in the mountains, with all their different hues, from a pale, lemon-lime to a deep shade of forest green. A foggy, early morning mist softened the green canopy and low-lying foliage. The dull, brushy understory was even showing signs of life with mint-green buds dotting its knee-high expanse between the finger ridges. To my chagrin, however, there were a few colors missing from the forest's palette as my eyes scanned the area from my left to the top of the ridge on my right. Important colors were absent, like white and red and blue, the colors of a wild turkey gobbler's head. I listened intently for the sound of drumming as my eyes strained to pick up any movement in the foggy laurel before me. Try as I might, I couldn't hear, or see, anything remotely resembling a turkey. Well, this wasn't the first time I had dreamed I could hear a turkey drumming this season. So, I clucked and purred with the V2, as seductively as I could, and closed my eyes. Unknown to me at the time, it would be the last turkey call I would make in 2004.

A few more peaceful minutes passed when suddenly my brain received electrical signals from the follicles in my inner ear, which it interpreted again as the faint sound of a drumming gobbler. Now I'm pretty dumb, but I'm not stupid. I wasn't falling for that again, I told myself. Nope, this headache and the overwhelming desire to kill a gobbler were just causing me to hear things. I wouldn't open my eyes, and I wasn't even going to call. I would just continue to rest and ...there it was! I heard it again...or did I? Keeping my eyes closed, I listened intently.

"VRRRRRRM," I heard faintly again.

I decided that it must be a gobbler and opened my eyes. Immediately I saw him. Seventy yards, directly in front of me, the gobbler was in full strut with his head up, looking in my direction. His skull cap was so white that it looked like it was illuminated in contrast to the gray, foggy, morning mist. His eyes were sky blue, and his waddles were so red that they defy description. Set against the chocolate brown background of his full tail fan, his head looked to be as big as a baseball. It was so colorful that it looked fake – like a painted porcelain replica. I just sat there watching him, every muscle completely locked in place except my heart and lungs which began to throb uncontrollably. I told myself to remain calm, as I watched the huge spring gobbler, ever so slowly, strut closer to my set-up.

"Just don't move," I kept repeating silently to myself. "The only thing that will mess this up is if you move."

At this point I would like to be able to say that I began to scratch in the leaves, or purr contentedly, or perform some obscure old Indian trick to bring the gobbler closer, but I didn't do anything. I just sat there motionless – laid back against the snake tree. However, what I had been enjoying up to this point as a comfortable place to sit was now my obstacle to overcome.

I always, and I mean always, sit with my left knee up and my shotgun resting on it before I begin to work a turkey. The butt of my gun always rests on my right shoulder, or at the very least in my lap, as I call. I do this to prevent the situation from occurring that I now found myself in. Because I had been approaching this entire morning's hunt with a "what's the use" attitude, I was sitting with both my legs extended flat on the ground, and my shotgun laying across my lap and left leg. Also, I was reclined backwards at about a sixty-degree angle against the trunk of the snake tree. The chances for me to be able to sit up straight, raise the shotgun from my lap to my shoulder, swing the gun forty-five degrees to my right, and train it on the tom without him seeing me would be basically impossible. The only thing in my favor was the gobbler was moving forward so slowly, that it took him a full ten minutes to cover the thirty yards I needed to get him into scattergun range. My mind raced through dozens of options I could employ during these long, tense minutes. Fortunately, I knew enough to quench any such notions that included a "John Wayne" maneuver. There wasn't any cover or trees of significant size between the gobbler and me that

I could use to conceal my movements from his keen eye. The tom wasn't spinning in circles either for me to use his tail fan as a screen. He was just methodically strutting in my direction and slowly raising his head from time to time to peer directly at me. I decided that getting the gun on the bird in one swift motion was out of the question. I had to coordinate too many movements. So I decided to make the task a two-step process. If the opportunity presented itself, I would sit up straight while bringing the shotgun to my shoulder, and rotate at the waist to my right. This would be step one. To accomplish step two, I would swing the gun to the right and point it at the bird, while trying to find and center him in my scope. You may have noticed that my plan is missing a crucial step – pushing the safety off. However, that part of the plan had already been done. I eased the safety off with the gun across my lap. If only I could figure out how to accomplish step one!

Normally, I get my shotgun pointed directly at a gobbler as soon as I see him. Then I follow his progress with the gun trained on him all the way into shotgun range. It is a special feeling like no other I get from any other kind of hunting – watching a big mature gobbler walking in your direction right down your gun barrel. With each approaching step the gobbler takes, my excitement seems to build. There have been times that I have actually prayed while watching a gobbler come to me down the barrel of my shotgun, thanking my heavenly Father for allowing me to see it one more time. But on this day there would be no such revelry, just the panic that suffocates a turkey hunter telling him he is going to miss his chance if he doesn't get his gun up.

Then it happened, out of nowhere, I heard a turkey running through the leaves... right at me. No, it wasn't the strutting tom; it was another bird, coming straight at me through a line of mature oak trees directly in front of me. I could only see the right leg of the turkey as he ambled back and forth racing to beat the big strutting tom behind him to my decoys. I couldn't see a beard on the running turkey, just one leg and parts of his tail feathers and breast, and I knew that the turkey couldn't see me either. This was my chance. I would have to swing my gun up into position quick because this second bird was about to be in my lap. I was painfully aware that any attempt to raise my gun on this second bird would spook the big tom still strutting just out of gun range into the next county, but hey, it was the last day of the season and one in hand is better than...well, you know. I began to quickly assess my situation. I had been assuming that this second turkey was a mature tom, I mean heck it's the last day of the season, and surely no gobbler is still with hens. What if bird number two was a jake? I would hate to spook a mature tom in order to train my gun on a jake. What if it is, beyond all reason, a hen? I would be sick for the next eleven months if I spooked big boy, and a hen wound up in my lap. As these thoughts cascaded through my brain, I saw the leg of a third turkey running at me behind bird number two! Now there were two birds that were going to run me over! I came so very close to jerking my gun up into position, but I didn't. I remembered telling myself, "Just don't move," at the first sight of the strutting toad, and I decided to stay put – gun in my lap. I came to this conclusion and convinced myself not to move at the remembrance of a Rio Grande turkey that I had killed about month earlier in Oklahoma.

The Oklahoma bird I refer to was a jake, which most of you know I don't normally shoot. However, I do make some exceptions. This bird was killed with only fifteen minutes left on the last day of my hunt. When I first saw the displaying jake at fifty yards, I elected to leave my gun barrel resting on my knee instead of bringing it to bear on the bird since, as mentioned, I normally don't kill jakes. I had decided to let him and his two jake buddies pass, and I let him strut right past me at fifteen yards. The three jakes stood around my lone hen decoy with the dominant one displaying for her. As I sat there watching, it occurred to me that I sure would like to eat a Rio Grande turkey. I also noted that his feathers were beautiful and would be perfect for some painting I wanted to do. Not to mention the fact that I had just driven two hours to hunt, paid a rancher a fifty-dollar trespass fee to hunt his property, and that I had purchased an extra gobbler tag for a second bird. So I decided to shoot the dominant jake still displaying fifteen yards to my left. The other two jakes were standing with him and there was no cover between the birds and me. I had to slowly raise my gun from my knee and swing it into shooting position without spooking any one of the birds. I just took my sweet old time, like a shadow moving along the ground. Eventually I had my gun in place and the crosshairs of my scope on the bird I wanted. An instant later, and one bird was lying on the ground at the base of my decoy, while two others were scrambling for altitude.

Recollecting this Rio Grande jake hunt now gave me the confidence to sit still and wait for the two fast-approaching birds to reveal themselves. If they turned out to be mature birds, I would try to do them like I had done the juvenile Oklahoma birds. If they were jakes or hens, I would still have the big tom coming my way. I didn't have to wait long to find out. Out from behind an old oak tree directly in front of me, a hen skidded to a halt in the leaves. She stood twenty feet in front of me, staring at me, eye to eye. A brief moment later, and the following bird emerged from behind the big oak and nearly ran up the back of the now motionless hen, which was trying to decide what I was. This third turkey was also a hen.

"Hens!" I thought, "You gotta be kidding me!"

I cannot describe the relief that swept over me. I had almost spooked a trophy gobbler to draw a bead on a couple of hens! I looked back at the strutting gobbler and determined that he was nearly within my self-imposed gun range of forty yards. Who would have ever believed that a Rio Grande jake from Oklahoma would help give me a chance at an Eastern longbeard in Virginia? That, my friend, is the epitome of a paradox.

As I began to gather my emotions and get it together, the hens made an abrupt turn to their right and walked straight to my decoys. I had remained still enough to alleviate the two female bird's fears. The hens walked silently around the dekes for a few moments and then became disinterested. They turned around and without a sound started running back to the real gobbler. The big tom slicked up and thrust his head straight up to watch the hens. He was spooked. Even though the hens hadn't putted or made any noise, the tom was concerned. He started walking over to the edge of the drop-off on my right to facilitate his exit, when his two hens stopped running and they started scratching the forest floor for breakfast. The hens were twenty yards from me, halfway between the tom and myself. The gobbler took note of his hen's activities and settled down somewhat, but not completely. He started to go back into strut, but would repeatedly lower his fan and raise his head. Finally, he raised his tail fan and locked it in the full-fan position, but he refrained from tucking his head down into his breast. The big, colorful gobbler just kept peering at me and easing his way to the drop-off.

I was in a fix. This old gobbler was spooked and fixin' to dee-dee. Three feet in front of the tom was a small, dead hardwood tree about two inches in diameter. I decided that my only chance for step one was when his head passed behind the tiny dead tree. Success would depend on doing step one smoothly and lightning fast. I quickly ran through my mental checklist…sit up, raise and shoulder the gun, rotate at the waist… sit up, raise and shoulder the gun, rotate at the waist. The moment of truth was here as he reached the small tree.

"Now!" I told myself.

Immediately I sat forward, and the gun came to bear as I turned toward the tom. Then as quickly as I had sprung into action, my entire body came to an instantaneous stop, and I froze in position.

"I did it!" I rejoiced internally.

Miraculously, the gobbler hadn't seen me, and the hens were feeding toward him with the large oak trees blocking their view of me! I kept watching the gobbler's tail fan as it would rise up and then go back down. As long as he kept raising his fan up, I knew the tom wasn't too spooked. I breathed a sigh relief.

"So far, so good," I thought, my heart pounding and breathing staggered.

I was so relieved to just have my gun up and the bird still there, that I had to force myself to think through step two. I would need to swing the gun barrel about thirty degrees to my right and get the tom in the scope, but there was no cover to conceal my move except two sapling pine trees, neither one with a trunk bigger than a broom handle and neither one with enough needles on it to fill a coffee cup. However, the two trees were both as tall as the big gobbler and only about five inches apart. I decided that my only chance for step two was when his head passed behind the two small pine tops. This was going to be a really tough, long shot. The gobbler had now decided to drop over the edge of the ridge on my right and out of sight, and he was no closer than forty yards. At least I had a chance.

The instant the nervous tom's huge head reached the first pine sapling, I swung my shotgun barrel in a controlled arc towards the twin "Charlie Brown Christmas Tree" pines. (Who says all that duck hunting can't help a turkey hunter?!) I was nearly panicked as my right eye found the proper scope relief and looked through the four-power optics. Instantly, I saw the gobbler's big blue-shaded eye pass between the two pine saplings, and I squeezed the trigger. It was a miracle just to get the shot off. If I had been just a tad slower, I would have missed my opportunity. It took a perfect swing and instant target acquisition to pull this off. It happened all in one motion. I didn't even see the crosshairs when I shot. I just knew that the gobbler's head was between the two trees and centered in the scope. This situation had all the ingredients of a missed gobbler.

After the shot's recoil, I jumped to my feet. I could hear the two hens' wings thrashing the brush and beating frantically to get airborne. My eyes, however, were fixed on the gobbler's position as I watched him drop out of sight, and I saw his full tail fan flip up in the air behind him. That full tail flip is a welcome sight to a spring turkey hunter. Missed gobblers, you see, don't throw up their tail fan before they run. They just run, all slicked up, or they take to the friendly skies. I stood motionless for just a second after the bird dropped out of sight and pumped another 3-1/2 inch, #6 Hevishot shell into the chamber of my 870.

With the big gobbler out of sight, my initial euphoria of taking him quickly turned to panic, as it sounded like the bird was running down the steep drop towards the bottom of the hollow. I began to run cautiously towards the thrashing bird, and soon I could see him flipping head over tail down the mountain. I couldn't tell if he was running and flopping or just flopping, but it was so steep that he was headed straight for the bottom either way. Now, I am forty years old as I write this, or so I am told, but when I was in my early twenties, I proved to myself and to one old gobbler that a wild turkey could not outrun me. They could outsmart me, outwait me, and outfly me for sure, but they could not outrun me. Well, forty or not, this bird wasn't getting away from me either. My cautious run turned into a combination downhill sprint, hurdle, and obstacle event. This wasn't just your average, everyday kind of downhill-hurdle track event either. No sir, this one took place with a locked and loaded, safety off, 12-gauge Remington in my hands. (Hunter's Safety Note – Don't try this at home.) This type of event requires the participant to hurdle fallen trees, break through small, dead saplings, and dodge trees too big to run through, all the while determining if you should shoot from the hip at the "butt-over-tin-cup" feather-ball hurdling below you. If there weren't already enough distractions as I hurdled down the mountain, I also became acutely aware that I was losing things as I ran. Things like the friction call and strikers that had been strapped to my leg. No matter though, those things could be found at a later date or replaced, the turkey couldn't.

I never did fire a second shot at the turkey, intentionally or otherwise, and I can only thank the good Lord for His grace and mercy in keeping me safe. The race came to an abrupt end when the big gobbler came to rest at the base of a large oak tree. The tree was at the very bottom of the mountain and only about seventy-five yards from private land. The gobbler was lying on his back with his head against the tree and his beard lying perfectly centered in the crease of his large breast. He was dead. All the commotion was just his nervous reflex after the shot.

I knelt down and thanked the Lord Jesus for allowing me to take the bird. After a short prayer, I examined the tom's spurs first. They were big and broken. They appeared to have been broken twice during his life and regrown, and yet they were still 1-3/8 inches in length indicating a bird at least five years old. Next, I took a quick look at his beard, which appeared to be about ten inches in length. I reached down to pick the gobbler up, and when I did, I knew something was wrong. This turkey was heavy – real heavy. I have hoisted my fair share of toms, but there was something noticeably different about this bird. I had never felt a turkey like this. It was at this very moment that the pieces of the puzzle started to come together for me in my mind. A gobbler with hens on the last day of the season; broken spurs that still measured 1-3/8 inches long, a turkey so smart he sensed danger when nothing had spooked him, and a bird that weighed well over twenty pounds on the last day of the season. It was at this point that I realized not what I had shot, but "who" I had shot. In all the excitement I hadn't even been thinking about The "Bus" – just about getting the gobbler. A shot of adrenaline surged through my body as the realization set in…it was him! I was literally in disbelief. I became so excited that I didn't know what to do with myself, and for lack of a better idea, I decided that I needed to get back to my set-up. I unloaded and slung my gun. Then, as I hoisted the monstrous bird over my left shoulder, I looked back up the mountain I had just come down. Dang it was steep! It was straight up! I looked at my watch and decided to time myself and see how fast I could climb back up to the top. It was 6:50 a.m. Without a single pause and buoyed by adrenaline, I reached the top at 7:00 a.m. Ten minutes of nonstop climbing straight up with one hand to grab trees and the other grasping the legs of The Bus. I was completely out of breath as I laid the big gobbler in the leaves at the top of the ridge.

After catching my breath, I stepped off the distance of my shot; it was forty-two yards. I then made a successful search for everything I had lost while running after the gobbler. I even found my spent shotgun shell. After loading all my gear into my turkey vest, I returned to The Bus with my Bible and license. I tagged the bird before praying. I remember praying on my knees at the bird's side and thanking my Father for putting two of these birds on the ark with Noah. I don't know why I thought to pray that, but I did. (Some of the guys I work with looked at me like I was plum nuts when I told them about my prayer and Noah's ark. It's a shame that people don't believe the plain truth of the Bible, but I know it is true and one day everyone else will too. Dear reader, I hope you'll take the time now to read the Word of God and come to know the God of the Word, the Lord Jesus Christ. He died in your place on the cross to provide forgiveness for your sins. His gift of forgiveness and a home in heaven is offered freely to anyone who will take it.) The rest of my prayer was very personal and will remain that way. It was a bittersweet moment in my life, kneeling beside a bird that once had seemed to be my nemesis; he now seemed to be my friend. I don't expect anyone to understand that – I don't understand it myself.

Before putting the large turkey into the game bag of my vest, I remembered that my decoys were still set up. Killing a big tom has a way of discombobulating the normal thought process of a hunter (even though it is well established that a spring gobbler hunter has no such "normal" process). Forgetting one's decoys when leaving the woods with a big gobbler over your shoulder is one of these anomalies, as can be attested to by my brother, Kevin. With Kevin's previous faux pas in mind, I walked into the swag that held my decoys. Until this point, all of my emotion had been stifled within. This is a rarity for me. When I take a trophy gobbler, I usually whoop, bellow, holler, squall, shout, or combine any combination of the aforementioned actions into a blurtation uninterpretible by man and unduplicatable ever again. In my most subdued form I will, at the very least, let out an elongated owl hoot, ah lah Eddie Salter. Heck, I'll do that when someone I'm hunting with kills a tom. This mental lapse on my part occurred to me as I made my way to the two decoys. I corrected my lapsus memoriae with the loudest owl hoot my diaphragm could muster, and for good measure, followed that with one of those combination blurtations previously described. I mention this loud outburst because three minutes later, as I began the hike back to my pickup truck, I bumped a large turkey off the roost – within two hundred yards of where I had killed The Bus. I couldn't see a beard on the large bird as it sailed off the mountain down into the private land bottom below, but it looked like a gobbler to me. Now go figure, what was this bird's problem? I know this wasn't one of the two hens I had in my lap, because they flew south and this bird was north of my set-up. I had probably passed under the bird in the dark when I walked in, and I never heard the turkey gobble or yelp. This crazy bird just sat on the roost all morning even after I shot, chased the gobbler into the bottom, hiked back up the mountain, wandered all over the woods looking for calls, strikers, and yelp markers (spent turkey shells), stepped off the distance of my shot, prayed and read my Bible aloud, owl hooted and squalled! Apparently I got into the bird's comfort zone when I walked under its roost tree in the daylight! Anyway it seemed a fitting ending to the kind of season I had experienced – messed up.

I was back at my truck by 8:00 a.m. Even though I was on a tight schedule, it was early enough that I could go out of my way and drive to a checking station with a certified scale to get an official weight for The Bus. On the way to the checking station, I stopped at two of my friends' houses, David Oliver and James Bryant. I knew David wasn't home, but I wanted to tell his wife, Tammy, and show the bird to his five-year-old daughter, Mary Jo. Mary Jo loves turkeys, and I carried her out to my truck in her pajamas. After letting her examine the bird, I plucked one of the bird's feathers and gave it to her. I explained to her that she could use the feather to tickle her daddy. After carrying her back to her mom, I told Tammy I wouldn't clean the bird until David had a chance to see him.

At James' house, he brought his three-year-old daughter, Olivia, out to see the bird. Olivia examined the turkey cautiously, and I plucked a feather for her to tickle her dad with. James took some pictures with his digital camera and asked me if I had weighed the turkey. I told him, "No," but that I kept a 50 lb. Shimano scale in my truck just for the purpose. He convinced me to get it out, and we weighed The Bus – twenty-four pounds and eight ounces. It was incredible. I figured he would weigh close to twenty-five pounds when I first picked him up, which is amazing considering the poor mast year we had, and the fact that it was May 15, the last day of the season.

In my experience hunting spring gobblers in the mountains of West Virginia and Virginia, the heaviest toms are always killed at the beginning of the season. The reason for this is somewhat obvious, but I will explain for those who read this and are not turkey hunters. Once mature gobblers begin to gather their hens during the onset of spring, eating is the lowest item on their priority list. Their days are spent strutting, loving, and fighting, although not necessarily in that order. I have watched mature gobblers do nothing but strut nonstop for hours with their hens. The only thing that will bring a gobbler out of strut is another tom "horning-in" on his harem, or a hot hen that approaches him from his group of concubines. Occasionally you'll see a mature bird peck the ground, or a blade of vegetation, for a piece of food that is probably more in his way than anything else. A gobbler in the spring is much like a teenage boy in school – the only thing on his mind is girls. While teenage boys may become sidetracked by cars, sports, or some other fanciful hobby, gobblers know nothing of such distractions. Hence, during the months of April and May in the areas I hunt, mature birds with hens begin to lose weight with the commencement of the breeding season. I would say a mature bird could lose as much as ten percent of his body weight during these months. In other words, a gobbler that weighs twenty pounds on April 1 might only weigh eighteen pounds come May 20. So, to take a gobbler on May 15 that still weighs twenty-four pounds means he probably weighed close to twenty-six pounds at the beginning of spring.

I left James' house for the check station and arrived there at 9:00 a.m. It had been two full hours since I had taken The Bus. The bird was so large, that the store's proprietor had to enlist my assistance to help him move other equipment from the periphery of the scale so the bird wouldn't rest on anything that could detract from his true weight. The certified scale recorded The Bus' weight at 21.96 pounds. This weight had no doubt been somewhat affected by the two-hour delay, and by the fact that all, and I mean all, of the bird's circulatory fluid (politically correct term for blood) was being carried around by me. Most of it was in my left pants leg and boot, but a generous portion was being held by my underwear, vest, and other articles of clothing. (This was a result of that ten-minute hike straight up the mountain immediately after the bird's demise.) Anyhow, just the fluid loss alone was good for about a pound of live weight. (If you think I'm kidding, take a look at the "graduation" picture at the end of this story – what appears to be reddish-orange on my pants legs isn't camouflage.) Enough explanation – he was heavy. The Bus is the biggest, heaviest turkey I have ever killed.

While at the checking station, I met a fellow turkey hunter who was purchasing a fishing license for his wife. The gentleman was in awe of the gobbler I had taken. After congratulating me and swelling my head with his admiration for the huge, beautiful turkey I had taken, he began to inform me of the disappointing season he had experienced. The kind man remarked that he hadn't killed a gobbler all spring, and that the turkey hunting had been so poor, he decided to just sleep in on the last day and go fishing instead.

Recalling my own poor season and the morning's decision to hunt instead of sleeping in, I thought to myself, "Now there's a man with some sense."

However, I left the checking station with the gobbler of a lifetime over my shoulder and a huge grin on my face. He, on the other hand, scuffled back to his truck and boat with a fishing license in his pocket and a disappointed look on his face. That is the difference between a turkey hunter and a member of the Tenth Legion.

On my way to the transfer station I made one final stop at another friend's house, Freddie Ambrose. Freddie's wife Carolyn had never seen a wild turkey before – up close that is. I figured this was a good one to show her. As we admired the bird in their front yard, I began to point out the beautiful features of a wild turkey gobbler. The sunlight caused his iridescent feathers to change from black to blue to green to red to orange. I showed her the turkey's beard, spurs, and his tail fan. As we appreciated the bird's beauty, I paused. The Bus' tail fan was abnormal. Besides the fact that it was the largest fan with the largest feathers I had ever seen, there was something else peculiar about it. The middle four primary feathers were barred – barred chocolate and white – like a wild turkey's primary wing feathers. I had only seen this a few times before. The first time I noticed it was on an old, 5+ year old tom that I had killed, and whose tail fan I had mounted. His primary tail feathers had this barring but just at the very base. The barring wasn't visible because it was shingled over by the secondary feathers. If I hadn't done the mount myself, I would have never known it was there. The Bus, however, was very different. His barring extended nearly the entire length of the primary feather until it reached the heavy black band near the tip. It was unique and special. I have talked to numerous turkey hunters and taxidermists about the barred tail feathers, and while the barring does occur on occasion, it is usually only at the base of the feather and is not visible above the secondary feathers. Another unique feature, which characterized The Bus, was his legs. The gobbler's legs had huge scales and were paler than the normal maroon shade exhibited by most wild turkeys. The large, pale-purple scales ran up the leg until they reached the knee, which had the more traditional reddish-pink color before the feathers began. A dyed-in-the-wool legion member, Barry Daniel, who I love to talk turkey with, and who has helped me to become a better turkey hunter, described The Bus' legs to me before I told him about them.

He asked me if they were pale with large scales, and I answered "Yup."

To which he responded, "That's an old bird."

I made the comment several times to my closest friends when describing The Bus that, "If he didn't already have a name, I would call him the Freak."

The "Freak" would not only describe his appearance, but would also be appropriate because of the Primos' "Freak" friction call I had used in conjunction with the mouth diaphragm to call him in.

Before I left Freddie's house, I plucked a feather for his wife Carolyn. Then I headed to the transfer station to unload my tires. After the tires were unloaded, I called my brother on a cell phone as I drove home. (Both of Kevin's kids had soccer games that day, and he couldn't take the morning off to hunt.) When Kevin answered the phone, I immediately apologized for what I was about to tell him.

"I hate to call you on the last day of turkey season all happy about killing a gobbler, when I know you haven't killed one this year and couldn't hunt this morning," I stated.

"You kidding? " he replied, "It's us against them, man. They have been winning, and that's one for us. I'm happy for you!"

He had a valid point, you know! I told him that I would be home in about twenty minutes, and he should really try to bring the kids to the house to see the turkey before their soccer games began.

"Is he a nice one?" he asked.

My response was simply, and I quote, "All I can say is…School's Out!"

Kevin knew immediately what that meant.

"You're kidding! You killed The Bus?" he asked excitedly.

"Yep, and he's unbelievable," I replied.

After pondering whether to bring the kids to see the gobbler for about a millisecond, he told me they would be there.

At the house, my wife, Lisa, sat on a stool in our rec-room and listened patiently as I relived the morning's events. I was sitting flat on the hardwood floor still in my blood-soaked camouflage. The Bus was lying on the floor next to me. (Yes you heard me right – the gobbler was in the house.) I bored her with the details of his size and unique features as I pointed them out to her.

Before anyone else arrived at the house to see the bird, Lisa and I took numerous pictures of him. The toughest one to get was a shot of him hanging from a limb by his spurs (hence the term "limbhanger"). The problem wasn't with the length of The Bus' spurs. The problem was his weight. All the branches would bend under his weight, and he would slide down and fall off. I finally had to hang him in an oak tree to get a branch stout enough to support him. With the photo session complete, I returned The Bus to his spot in the floor of our rec-room.

"Are you going to have him mounted?" Lisa asked.

"No, we can't afford it, and I want to eat him," I said. "Besides," I continued, "I've been plucking his feathers all morning and giving them away." (This is not something you do to a bird you plan to mount.)

Lisa's sister, Christy, was the first to arrive as word of the big gobbler spread through our family.

"You're going to mount him aren't you?" she asked.

"No," I replied, "I'm gonna eat him."

Shortly thereafter, Lisa's parents arrived. They asked me the same question, and I gave them the same answer. What was this, some kind of conspiracy? Then Kevin arrived with Katie and Caleb.

After reliving the hunt for about the sixth time with them, Kevin asked, more in the form of a statement than a question, "You are mounting him?!"

"No," I said exasperated. "I'm not mounting him, I'm eating him." (These are words Kevin understands well, as I have heard them uttered from his own mouth every time I try to egg him on about mounting something he has caught or killed! Kevin has even learned to apply them to his son Caleb's requests for such treatment of his fishing and hunting conquests). "Besides," I resumed, "I've already got two ducks and a Rio Grande turkey at the taxidermist. Not only can I not afford it, I don't know where I'm going to put them all."

Kevin told me it didn't matter, and that I was getting the turkey mounted. He would pay for it.

"That's about a five-hundred-dollar decision," I warned him.

To which he said it would be my birthday and Christmas present for the next five years.

"You have to mount a bird like that," Kevin remarked, "With all the history you have with it, you just have to."

Dang, I hate it when he's right! Everyone left the house, and I showered and changed to take the kids from church to the Safari Park.

David Oliver called me at 9:00 p.m. to hear about the bird. I told him it was still in the house, and I had kept my word not to clean it until he saw it. David said he was on his way. Despite his wife Tammy's objections to showing up at another's house so late at night to see a dead turkey, David arrived at my house around 10:15 p.m. In great detail I expounded the story one more time, and we admired the bird together. David told me that he had spent one hundred hours hunting this bird himself, and then wanted to know if I was going to mount it…go figure! Turkey season was now officially over in Virginia, but we talked until 11:30 p.m. about nothing else. It was so late when David got ready to leave that I didn't feel like cleaning the bird. So, I double bagged The Bus in thirty-three-gallon trash bags and put him in the freezer – just like you would a bird you planned to have mounted…hmm. As midnight approached, Lisa and Tammy both had to be wondering what was wrong with their husbands. Of course, Lisa already knows. (Tammy, if you read this be forewarned – this is only the beginning. I have diagnosed David with a case of legionnaire's disease – the turkey hunting variety. The disease is in its early stages, but it is incurable. You'll have to come to terms with the fact that the man you married is now a bonafide, genuine "golly-turkaconous-freak." All we can do now is hope that Mary Jo and McGuire don't contract the severe disorder from their dad. The pushbutton turkey call I gave to Mary Jo for Christmas probably won't help though!) For those of you who don't know David and Tammy, please just ignore the last few sentences.

So I guess you are probably wondering, "Did you have the gobbler mounted, or did you eat it?"

To which the answer is, "Yes!"

A few days after killing the gobbler, I talked to Mike Gray, my friend and taxidermist in Richmond, and asked him if he split his turkeys for mounting down the front or back. He told me down the front – just what I was hoping to hear. I then asked him what he thought about me splitting the gobbler down the front to remove its breast before sending the bird's carcass to him for mounting. He told me that he trusted me to do a good job and just to make sure that I didn't get any fluids on the bird's feathers. So I thawed the bird out for an entire day (it took forever for the bird to thaw enough to clean), and Lisa helped me skin the breast out at 11:30 p.m. that night – I think there is a "you might be a redneck" joke in here somewhere! I am so glad I decided to breast the gobbler. Not only because he was delicious and provided two meals for my family, or because after hunting him for five years it would have been a disgrace not to, but because there was one more enigma in the story of The Bus that I was unaware of, until I cut the meat from his breast. The Bus had been shot before. I removed a half dozen fine-shot pellets from the gobbler's left breast. The shot was encased in a sort of tissue pouch located between the breast muscle and his skin. I showed the shot to Lisa after I removed it from the gobbler.

"Oh, are those your BBs?" she asked casually.

"No, these shot are on the wrong side of the bird," I replied. "The gobbler's right side was facing me when I shot him. "Not only that," I continued, "They are too small and too old to be my shot, and the meat is undisturbed on the bird's left side. It's not even bruised."

Lisa asked me the obvious question, "Have you ever shot at him before?"

I told her that I never had, and that David hadn't either – but someone sure had, a long time ago. I would have never known if I had just sent him to the taxidermist.

It is somewhat amusing that in a strange sort of way The Bus got the last laugh in this saga. This gobbler managed to get the better of me one more time, even after he was dead. These detailed stories that I write must, at times, seem unbelievable. I firmly attest that they are true, whether believed by the reader or not. Actually, I don't think I could make this stuff up. What follows is a case in point. At the time that I killed The Bus, I was in great physical shape. You have to be to hunt the places that I hunt. Even if I wasn't in shape before the opening of turkey season, I was at the end of it. I had been climbing the mountains and ridges in the counties near my home for six straight weeks pursuing longbeards.

However, on Sunday morning, the day after I killed The Bus, I had trouble getting out of bed for church. This trouble was not because I was tired, but because the quadricep muscles in both my legs and the gluteus maximus muscle in my left…you know what, were so sore and stiff, that they hurt too bad to move. Recall that in his death throes, The Bus went all the way to the bottom of the mountain, forcing me to follow if I wanted to get him. The steep climb to return to the top with him over my left shoulder resulted in my painful condition. My muscles continued to hurt until Thursday. I would wince all day at work climbing steps and ladders on the job.

I laughed to myself thinking, "He won again. After our last encounter, his worries are over, but I'm still in pain!"

Let me tell you though, it was a hurt that felt so good. The Bus couldn't even expire like a normal turkey and just let me walk over and pick him up. No, even after he was dead he had found a way to get at me!

It has been almost a year since that fateful day that I harvested the toughest gobbler I have ever taken. I hunted The Bus twenty-eight times over the course of five spring gobbler seasons – eight times alone in 2004, the year I killed him. I still can't believe I did it. All the times that I should have killed this bird – he slipped away, and the day that I killed him – he should have gotten away. I am also saddened that it is over, my battle of wits with this magnificent game bird. He beat me fair and square and frustrated me so many times that I was ready to just give up on him. He made me throw things not meant to be thrown, say things not meant to be said, and do things not meant to be done. As the name that I gave to him implies, he taught me many turkey-hunting lessons. I'll miss his gobble and his dastardly tricks this coming season, if the Lord allows me to live and hunt again.

Some would ask me, "How can you hunt for a creature and then when you kill it, feel bad about it?"

To which I would say that if I didn't hunt for them I would never truly get to know them. Oh sure, I could take to the woods with a camera and observe them pass by me and take their photograph, or I could hear their gobble and videotape their behavior, but until you hunt them you are just an outsider to their world, a tourist of sorts, intruding on their property and in their home – a spectator content to sit back and watch the game with no involvement or bearing on its outcome and no relationship with its players. This is not the case with a hunter. When I entered those hardwood ridges that The Bus called home before dawn, I had a right to be there. I belonged there as much as any other creature. I knew this turkey personally. I learned his mannerisms and his routine. I learned his escape routes and his water holes. I met his family and spent countless hours in his home. And every spring for five years he bested me, a gobbler with a brain not much larger than a pea, and I with all the best camouflage, equipment, decoys, and calls available. He was amazing. I honored him when I killed him by serving him to my family, which is what the Bible calls for in Genesis 9:3. I will never forget him. The feathers and skin that he lived in will be mounted in my rec-room in full strut, reminding me of the very first time I ever laid eyes on him on May 13, 2000. I'll never hunt The Bus again, but there will be another wise, old gobbler that will undoubtedly take his place in my spring hunting pursuits. Like The Bus, he will outsmart me repeatedly and seem impossible to kill. I'll lie on the ground pounding my fist in the dirt, or I'll throw my hat down, or both. I'll probably name him too, something like $#%^@###. In the future though, I'll have an advantage that I have never had previously. I'll remember the day that I just wrote about, the day I killed The Bus. It will encourage me to never give up, for The Bus has set the standard that I will judge all other turkeys by. Yes, there will probably be another named, unkillable gobbler in my future, but only if I am lucky.

I'm still not sure why I drug myself out of bed with a splitting headache on May 15, 2004, but I sure am glad that I did. You never know when the memory of a lifetime will be made. And just so you know, sometime during the ten minutes that elapsed between seeing The Bus at seventy yards and pulling the trigger when he was at forty-two yards, my headache went away.

School's Out!

The "Bus"
Graduation:
May 15, 2004

The "Bus"

Date: May, 15, 2004
Time: 6:50 a.m.
21 lbs. 15 oz.
10 inch Beard
1-3/8 inch Spurs

Hitman

–

The Osceola Gobbler

Preface

It was a cold day in mid-March, and I was working in my office at my job as an engineer for a large paper company in Virginia. In approximately one month I would be traveling on vacation with my brother, Kevin, to the state of Nebraska, where we planned to hunt for Merriam's spring gobblers. I had been planning this trip for nearly a year and was beginning to froth with excitement as the departure date drew near. My entire focus was being directed to this Merriam's hunt, because a wild turkey Grand Slam hinged on the hunt's success. All that changed, however, when the phone in my office rang. As I answered the phone, innocently enough, I had no idea that a business call would prove to be the catalyst for changing my life as a spring gobbler hunter.

The phone call was from a business colleague, Gordon Jarrett, who worked at a company located in Florida. I had worked with Gordon on numerous occasions in the past, as his company supplied me with technical measuring equipment for several of our mill's processes. Gordon had been a huge help to me in previous years by providing me with technical support over the phone. After working together for several years via telephone, I finally had the privilege of meeting Gordon face to face. He had flown to Virginia to make a joint presentation with me to our mill's management about an upgrade to the equipment his company supplied us with. Upon his arrival at my office before the meeting, Gordon perused the framed 8x10 photographs hanging on the wall above my desk – two of which were of my brother and me with gobblers we had taken. Gordon asked me about the pictures and remarked that he was a spring gobbler hunter too. At that moment our relationship changed from a strictly professional one to a personal one. We had worked closely together over the years without either one of us ever discussing personal interests, but now I knew why we got along so well – Gordon was a legion member! In fact, on my first trip to the Sunshine State to hunt for an Osceola, it was Gordon who had arranged to secure an extra hunting permit for my use. He had also met me, provided me with a topo map of the National Forest area I would be hunting, and showed me where to start hunting. Although my first hunting trip to Florida was unsuccessful, it laid the foundation for a future trip, a trip that resulted in my taking of "Turkulese – The Osceola Gobbler."

Due to a change in my job responsibilities, I was no longer responsible for the area of our paper mill which used the equipment supplied by Gordon's company. So when I answered the ringing phone at my desk that fateful March day, I was surprised to hear Gordon's voice on the other end. Gordon explained that he needed to speak with the engineer now assigned to the area of the mill using his equipment, and the only phone number he had was mine. It just so happened that the gentleman that Gordon needed to speak with was on another line sitting next to me. I told Gordon to hang on for a minute, and I would hand my phone over when his call was complete. Of course, since we had a few minutes to kill while we waited, we struck up a conversation. Now, it is mid-March, Florida turkey season is in progress, and I am about to leave for a crack at a Grand Slam. Take a wild guess as to what topic we chose to discuss.

You got it – The current trend of American manufacturers to use linear electronics in control systems. Now if you believe that, you apparently give me much more professional credit than I deserve. Of course we talked about turkey hunting!

Our conversation, while waiting for another engineer to finish his telephone call, would be a providential engagement. I personally am convinced that the phone call did not take place by mere chance, but by divine appointment. The story that follows is an account of the Lord's blessing to me and the start of an unbelievable spring gobbler season: a season in which I would not only complete my first Grand Slam, but unbelievably record a second slam in a single season.

Hitman

"So where are you headed to this year in search of your Grand Slam?" Gordon inquired of me, as we passed the time chitchatting.

"Nebraska," I replied, "In search of a Merriam's. It's the last one I need to complete my slam," I said before questioning Gordon. "How's the hunting been there in Florida thus far? Are they tearin' the bone out of it yet?" I asked.

"The season's not in yet," was Gordon's response.

I have to tell you I was surprised. I thought for sure he had been hunting for at least a week.

"It's late this year and permits for the first week don't start until March 24," Gordon explained.

"The twenty-fourth? Man, that is late," I agreed. "That's Easter weekend isn't it?"

Gordon answered, "Yeah, I believe it is."

"If I had known that opening week was Easter weekend, I would have applied for a permit and tried to come down," I said half seriously. "By the way, how did you do on permits this year?" I asked.

"Not too bad," he responded, "I managed to get permits for most of the weeks."

"That's great!" I stated, and then jokingly added, "You don't have any extras do you?"

"I could probably get one," Gordon responded before asking me, "Why, are you thinking about coming down?"

"Lisa and I are both off for Easter and have a four-day holiday," I replied. "It would have been an ideal time for us to come to Florida, especially if I could have hunted," I concluded.

At about this time, the engineer that Gordon wanted to speak with completed his phone conversation and hung his phone up. I motioned to him to pick up my phone and told Gordon good-bye and good luck hunting.

Gordon replied, "Let me know if you want me to try and locate a permit for you."

I told him in closing, "I'll talk to Lisa, and I'll let you know," before handing the phone to Gordon's intended contact.

A short explanation regarding Florida's hunting permits is in order here. I wouldn't want you to think that Gordon or I were doing anything illegal trying to locate and secure hunting permits that the state of Florida issues by lottery-type drawings. To hunt on public land in the Sunshine State a person must obtain a quota permit. A quota permit is issued for only one week of the season. (The permit for the area I typically try to hunt isn't even valid for a week, only the last four days of the week.) These permits are applied for in November and a drawing takes place in early December. The fortunate hunters that are selected at random by computer are issued permits. Once a permit has been obtained, a hunter may elect to give his permit to another if he decides he doesn't want to use it. (In other words the permits are transferable.) Permits may be transferred to either resident or nonresident hunters with a valid Florida hunting license. The only thing that would make the transfer of a permit illegal is if one party tried to sell it to another. Selling permits is strictly forbidden. (I will tell you that hunters as far away as Maine who wanted to buy a permit that I had drawn have called me. They had seen my name posted on the Florida Wildlife Commission's Internet site showing the successful turkey hunting quota permit recipients.) Being a resident of the state, Gordon talks to local hunters who draw permits and then decide not to use them. The reasons they offer for giving up their permits are varied, but they usually range from "too many bugs," "it's too hot," "my son has a game that weekend," "the snakes are just too bad this year," and "I didn't realize that it was Easter weekend, and we have other plans" – the last one is the one I really like. I feel it appropriate to point out here that the only people giving up their quota permits are the normal ones. Legion members wouldn't dare feign such weak excuses. So that is how Gordon manages to come up with permits for just about every week of the Florida spring gobbler season. If he tags out, he just gives the extra permits to someone else. (Tagging out on Osceola gobblers hunted in the swamps of Florida's National Forest isn't exactly what you would call easy. In fact, you might call it impossible.)

After my impromptu phone conversation with Gordon, I did two things. First, I double-checked my calendar and schedule to be sure I was off on the opening days of turkey season in Ocala's National Forest. Second, I phoned my wife, Lisa.

"Hey, Hon, how would you like to go to Florida over the Easter holiday?" I asked her enthusiastically.

"I would love to, but you wouldn't be able to hunt if we went would you?" she replied.

Why does she always assume my ideas are somehow centered on hunting? Can't a loving husband just be spontaneous and surprise his adoring wife of sixteen years with a weekend getaway for two? I mean what woman wouldn't want to leave the snow and ice for a few days of fun in the sun? OK, you're right in agreeing with Lisa. I'm full of it – but you have to admit it was a nice try, right?

I filled Lisa in on Gordon's offer to try and find me a hunting permit. She and I discussed the possibility of making the trip on such short notice. We only had a week to decide and make the travel arrangements. The two of us discussed many of the obstacles that had to be overcome in order to make the mini-vacation a reality. This would be the first of about three long discussions focusing on if, and how, we could do it. Lisa's only stipulation for making the trip was that we fly to Florida in lieu of driving. A stipulation I was in agreement with, as I was staring a three thousand mile round trip to Nebraska in a four-wheel drive square in the face. We agreed to pray about the decision, and trust the Lord to direct our path if it was His will that we proceed.

Now if you are not a Christian, you will have trouble understanding what I am about to relate. (If you are not a Christian, dear reader, my greatest prayer for you is that you will accept Jesus Christ as your personal Savior before it is eternally too late. Nothing in the world is more important than your soul.) The Bible teaches that a Christian should always put God first, others second, and himself last, in the priority he places on decisions he makes. The Bible also clearly states that a Christian should commit his way unto the Lord, and in return, God will direct his paths. While the hunting story that follows may not appear to the casual reader as something spiritual, it is indeed fraught with spiritual principles and outcomes. When Lisa and I agreed to pray about our decision, it was the best possible thing we could have done. As my account of a simple turkey hunt will relate in the pages that follow, our prayers were certainly answered. God would direct our path to the state of Florida, and in His own mysterious way, put me in a position to be eye to eye with the gobbler of a lifetime.

I should continue by listing several of the obstacles that Lisa and I had to overcome in order to make a spur-of-the-moment trip to Florida. Financially there were several, as we were operating on a tight budget. Airfare would cost us $1000, the motel would cost $400, a rental car would be $500, and my hunting license would run $180. Of course this didn't include meals and entertainment. So we were looking at a $2500 price tag for the weekend.

The airline tickets were another problem all their own. Deciding to travel to Florida one week before departure only allowed for purchasing premium, non-refundable airline tickets, and because the week we wanted to travel coincided with Easter and Spring Break, there were basically no flights available. In order to get a flight, we each needed to take another vacation day from our jobs so we could fly on Thursday instead of Good Friday. To be able to get the extra vacation day, Lisa and I discussed canceling our yearly weekend getaway to celebrate our anniversary. (We both had scheduled a vacation day on the Friday before our anniversary to facilitate that trip.) With our bosses' permission, we could reschedule the vacation day from our anniversary trip to accommodate a trip to Florida on Thursday. There were numerous other headaches that we had to consider as well, but I won't bore you any further. Suffice it to say that we were pretty undecided if it was worth all the expense and hassle.

The next day (a Friday), Lisa phoned me as I was on my way home from work. She had talked to a travel agent who had informed her that there were only three airline tickets available on any airline to Orlando International Airport. The travel agent told my wife that if we didn't book the tickets in the next hour, we could probably forget any chance of flying to Florida. Lisa wanted me to tell her what to do, as we hadn't decided whether to go. I told her that we didn't even have permission to be off the day of the flight, and that we needed to do that first. So I hung up with Lisa, and I called my boss at his home and asked for permission to move my vacation day, which he graciously allowed. Lisa's boss did likewise. When we spoke again by phone Lisa was even more urgent about the ticket situation.

"No," I told her, "We haven't had time to discuss it fully, and we just need to pray about it over the weekend. If it is the Lord's will that we make the trip, the tickets will still be available on Monday," I concluded.

Lisa sighed in agreement as we ended our conversation.

After much discussion during the weekend and an unsuccessful search for plane tickets online, I told Lisa on Sunday evening that I would leave the decision up to her. I was "OK" with going to Florida for the weekend, and I was "OK" with staying home and pocketing the $2500. The phone in my office rang around nine o'clock on Monday morning. It was Lisa.

"You're not going to believe it," she said. "I got the tickets and they were twenty dollars cheaper than they were on Friday!" she continued in a bubbly tone.

"So I guess we're going to Florida, huh?" I replied.

Lisa responded excitedly, "Yep. Now I have to make some appointments for the tanning bed!"

I suggested that a motel and rental truck would be a better selection for her next phone call, but she quickly informed me that the motel reservations were made and the travel agent was trying to find us a four-wheel drive vehicle to rent.

That woman of mine is all right!

I purchased my hunting license online that same day and called Gordon. I don't think he was too surprised to find out that I was coming to Florida. He told me that he had indeed secured an extra quota permit from a gentleman he worked with. The kind soul that gave up his permit "didn't realize that it was for Easter weekend, and he had other plans." I told you that was my favorite excuse!

I filled Gordon in on our itinerary so I could plan to meet him and get possession of the permit. I told him that the only flight we could get departed Roanoke at 6:00 a.m. We were scheduled to arrive in Orlando at 8:50 a.m. after a short layover in Charlotte, North Carolina. He said it was "all good" to him, and we bid each other farewell, each looking forward to seeing one another again.

I called the airport in Roanoke and the airline our flight was booked with to make certain I was properly educated about the correct procedures for declaring and traveling with a firearm. Standard procedure for checking a firearm along with one's baggage required you to arrive at the airport at least two hours before your

flight, in order to clear security. The Roanoke airport, however, didn't open until 5:00 a.m. so I was a little concerned about having enough time before my six-o'clock departure.

The travel agent helped Lisa to reserve a rental car, as no 4x4s were available. I was somewhat concerned about renting a car because of where I intended to hunt. Not to worry though, I told Lisa I would walk as far as I had to in order to hunt gobblers in the swamp. Everything was falling right in place, and we were both getting excited. We packed our suitcases, I readied my hunting gear, and Lisa attended tanning sessions each day before the trip. The only problem at all was with me trying to decide what gun to take, and how to pack all the hunting clothes and gear I needed in such a small suitcase!

I decided to take my old turkey gun. The gun I refer to is a Remington 11-87 Special-Purpose turkey gun chambered for three-inch shells. It is completely camouflaged from the factory and is outfitted with a scope, just like my 3-1/2 inch gun, which I normally use. This gun is nearly infamous from its many appearances in the turkey hunting videos that my brother and I use to make. I decided to take it for three reasons. (By the way, you may be wondering at this point why on earth I am boring you with all these dumb details and not just getting on with killing something. – A valid point that I have asked myself even as I type this. Just trust me that every detail I share is for a reason. Reasons that will all play a part in the outcome of this hunt.) Now where was I? Oh yes, the three reasons: 1) The 11-87 has a very short barrel, which allowed me to take a smaller airline-approved gun case, meeting the airlines restrictions on case size; 2) Should something happen to my gun during the flight: i.e., lost, confiscated, stolen, I wouldn't be jeopardizing my main turkey gun, which was going to be needed for my Merriam's Grand-Slam hunt in Nebraska; and 3) On previous hunts, everyone in Florida laughed at my 3-1/2 inch gun because in the swamps you can't see much over fifteen yards most of the time, and a big magnum is just overkill. So there you have it, an engineer's approach to gun decision-making.

After church on Wednesday night, the eve of our flight, I packed our 4-Runner with the suitcases and my 11-87. We turned in to bed early and set the alarm for 3:00 a.m. We planned to get showers in the morning and leave the house no later than 3:45 a.m. I told Lisa it would be better to be at the airport waiting for it to open, than to be late and have trouble with the gun issue. We were both excited as we pillowed our heads.

The alarm sounded at 3:00 a.m. as expected. I awoke and was praying before getting my shower, when the phone rang, unexpectedly. Lisa asked me who it could be at this obscene hour of the night. I remarked that if it was the mill, I was going to have to get someone else to help them. I answered the phone, only to hear a pre-recorded message:

"Due to the unavailability of the flight crew, your flight #XXXXX has been delayed. You will be contacted shortly with new flight information. Please call 1-800-XXX-XXXX if you need further assistance."

I hung up the phone and gave the bad news to Lisa.

Then I said, "Well we might as well get a little more sleep until they call."

It was a nice thought, but we couldn't sleep. At 3:15 a.m. the phone rang again.

"That's them calling to tell us our new flight plans," I said as I reached for the phone.

Instead of the news I was hoping to get, I heard the exact same recording as before. It then dawned on me that one call was for me, and one was for Lisa. Then something else dawned on me.

"If our flight is delayed by more than thirty minutes, we will miss our connecting flight in Charlotte, and we already know that there are no more flights available to Orlando!" I blurted out.

My mind started racing, wondering if we could drive to Charlotte, four hours away, in time to catch our 7:30 a.m. flight there, but I resigned myself that there was just no way.

Fortunately, I had somehow remembered the 800-number given by the recording, and Lisa called it for assistance. After a long fifteen minutes on the phone with a customer service representative, I could see Lisa's soft, glowing tan starting to turn red.

"What do you mean we can't get a flight until Saturday afternoon? That won't do us any good, and our vacation will be over! That's just not right!" Lisa exclaimed visibly upset.

My poor wife seldom gets that upset, but after all she had done to make our arrangements and get all tanned for the trip, she was not a happy camper at 3:45 a.m. My mind began to race again. After reviewing about three different options, I decided what we were going to do.

"Tell her we want our tickets refunded," I said to Lisa, who was still on the phone.

Due to the airline's problems they agreed to refund our "non-refundable" tickets. When Lisa hung up the phone, she looked as if she was about to cry.

"Don't worry," I said to her, putting my hand on her shoulder, "We are going to drive to Florida!"

I told her we were already packed, the trip would take about twelve hours, and if we left by 4:30 a.m., we would be in Florida in time for supper. Lisa didn't even hesitate to say, "Yes."

We hurriedly got ready, and since I would be driving now, I was tempted to throw in a bunch more hunting gear and my 3-1/2 inch turkey gun. I decided that there was no time or sense in that. I did decide to throw in my trusty coffee pot that travels the country hunting turkeys with me though. We got in the Toyota and prayed before leaving. I thanked the Lord for the circumstances that had occurred, trusting it wasn't His will for us to be on that plane. I concluded my prayer by asking Him to provide safety for us as we traveled. After praying, I looked at the time…it was 4:40 a.m.

The drive to Florida was one of the best Lisa and I have ever had. We had great weather, mild traffic conditions, and we really enjoyed one another's company.

Along the way we phoned family members by cell phone to alert them to our change in plans. We also used the cell phone to cancel the rental car we had reserved. I remarked to Lisa that by driving we were saving $1500, and that is probably what really made the trip enjoyable. Before we knew it, we were pulling up to the Comfort Inn at Mt. Dora, Florida. I looked at the time, and I kid you not, it was exactly 4:40 p.m.! It had been twelve hours to the minute since we had pulled out of our driveway! It had also been two years since I had been to Mt. Dora. The last time I was there I had harvested "Turkulese." Just pulling in to the motel parking lot brought back a flood of memories. I was so glad to be back in Florida, and I was really looking forward to revisiting the swamp and sitting at the exact same tree where Turkulese made his final mistake.

When I finally got in touch with Gordon, it was after 5:30 p.m. He wanted to know what had happened to me, as I had missed our previously arranged meeting time by about five hours. After explaining the airline debacle to him, Gordon chuckled in sympathy – he himself being a veteran business traveler.

My plans for the entire day had been shot due to driving. Not only had I missed my meeting with Gordon to get the permit, I had also missed my chance to scout the area where I had killed Turkulese and plan my hunt for Friday morning. (You don't want to just wander into the swamps of Florida in the dark without scouting the area after not being there for two years.) Gordon offered to come to my motel room and drop the permit off because he was going out to dinner with his family. They would be passing by our motel on the way to the restaurant. He also had some good news for me.

"My son, Jesse, killed his first longbeard this morning," Gordon said proudly.

"That's great!" I replied, telling him that I couldn't wait to see them when they arrived.

A knock on our motel door an hour later heralded Gordon's arrival with his wife and youngest son, Jesse. As soon as I opened the door to let them in, Jesse pulled a nine-inch beard from his pocket and extended it for me to see. He was so proud of his turkey, and who wouldn't be? I personally know a whole bunch of grown men who would love to have that Osceola notched on their shotgun. Gordon and Jesse then related their morning's hunt to me, telling me about numerous gobblers they had seen using a newly created "chop." Gordon described for me how two mature gobblers had come to his calls but wouldn't commit to his decoys. Because of the bird's actions, Gordon took the time after his morning hunt to build a blind out in the chop where the birds had hung up. Jesse's bird, on the other hand, had literally flown in to his calls. I congratulated Jesse on his fine accomplishment and thanked Gordon for the permit he had secured for my use. Before they left for the restaurant, I gave Gordon a turkey hunting DVD that I had bought to show him my appreciation for his kindness to me. As they prepared to leave, Gordon asked me to join him in the morning and to hunt the chop with him. (A chop is what Floridians call a clear-cut.) I thanked him for his offer but politely refused. Gordon wouldn't give up asking me though. Each time I would decline the invitation with a different reason for why I didn't want to hunt his area or interfere with his hunting, and each time he would ask me to come with him anyway. Finally, I offered to go with him and call for him, thinking that might be what he wanted. However, it was not. Eventually, Gordon told me why he kept asking. He didn't want me to sit with him; he wanted me to park next to him.

Gordon then explained that the chop he had found had been cut recently and then burned, as is common practice in the bug, snake, and palmetto infested Ocala National Forest. This chop was very large and had created a perfect spot where turkeys could congregate to feed and where gobblers could strut. Gordon knew some other hunters were accessing it by boat from the rear already, and he was afraid more hunters would be coming in from the road and ruining it in a matter of days. His thinking was, if I went with him and parked my truck next to his, that it might discourage someone else from hunting there. Gordon hoped that it would appear as if the public hunting area was "crowded" already. I was getting a little embarrassed at turning down his offer, especially since he had gotten me the permit. All I wanted to do was sit where I had killed Turkulese and remember that special day; I didn't really expect to have much luck hunting. As I thought about what to do, I knew that I should volunteer to help Gordon.

"Okay," I finally said, "What time do you want to meet in the morning, because I have no idea where this place is?"

Once we worked out the arrangements for our pre-dawn rendezvous, Gordon hit me with another news flash.

"The chop we are going to hunt borders a United States Navy bombing area. I just wanted you to know ahead of time."

Now I knew why he was so worried about multitudes of people flocking to the spot to hunt – detonating bombs are probably good locator calls!

When the door closed behind Gordon as he left the motel room, I looked at Lisa and just shook my head. I wasn't so happy anymore; it had been a long day. I had been so looking forward to reliving my old hunt, and now I was punting that plan to hunt an area I knew nothing about. I told Lisa that I was only doing it to be kind (you know – put others first). It seemed reasonable to give up one of the two mornings I had to hunt, in order to help Gordon, since he had gone out of his way to help me. So what if I spent one of my two mornings bumbling around in a swampy area bordering a chop that I had never seen; I could still hunt the area where I had killed Turkulese on Saturday, right?

I then told Lisa half-heartedly, "If I hadn't already killed an Osceola, there is no way that I would be doing this," as we prepared to exit the motel room to embark on our own dining excursion.

I awoke when the alarm sounded at 4:00 a.m. After morning devotions, I had just enough time to dress and get my coffee before leaving to meet Gordon. As I left the Comfort Inn parking lot, it was raining – imagine that. We met at a quick-stop located fifteen minutes from the motel at the appointed time of 4:30 a.m. I followed Gordon's truck for the next forty minutes as he led the way to his "new-found" hunting spot. The first twenty-five minutes of the drive were by paved roads; the last fifteen minutes were driven off-road through the red sand of Ocala's National Forest. At one point, the sandy road we were traveling came to a seemingly dead end, a dead end with a ten-foot high chain link fence facing the road – a chain link fence with metal warning signs fastened to it – signs stating things like "No Trespassing – Property of U.S. Government," and "Danger – Unexploded Ordinances," or "Keep Out," and "Bombing Runs In Progress." This hunting experience was definitely going to be a first for me, although I figured that hunting gobblers next to a bombing area should improve my credit rating as a legion member! A sharp turn led us along the bombing area fence to the intended parking location, and I pulled my 4-Runner alongside Gordon's truck. We were early, and no one else was parked there. So far, so good.

Gordon and I spoke with hushed voices, as we extracted guns and gear from our vehicles, before quietly closing the doors. We began our walk to the chop along an old road. The road was in good shape making the walk easy, and the rain had eased up to a drizzle.

After a short five-minute hike, Gordon stopped and said, "Well, here I am. This is where my blind is located."

There was just enough gray light starting to show through the overcast pre-dawn sky for me to make out the shapes of a tree line in the distance. I felt a little awkward, as I asked Gordon what he thought I ought to do. He then proceeded to explain the layout of the land behind the chop. He referred to this area as the "prairie" and told me nobody would be in there.

"I know you like to walk a lot, and that place would be perfect you," he said. "You might have to wade through the water to get there though," he cautioned.

I don't know that up to this point in my turkey-hunting career there had ever been any obstacle that I wouldn't have overcome to get to a gobbler. Now, however, I believe I had discovered one.

Although I didn't say it out loud, I was telling myself, "There ain't no way I'm wading seventy-five yards through waist deep water in the dark, in a swamp, without waders, not knowing where I'm even going."

Now, if it was light enough to see, and there was a gobbler screaming from the roost back in the "prairie," well then that would be a different story. As it was, it wasn't about to happen. So I looked around the perimeter of the chop trying to decide what to do before it got light enough to see. About five hundred yards from where we stood I could see a line of trees jutting out into the chop. I asked Gordon if I went to the point formed by the trees jutting into the clear-cut, if that would be far enough away from his blind so as not to interfere with his hunting.

"Oh sure," Gordon replied, "That's plenty far enough away. In fact," he continued, "That is near where Jesse killed his turkey yesterday."

"Great," I thought sarcastically to myself, "that spot is probably janked-up already."

Gordon further explained that there was a large dip between where we stood and the line of trees barely visible in the distance. Gordon had one final piece of advice for me.

He informed me that, "During my hunt yesterday, I heard a shot in the far back corner of the chop."

Gordon surmised that the person who fired the shot had come in by boat and would be there again during our hunt. He warned me to stay away from that side of the chop. Not knowing what else to do, I decided to head for the point of trees, set out some decoys, and wait for daylight to decide what my next move would be.

Before leaving, I turned to Gordon and asked, "What is the best way for me to get there?"

Gordon responded by telling me that the forest service had bulldozed a large firebreak around the perimeter of the chop, and I could follow it all the way around. I shook his hand, thanked him, and wished him luck, before striking out on my own.

As I began my walk along the firebreak, I was still feeling a little frustrated with the situation. I do not like to just up-and-hunt a spot without some measure of scouting beforehand, but what was I gonna do? I tried to console myself as I made my way through large water holes and over downed trees along the dozer trail. I mean look at the bright side I told myself. I was helping Gordon; the rain had all but quit; I at least had a place I could find and start to hunt; and, after everything we had gone through to get to Florida, I was finally here and about to start my 2005 spring gobbler season – a season that would hopefully result in my lifelong dream of a Grand Slam. Yeah, I was convinced there were way too many positives to be getting all bummed out so soon. All that thinking also served to keep my mind off snakes, as I made my way along the snake haven disguised as a firebreak at the edge of the chop. The fact that I was walking without the aid of a flashlight probably also helped in my not worrying about the snakes. You know the old saying, "Ignorance is bliss!"

I hadn't quite made it to the line of trees yet when something caught my eye in the clear-cut. In the faint light, I could barely make out what looked like a small tree. I was still sixty yards from the point of trees I was trying to reach, and I was standing at the back of a "U-shaped" bend in the firebreak. I started to dismiss checking out the lone tree, and then changed my mind. I climbed out of the firebreak and made my way to the tree, which turned out to be a live oak tree with two trunks. The tree had a sort of fork at its base with two small trunks, neither of which was bigger than a one-pound coffee can in size. The tree wasn't very tall and somehow had survived the clear-cut operation, the prescribed burn, and the bulldozer. The 'lucky" tree had a bunch of brush and small branches at its base, which needed to be cleared away if I was going to use it as a backrest. Again I started to pass on it and head for the tree line, and once again I changed my mind.

"This is it," I told myself, "We're setting up here."

The little forked tree was an anomaly in a vast, wide chop that was at least one thousand yards long and one thousand yards wide. The advantage that the little tree provided me was it put me out into the chop with a little cover. It didn't put me much more than twenty yards into the clear-cut, but twenty yards could be the difference between a hung-up bird and a dead bird.

After pruning the branches and throwing out the brush, I kicked out a bare spot at the base of the tree. I got out my small, portable blind and staked it into the ground around the base of the tree. Normally I wouldn't have done this, but due to the rain, I employed it. I was tempted to put my camo umbrella up but decided to hold off unless it started raining heavily again. (When hunting turkeys in the rain, I almost without exception use this set-up. I stake out the small blind at the base of a tree and then put my umbrella up just above my head where I sit. This setup keeps me dry for the most part and also allows me to move my hands and legs without being seen. This is important because when it is raining a spring gobbler hunter has two problems: he can't hear an approaching gobbler's footsteps, and many times birds won't gobble as much, or at all, and they will approach silently. All this silence on the gobbler's part can catch a turkey hunter off guard. All it takes is one small move by the hunter to be seen by the turkey and there he is – gone! The blind helps conceal some of the hunter's movements if he is careful. The little blind I use is very small and light, and it fits easily in my hunting vest, so it doesn't interfere with my running and gunning for gobblers. If you have read my story about "Loverboy," the Rio Grande gobbler, you will understand that my small blind is lighter now than it was when purchased because it has a large swatch of material cut out of it, when once it was needed for a face mask!)

With my blind in place, I pulled my trusty decoys from my hunting vest. I stepped off seventeen yards from the blind and placed the decoys off slightly to the left. I had given both my aggressive jake and hen decoy brand new paint jobs back in January. I had also made new metal stakes for them in my welding shop. The new stakes had pins in them that would only allow the decoy to spin about a quarter turn before the pin would stop the decoy from moving. I had done these things in preparation for my Merriam's hunt. I was concerned that high winds in the Husker State would cause my decoys to spin, making them look unnatural.

I placed the jake decoy about six feet behind the hen and had both them facing away from me to my right. Satisfied with my decoy placement, I returned to my little nest at the forked tree.

It was now 5:30 a.m. as I took up residence at the base of the small tree. After readying my gun and gear, I closed my eyes in prayer. Even though I was excited about my first spring gobbler hunt of the year, I hadn't forgotten what day it was – Good Friday. My prayer that morning dwelt a little longer than normal on thanking my Savior, Jesus Christ, for dying on the cross for my sins. Lisa and I had watched "The Passion of the Christ" just a couple of days before leaving on our trip, and the images were still fresh in my mind.

Daylight finally came at about 6:00 a.m. I wanted to start calling so bad, but refrained. I don't know if all turkey hunters experience the same feelings as I do, but I am always a little nervous before making the very first call of a new season. It's a great feeling though, being nervous and excited at the same time. Finally, I couldn't wait any longer and at 6:08 a.m., I began the 2005 season. I started with soft clucks, then moved to tree yelps, then flock talk on the roost, and eventually a couple of flydown cackles. I was using a Woodhaven "V2" mouth diaphragm and a Primos "Freak" friction call to simulate all this bird noise. Unfortunately for me though, I began the 2005 season alone. I got no response to any of these imitations, no matter how well I performed them. I just sat back and relaxed and called a little, like a hen that was already on the ground. And then it happened, at 6:40 a.m. I heard my first gobble.

It sounded like the bird was roosted at the far side of the clear-cut from where Gordon and I had come in. I could see the tree line, which appeared to be composed mostly of pines. It was at least another five hundred yards off to my right. To help you understand the layout, let me explain it like this: Think of the clear-cut like a square clock – one thousand yards tall by one thousand yards wide. I am sitting at six o'clock and facing toward twelve o'clock. Gordon is five hundred yards to my left somewhere around nine o'clock, and the gobbler is roosting five hundred yards to my right at three o'clock. Directly behind me is the firebreak, then a small strip of trees and palmettos. Behind the palmettos is a large body of water, and behind the water is a large bayhead, or forest, or "prairie" – I'm not sure which. Hopefully this mental picture will help you with the rest of my account.

I waited a minute before calling back to the gobbler. I sat silently because I wanted to see if he was gobbling on his own or if possibly another bird would answer him. When nothing else sounded, I plain yelped with my mouth call. "Garrrobble" sounded back from the tree line far to my right. There was no question where this bird was; he was definitely roosting in the pines bordering the chop five hundred yards away. I waited for another minute and then called again just to see how interested he was. Again the gobbler answered me immediately. It was amazing being able to hear a turkey that was so far away. The bare clear-cut, however, had no trees or obstacles to interfere with the traveling sound waves emanating from the breast of this Osceola tom. I guess he could hear me just as well. Believe it or not though, I wasn't really all that excited. This bird was just too far away to work, and he was near the area that Gordon warned me to stay away from because of the boat hunters accessing it. Part of the reason I was calling to the gobbler was to see if he was gobbling at me or perhaps at someone else's calls. After he answered a third call from my V2, I decided to shut up. I knew that he was definitely responding to my calls. It was early, and he was still on the roost. I was afraid that if I kept him gobbling, one of the boat hunters might ease up under him and "pick a little limb fruit." So I quit calling and just sat there not really knowing what to do. I wanted to call to the other gobblers that I hoped were nearer to my position, but I didn't want to continue encouraging the boisterous tom to give away his roost location five hundred yards away.

Another five minutes passed with no turkeys calling anywhere. What the turkeys lacked in enthusiasm, the other large birds of Florida's swamps made up for. Two great blue herons came sailing straight at me and nearly clipped me, as they passed by me on my right and landed in the water behind me. Those two jokers made a racket when they came in. Not to be outdone, two sandhill cranes, with their red heads blazing, came barreling across the chop toward me next. They cackled and screamed their way past me on my left, raising a ruckus like only sandhill cranes can do. The tree I had decided to sit under needed an air traffic controller. I knew now why Jesse's bird had flown in to him the day before! Other birds were also calling and making their presence known. I heard pileated woodpeckers, a red-tailed hawk, one barred owl, and crows – lots of crows. With all the other birds letting it all hang out, Ol' Tom finally had to cut one loose.

When he gobbled this time though, I could tell he was on the ground. It sounded like he had flown down and moved toward the back corner of the clear-cut to my right. This wasn't good because this is where Gordon heard someone shoot the day before. Since the bird was on the ground now, I had no further qualms about trying to call to him, and call to him I did. He only answered me once or twice, and that was it. My first turkey hunt of the year wasn't looking too good for me at this point.

I eased up on my calling and just sat scanning the clear-cut for any sign of life, while listening intently to all the different species of birds singing and calling. As my eyes worked their way back and forth across the chop, something caught my attention on the horizon, three hundred yards away to my right at the one-o'clock position of our imaginary clock. I wasn't sure what it was, but I didn't think I had seen it before. The chop was cut and burned bare and now had small green palmettos and other green plants starting to regrow. The bright-green chutes extended from the charred, black sand, and under the overcast sky, they seemed to have a soft, green glow. Scattered randomly throughout this green blanket that was threatening to cover the chop were various fallen logs and stumps, many of which were burnt black. What had caught my attention, however, appeared to be a car tire standing on edge. I could faintly make out a round, black form on the crest of the clear-cut's horizon. As I strained to study it, I noticed what looked like a small, white dot in the center of the tire.

"That almost looks like a gobbler in strut," I thought to myself.

I started chuckling. I wanted to see a gobbler so bad that I was seeing a mirage. Whatever it was, it definitely wasn't moving. Mirage or not, I decided to call just for kicks and watch to see if it moved. I yelped and then cut on the mouth call. I could not believe what I saw. The little white dot moved from the center of the "tire" outside the tread to the left, and then returned to the center of the tire. About a half second later I heard the gobble. I was absolutely stunned; it was a gobbler!

It took me several seconds to compose myself, as I was bewildered and somewhat in a state of shock. After convincing myself that I wasn't seeing things, I experienced a dilemma that I had never encountered before during a turkey hunt. I didn't know how I should call to the bird. I hadn't been calling much at all, and the bird had come a long way already. He had flown down from the roost and covered about two hundred yards to get to his present vantage point. He could not only be heard by every turkey in the surrounding area, but he could see, and be seen, throughout the chop by any hen looking for a date. Calling aggressively is what I wanted to do, but I was afraid it might spook the bird. He was at least two hundred and fifty yards away, maybe three hundred, and although only a small speck along the crest of the clear-cut, I could see him and watch his movement. He was too far away for soft calling, so I had to decide whether to yelp or cut. It was an unusual situation to have a gobbler answering my calls from so far away, and for me to be able to hear him answer and see him coming. I mean you would have trouble beating this long distance scenario out west, and here I was faced with it in Florida of all places! If you're going to be a turkey hunter, one thing you will learn to do is make decisions. Sometimes we make the right one, and other times we make the wrong one. Some days it seems you can't do anything right, and some days it seems you can't do anything wrong. I haven't had as much experience with the latter as I have had with the former. In fact, I've become a sort of expert at messing up. There was a lot riding on the decision I was about to make, cut or yelp?

Of course, I decided to cut. The gobbler? He decided to gobble. The more I cut the more he gobbled. And then he did something better than gobbling. (I know that sounds impossible.) The tom left his strutting zone and started coming my way. He wasn't coming directly to me, but he began moving from my right to my left, following the crest of the chop. I would watch him move slowly for several seconds, and then I would call. Sometimes he would stop and gobble at me, and sometimes he would remain silent while methodically moving closer. After watching him ease along the horizon for several minutes, something brown caught my attention in the clear-cut, below and behind the tom. It was the full tail fan of another gobbler.

Well let me rephrase, it was almost a full tail fan. Dead smack in the middle of the gobbler's fan, there was a feather missing. It reminded me of a kid's smile with his front tooth missing. This "toothless" gobbler had come from the same roosting area as bird number one. However, this second bird was coming right to me. He was strutting in my direction as fast as he could come. The only thing slowing his progress was the occasional fallen log he encountered. Not to be deterred, the tom would climb up on the log and drop off the other side, strutting the whole time! As the big "toothless" bird closed the distance to one hundred and fifty yards, big-boy up on the hill had a change of heart concerning his game plan. He now found his route a bit circuitous, and decided to opt for the direct route as chosen by his competition. The first gobbler now came straight down the slight grade to me. He dropped out of strut and started running through the chop until he finally drew near to Toothless.

When the two gobblers were within ten yards of each other they both slacked off the pace, and both resumed strutting as a full-time occupation. When this occurred they were still about one hundred and twenty-five yards from me. In the open chop though, I could hear them spitting and drumming as they strutted ever closer. I had been calling the entire time as they approached. I was letting their body language and gobbling determine when and how to call. I don't think it mattered what I did on that V2 mouth call, they were sold. I had started the morning thinking I was probably wasting my time, and now here I was, one hour into my hunt, experiencing what every spring gobbler hunter dreams of: two mature gobblers strutting, gobbling, and coming – all in plain view! I was really getting excited. My gun was in position, and when they reached seventy-five yards I pushed the safety off. I have written in the past how sometimes in these situations I pray and thank the Lord for letting me experience a gobbler coming down my shotgun barrel one more time. I said just such a prayer at this point.

The gobblers could easily see my decoys now, and I knew that at any minute one or both of them was going to rush that jake of mine. I was only soft calling to the toms now with clucks and purrs. They continued their approach with Toothless in the rear until they reached the sixty-five-yard mark. For some reason, when they hit that spot they wouldn't come any further. They just continually spit and drum while strutting back and forth in front of the decoys. I was really perplexed. I could understand this behavior if I had only placed a hen decoy before them, but with a puny little jake decoy there should have been some "mean-walkin'" taking place. I tried calling to them more excitedly to break them. The longbeards would gobble at me from sixty-five yards away, but they just wouldn't commit the last twenty-five yards I needed. In fact, I began wondering where in the heck my big 3-1/2 inch Remington 870 was. So much for not having a shot at more than seventeen yards in Florida! I was sitting against a tree in a chop, which allowed me to see half the county! Who would have guessed? The gobblers kept their sixty-five-yard buffer between us for an eternal five minutes, and then they began strutting away from me to my left. I was sick. What is it about these Osceola turkeys? Do they have this habit of getting you all excited only to exit stage left and leave you holding an unfired shotgun? I had wanted to spend the morning reliving my Turkulese hunt, and now a pretty good facsimile was taking place. I used every trick in the book trying to get those two birds turned around, but it was useless. I lost sight of them at 7:15 a.m. when they went into a low place in the chop behind a dune to my left. They kept gobbling at my calls, and I could still hear them spiting and drumming, even though I could now no longer see them. There comes a time in an unsuccessful turkey hunt when you're not quite ready to give up, but deep down you know it is over. This was that moment for me; I kept calling to the gobblers, who answered my every call as they continued to move farther away. Finally, I threw in the towel. There was no use in continuing, and I was getting tired of calling – if you can believe that.

I was so frustrated with this outcome. I had called those birds off the roost a bleepety-bleep five hundred yards away, and you mean to tell me that they couldn't muster another twenty-five yards? What was the matter with those gobblers anyway? Were they some kind of wimps that were afraid to take on a girly-man jake? Heck there were two of them, they could have double-teamed the little guy! I had just been on another Osceola roller coaster, from no chance in the morning, to an unbelievable sure thing, to jack squat to show for it.

And then I got an idea – a devious, wicked idea. I could still hear the gobblers drumming behind the dune, which was about forty yards to my left. I was going to run to the dune, crawl to the top of it, and introduce one of those wimps to my 11-87. It was a foolproof plan. They would be in easy gun range from the top of the dune, and there was no way they could hear me approach in the wet sand. There weren't even any trees for them to run behind – it was a slam-dunk! There was only one small problem with my plan; that's not the kind of turkey hunter I am. (Although as agitated as I was, the thought of crossing over to the dark side and "bushwhacking" one of them did cross my mind.) Instead, I decided to let the birds go. It sounded as if they were heading straight for Gordon's set-up, and I intended to let him have them. The way I saw it they were his birds anyway. In fact, as I thought about his encounter from the day before with "two gobblers that stayed in the chop and wouldn't come to his decoys," I was nearly convinced that these were the same two birds. They certainly fit the "M.O." No, I would just sit and wait to hear Gordon's gun go off, and then I'd get a good look at one of them. I started to feel a little better about the situation, convincing myself that I had called those birds off the roost five hundred yards away for Gordon to kill. That would certainly be an acceptable payback for getting me a permit. As I sat there contemplating these things, a large crow flew into the chop behind the dune to my left and landed on the top of a spindly little tree that had no branches. As the small spine of the tree swayed under the weight of the crow, he hammered a "caw, caw, cawww," from his perch. The two wimpy toms shock gobbled in unison at the black raven. They sounded like they were about one hundred yards away from me now, still on a collision course for Gordon's blind.

With the two birds I had been hunting gone, I wasn't sure what to do next. The sky was overcast and foreboding, but the rain had stopped completely. I began to contemplate leaving my position on the chop and heading for the wooded area beyond the water behind me. Thing is, I didn't know how to get around the water, and I really didn't want to wade it. I decided that it would be foolish for me to leave my spot in the clear-cut just yet. After all, I had called two birds in close to my little tree. With all the calling that both the gobblers and I had done, and with sound carrying so well across the open chop, surely other birds had heard the racket we made. Another gobbler may try to sneak in and check out the situation I mused. So I stayed put and continued calling about once every five minutes.

I had tried every trick in the book to no avail. However, I have a motto: "When every trick in the book fails, get another book." So sometime around 7:45 a.m., I switched books, so to speak. Actually, I switched calls. Now there is no such thing as a perfect turkey call, nor is there any such thing as a magic turkey call that will work every time. However, not all turkey calls are made the same, and some are better than others. Like anything else in life, the better ones usually cost a little more. At this point during my hunt, I removed from my vest a new friction call that, heretofore, I had never used on a turkey hunt. The call was custom made and was the most expensive call I had ever bought, carrying with it a price tag of seventy dollars. I had used the call frequently during practice sessions, but had never hunted with it. Several women in the Clifton Forge, Virginia area are probably still mad at me for demonstrating the call at one of my turkey hunting "Roost" parties. All of these women share something in common: they are closely related to friends of mine by marriage. After the get-together at my home, several of my friends "just had to have one" once they had heard the call's unbelievable sounds. The call is a slate-type model with a crystal striking surface and a cherry sound board. When run properly, the call produces a yelp with an extremely high-pitched front end that drops off sharply to a deep rasp. The call seems to literally ring in my ears when I practice with it. I had always hoped that it would have

Severe Gobbler Disorder

the same affect on an old longbeard, once I employed its use in the turkey woods. Now, for the first time ever, I was going to do just that. Along with the new book's recommendation for a new friction call, it also called for a new mouth call as well. I pulled a MAD Calls "Metcalf Cutter" diaphragm from my vest and slid it into my mouth. As far as I know this was the first time for me to ever use that particular style call from MAD. So there I was ready to break in two new calls on the hardheaded Osceola gobblers of Marion County, Florida.

I started my calling sequence with the friction call. As I applied pressure to the surface of the call with my laminated striker, it rang out those beautifully high and raspy notes as previously described. Before I even had a chance to admire my handling of the call in a hunting situation, the woods around the chop erupted with gobbles. One deep gobble boomed from the woods across the water behind me. Another, which sounded like a jake's gobble, came from the woods far down the edge of the chop to my right. A hen also answered me with yelps of her own somewhere near the jake's location. The other two gobbles that I heard came from guess who? Yep, Toothless and his buddy answered me from way up near Gordon's blind. I couldn't believe the response that call had brought. I had been calling for the last half hour without so much as a peep from any turkey; now they were answering me from everywhere. I continued to employ the use of the friction call and the mouth call to sound like two hens "carrying-on" in the chop. My senses went on full alert as I considered the possibility of the gobbler behind me flying across the water to get to the clear-cut. The way those birds answered me, I just knew something was about to happen. Unfortunately, and as usual, I was wrong. I had backed off on my calling because I was convinced the birds would come to me. Since nothing had showed up, I decided to try the "magic" friction call again. I ran the crystal again, but this time I got nothing in response. Dang, I was aggravated. As I looked at my watch it was now exactly 8:00 a.m.

"That's it," I thought to myself, "I'm outa here."

I hadn't heard a gobble in over fifteen minutes. It was clear that nothing was coming my way.

"I need to get after the gobbler that had hammered away at me from the woods across the water behind me," I told myself.

If I didn't make my move soon, he was liable to be gone by the time I found my way into his lecht. Every fiber of my being wanted to get up right then and take off after him. The only thing that was stopping me was my rule, my "fifteen-minute rule." This rule that I invented was designed by me to make me sit still after making a call. The "fifteen-minute rule" works like this: If any turkey answers my calls during the course of a set-up, then I cannot leave the set-up for at least fifteen minutes after making another call – whether the last call is answered or not. The fifteen-minute rule forces me to make sure that a gobbler which has decided to sneak in has the opportunity to make himself visible before I get up to leave and spook him. I developed this rule after numerous occasions when I had given up on a bird only to spook it by leaving too soon. The rule was conjured up for situations just like the one I found myself in now. With the fifteen-minute rule now in play, I could not leave my set-up until 8:15 a.m. – that is provided I didn't make any more calls. If I did elect to call again, then the fifteen-minute-rule clock would be reset to zero and would have to be started again from scratch. Those fifteen minutes passed so very slowly. I kept looking at my watch fretting about the gobbler in the woods behind me.

When 8:15 a.m. finally arrived, I started to doubt my decision to leave. I knew those gobblers had been all fired up. I was still having trouble believing that nothing was working my way. Almost with a sigh, I convinced myself to make one more desperate plea. Reluctantly, I shifted the diaphragm call from my cheek to the roof of my mouth. I used the Metcalf Cutter mouth call to make my final attempt at dragging a response from one the gobblers that had answered me previously. After completing the calling sequence, I sat there listening intently. In the infamous words of Yukon Cornelius, "Nuttin!"

"Dang it man," I thought to myself, "Now I have to wait another stinkin' fifteen minutes before I can leave!"

Let me tell you, I was real happy with myself. I now had to stay put until 8:30 a.m. to satisfy my self-imposed legislation.

With a new fifteen minutes to kill, I decided to start packing up my calls and strikers that were strewn about me in my nest behind the blind. I separated mouth call reeds with toothpicks and neatly returned everything to its proper location in my hunting vest. I also kept tabs on my wristwatch like a kid watching the clock in his classroom on the last day of school.

"C'mon 8:30," I kept thinking.

When 8:30 a.m. finally arrived, it did so with me literally watching the second hand on my watch strike twelve. As soon as it did, I stood up. I stretched and leaned my shotgun against the tree I had been sitting at for the past three hours. I then turned completely around to view the woods and water behind me, in an effort to try and locate an entrance into the wooded area where the gobbler had been earlier.

"How was I going to get across that water?" I wondered.

When I stood to survey the area behind the chop, I did so with my headnet still up and my mouth call still in my cheek. Normally, I would pull my headnet down when getting up to move to a new location. In the mosquito-infested swamps of Florida, however, a headnet does more than disguise a hunter's face from the view of a wild turkey. It also serves as protection from the biting bugs that constantly harass him. Leaving that headnet on would prove to be a critical decision. Also, before I stood, I slipped my vest's shoulder straps off my shoulders so the vest would remain on the ground as I stood. So I am standing with my vest on the ground, my gun leaning against the tree to my right, and my back towards the chop I had been watching all morning. I just couldn't figure out how to move on that other gobbler I had heard behind me earlier. As I was standing there looking over the water, I thought I heard something. It sounded like a gobbler spitting and drumming. Only moving my head, I snapped it around for a look over my left shoulder into the clear-cut, half expecting to see a gobbler strutting. Unfortunately, there was no such sight to behold, just the same old barren chop I had been staring at for the past hour and fifteen minutes. I turned my head back around to resume studying the area behind my blind.

"You want to kill a turkey so bad you're hearing things!" I told myself.

Several seconds went by when again I thought I heard the drumming of a strutting gobbler. This time though I wasn't about to turn my head around.

"I'm not falling for that again," I thought.

I decided to just stand still and listen really close. Twice more I could have sworn that I heard the faint sound of a drumming gobbler. I lowered my chin to my chest and strained to hear the sound again. "Fittt...Baaaaaroooomm," sounded audibly behind me.

"That was definitely a gobbler!" I told myself. "He must be behind the dune like Toothless and his buddy were earlier," I thought. "I could hear them drumming but couldn't see them either. I had better get turned back around and get my gun ready," I convinced myself.

Before turning or sitting, I decided to take a look over my shoulder just to make sure the coast was clear. As I eased my head around to peer over my left shoulder once again, I just about messed my pants, because the coast was anything but clear.

The vast green and gray chop before me now held two large gobblers in full strut, with their large, black bodies backed by wide brown tail fans, and their red, white, and blue heads tucked into their breasts. It was the sight I had been looking for all morning. The two longbeards were already in gun range about forty yards away, and even better, they were coming as fast as a strutting gobbler can move. Also of note about these two monster toms, they were the same two gobblers from earlier. I knew this because the gobbler in front was Toothless, his missing tail feather leaving no doubt as to his identity. The only problem now was that I was standing up, facing away from them, with my shotgun leaning harmlessly against the tree. I was stuck! Whatever reason they had had earlier for not coming to the decoys had been definitely overcome now, as they marched straight at them, and at me for that matter. I was ready to cuss. If they had been two minutes earlier this would have been perfect. Instead, I was caught with my pants down, so to speak.

I had no other recourse than to just stand completely still with my head turned as far as it would go to my left and watch the gobblers advance from over my left shoulder. They were huge! As they closed the distance towards the decoys, I noticed that the bird in the back had a rope for a beard. It appeared to be at least eleven inches in length, and it was very heavy. I made up my mind at that very moment that if somehow a miracle happened, and I was able to get a shot at these birds, I was going to try for the gobbler with the eleven-inch beard and the full tail fan. I had never killed a gobbler with a legitimate eleven-inch beard, and I would probably mount the bird's fan for my wall. Since they were probably the same age, it made sense to me to try for the back bird. I always try to harvest the dominant gobbler when faced with a shot at multiple longbeards. I had intuitively decided from my encounter with these two birds at daybreak that Toothless was probably the dominant bird, although I couldn't be sure about it. Neither one really did anything to clue me in on who the boss was. They acted like carbon copies of each other, with neither one out-strutting the other. I took them both to be two-year-old birds. I couldn't see their spurs due to the black char and sand remaining from the burn, and since they had showed reservation at approaching my aggressive jake earlier, it just made sense to me that they were two years of age. All this planning of mine was a mute point. Getting a shot at them now was just about an impossibility. I couldn't move a muscle, let alone reach for my gun, turn around, and somehow get a shot at them. So I just stood there, stock still, thinking about what I would do if I could.

When the two gobblers reached my decoys, they were less than twenty yards from me. Toothless strutted right past the jake and stopped about fifteen yards from me, positioning himself between me and my decoys. The other gobbler's true identity was then revealed. This second bird was apparently the Osceola turkey's version of a "hitman." This was the bird that had gobbled originally from the roost, and the one that I had spotted looking like a tire at the top of the clear-cut's horizon at dawn. I'm not sure if he was the brains of the operation, but he was definitely the muscle. Unlike Toothless, the Hitman, with his full fan and eleven-inch beard, didn't strut past the jake decoy. Instead he strutted right to it.

While this was taking place, I had made up my mind to do something about the predicament I was in. I decided that I basically had no chance to kill one of these birds, so why not try something insane. After all, insane is something that I excel at. The crazy plan I concocted was to start moving downward as slowly as I could. I would try to mimic a shadow moving down a wall; with my movements so slow they would be undetected. I was concerned about several problems with this plan, the toughest one being able to remain still as my thighs would surely begin to burn, if and when I was able to reach the half-squatting position. I decided to worry about that when the time came – if I was fortunate enough to even get that far. What the heck did I have to lose by trying? So with my head cocked completely to the left, and my eyes fixed on the gobblers, I nervously began my descent.

When Hitman reached the jake decoy, his posture changed. He moved his head from its tucked position in his breast and raised it to look directly into the eye of the jake. He dropped his tail fan from the erect position to about half-mast, and walked head-on at the decoy. As he neared my fake gobbler, Hitman slowly stretched his right wing out to his side while angling himself slightly to the right. Upon reaching the aggressive looking youngster, Hitman slowly raised his right wing and then in a flash, used it to smack the decoy right in the head. The force of big gobbler's blow spun the jake decoy violently to one side before it hit the pin that I had installed to limit the decoy's travel in windy conditions. When the decoy hit the pin, it naturally "snapped back" to its original position facing the menacing longbeard, which was standing in front of it. It was almost as if the little guy took the big bird's best shot and snapped right back in front of him like, "Is that all you've got?" Apparently, I'm not the only one who got that impression from the decoy's movement, because Hitman "went off" when that decoy came right back to the same spot. Why the nerve of this little punk embarrassing him like that in front of his running buddy, Toothless! I'm telling you the truth, I believe I could see the anger well up in the gobbler's face, as he went berserk attacking my little jake.

If I wasn't in the throes of a leg-burning, undetectable descent, I'm sure I would have been laughing at the antics of the furious gobbler. As it was, I had my hands full executing my extreme maneuver downward. Twice during my grueling attempt to get to the ground I was spotted by Toothless. Both times he slicked up from strutting and stood there with his head cocked in my direction, watching me intently with one eye, from about thirty feet away. As interested as he was in determining if the funny looking tree behind him had moved or not, he couldn't stay focused on me for long because of Hitman's pummeling of the jake. Hitman was screaming fighting purrs as he attacked the decoy. Try as he might to keep his eye on me, the ruckus behind Toothless would eventually capture his attention, and he would resume strutting. When he did, I would resume breathing, but just barely. Toothless would spread out and turn back towards the beating taking place near the edge of the chop. I would resume my descent.

The beating had turned to flat out murder. Hitman had knocked both decoys, the hen as well as the jake, flat on the ground in his fit of rage. This took some doing, since I had set the jake approximately six feet behind the hen. The furious gobbler was jumping up in the air and coming down on my flattened jake decoy hitting it with both of his wings and spurring it with his hooks. His uncontrollable anger had caused him to flatten the innocent little hen decoy by accident. Anyway, I hope I am conveying to you the aggression and fury displayed by Hitman. He was kickin' butt and takin' names, and I was almost down to my knees.

About one week before this trip to Florida, a turkey-hunting friend of mine asked me if I had ever watched a gobbler attack my decoys.

"Nope," I said smugly, "I'm not out there to make a National Geographic documentary of turkey behavior. I'm out there to kill them. I never let a gobbler get close enough to my decoys to fight them, because as soon as he is in good gun range, I bust him," I finished telling my friend.

Well, I couldn't say that anymore, and it's a good thing too. Hitman was so engrossed with busting that jake that he never saw me move, and it was his fighting that kept redirecting Toothless' attention off of me. And then it happened; I finally reached the ground undetected! I was on my knees with my back still towards the gobblers and my head still turned looking over my left shoulder. My next move was to get my shotgun.

Without taking my eyes off the gobblers, I eased my right hand slowly along the ground until I felt the butt stock of my Remington. I slowly worked my hand up the stock until I had a hold on the comb. I was able to get away with this movement courtesy of the little ground blind I had set-up because of the rain. Even though it only provided a small amount of cover, it was proving to be a lifesaver. With the gun in my right hand and my eyes locked on the gobblers, I started to lift the autoloader away from the tree and bring it towards my lap. "Clang – Crunch!" – that is a good description of what I heard next as the gun slipped from my hand and fell to the ground, wedging itself between the two small liveoak trees! For the second time in a five-minute period I just about messed my pants. Toothless just about messed his too. He slicked up again and put his now familiar eye on me for the third time. I was so nervous. I just knew I had blown it this time.

"I'm the Bad News Bear of turkey hunters," I thought, holding my breath and hoping Toothless wouldn't spook.

Unbelievably, Hitman bailed me out again, as he continued stomping the life out of that decoy. Toothless turned to look at the jumping gobbler and resumed strutting.

"Whew that was close!" I thought, as once again I slid my hand along the ground feeling for the shotgun.

It took me a second to free it from between the two trees, and this time I had a death grip on it with my right hand as I guided it away from the trees and across my knees. My left hand then moved slowly to take its proper hold on the forearm of the 11-87. I now had my shotgun in my lap with both hands holding it properly. I pushed the safety off, and even though my head was still looking over my shoulder at the gobblers, I believe a smile came to my face.

"I've got them now!" I thought triumphantly.

Even though I was on my knees with my back toward the gobblers, I knew I could spin around and get a shot at them now, even if they spooked. The fact that I had my autoloading shotgun also served to comfort me, because even if I missed a shot at a running bird, I had two follow-ups at the touch of the trigger. My confidence was further buoyed by the fact that there were no trees or cover for the turkeys to put between themselves and me should they deem a hasty retreat necessary. However, despite all this confidence and my uncontrollable excitement anticipating a chance to finally take a shot at one of these two longbeards that had frustrated me all morning; I had enough sense to do absolutely nothing. Everything was in my favor now, and I decided to just be patient. So I sat there on my knees watching the birds over my shoulder – Hitman was still flogging the lifeless jake and Toothless was strutting. Both gobblers were purring, but Hitman's purrs were furious.

It didn't take long before Toothless, in full strut, turned toward Hitman. This caused his butt to turn towards me, and his tail fan blocked the heads of both birds even though it had the large gap in the center. It was the opportunity I had been waiting for. In one quick motion, I spun around from off my knees and sat flat on my butt, while at the same time bringing my shotgun to bear against my right shoulder. My head settled in on the gun's butt stock and my right eye peered through the scope settling the crosshairs directly on the tail fan of Toothless. Neither turkey saw or heard a thing! He was mine now! I just sat there, gun at the ready, safety off, waiting for the right moment. Both gobblers were less than twenty yards from me, and Toothless was between me and Hitman. Hitman was still the bird I wanted to take, not just because of his fan and beard anymore, but in defense of my trusty jake. My breathing had become steadier now as I waited for something to happen, and then Toothless strutted slowly to my right, exposing Hitman to my gun barrel.

Hitman was standing directly on top of my jake decoy when Toothless eased out of the line of fire. I moved my gun slightly to center the crosshairs on the big Osceola's waddles. Hitman was looking directly at me and saw the movement. He raised his head a little higher to get a better look at me, and I touched the trigger. "KABOOM!" The 11-87 barked once, and Hitman's worries were over. He hit the ground in a lifeless heap right next to my dead jake decoy. Every pellet from that 1-5/8 ounce load of Hevishot No. 6s launched from its three-inch shell hit that bird in the head and neck. I mean I don't think it knocked a single feather from him! That ol' 11-87 of mine is just plain nasty!

At the sound of the shot, Toothless did his best impression of a roadrunner. He came out of strut and in the same motion was off to the races. He took a course straight away from me to the right of the decoys. Remember that I said earlier that I still had my mouth call in my cheek? Toothless had made it about ten yards by the time I was able to get my mouth call positioned properly to use. He stopped just past the decoys to look back, and I cut loudly to him on the mouth call. "GARRROBBLE!" He thundered back, hesitating at what to do next. I cut to the gobbler again, and immediately, he dropped back into full strut! It was awesome! He was standing there strutting no more than thirty yards away, and I had my gun sights resting on him! I cut to him again and though he refused to gobble, he started strutting back in my direction. It was actually kind of funny. I mean just a few minutes before, there had been four turkeys standing there (albeit two of them were decoys). Now three were lying flat on the ground and only Toothless remained. It must have made him feel larger than life, because he was full of himself strutting around the fallen birds.

When I first related this story to my friends and family, many of them asked me the obvious question, "Did you shoot him too?"

My reply?

"No, I didn't shoot the gobbler," I said with a grin, "But let me tell you…I had all the slack out of the trigger!"

It took all the moral fortitude I had not to bust this gobbler too, after the way he had aggravated me throughout the morning. Refrain I did though, as I was only legally allowed to take one bird on my permit. I was content to save this bird for Gordon.

Toothless was pretty content to just continue strutting, until my dead gobbler started to move after lying motionless for a minute. My dead bird started to flap his wings as a reflex action common to dead turkeys. As he beat his lifeless wings, he was slowly flopping along the ground straight to me. This startled Toothless at first, but then his caution gave way to bravado. He started chasing my flopping bird, while maintaining his strutting posture. (I know that technically he was displaying and not strutting – strutting just sounds better!) Hitman flopped almost into my lap. He continued flopping until his progress was impeded by two, fallen logs, which he managed to wedge himself between – only twenty feet in front of me. Hot on his trail was Toothless. When Hitman finally stopped, Toothless strutted up to the fallen trees and jumped up on one of them to peruse his fallen companion. Toothless stood on the log overlooking Hitman cautiously for about ten seconds, and then he slid off the log onto the back of my gobbler. Toothless then proceeded to strut while standing on Hitman's back, and shortly thereafter decided to attack the lifeless bird. Toothless began pecking my gobbler's neck and head repeatedly. Each time he would actually pick my bird's head up off the ground, before dropping it and attacking it again.

"That's one heck of a way to show respect for an old friend at his funeral!" I thought, chuckling to myself.

I was content to watch the gobbler's antics for a short time. Eventually though, I decided that there was no sense in letting him "tear up" my hard won prize. I hadn't knocked a single feather out of the bird, and Toothless was plucking them left and right. While all I planned to use from the gobbler was his tail fan, I decided to put an end to the living bird's fun. I did so by raising my head away from the stock on my shotgun, which was pointed right at the bird less than ten steps from me. When my head moved, Toothless putted once and came straight to attention. For the fourth time in five minutes, he was slicked-up and staring at me eye-to-eye. This time though he was doing it while standing on my turkey's back! Confused once again as to what I was, he continued to just stand there motionless, peering at me with his left eye. Now it's not often that a turkey hunter has the opportunity, let alone the desire, to choose any method he wants to purposely spook a mature gobbler. This was unfamiliar ground for me. With all the options at my disposal, I chose the following:

I simply looked the gobbler straight in the eye and politely said, "Good Morning!"

Whew Boy! You should have seen that gobbler freak out! He putted, jumped the log behind my gobbler, and took off running like a bat outta…you know the rest. When he had gone about twenty yards he stopped and looked back at me over his left "shoulder," like, "What in the heck was that?" The gobbler took off running for another few yards before stopping once again and looking back at me. I decided to stand up and get out of my little nest. When I did, Toothless let out another "putt" and proceeded to run full speed all the way across the chop away from me. I watched him run for two hundred yards without a single misstep before I lost sight of him. I laughed the whole time I watched him go.

As I stood to retrieve my turkey, I was one happy boy. Against all odds, I had killed another mature Osceola gobbler. The only reason I was even here, instead of hunting in the swamp trying to reminisce about my hunt for Turkulese, was to help a friend. Now, I had not only killed a turkey, but I had just experienced a hunt that would rank equally with, if not better than, that of Turkulese! It had taken me one hour and fifty minutes to kill Turkulese, who succumbed to my shotgun at 8:30 a.m. Hitman, now, had taken me exactly two hours to kill, succumbing to my Remington at 8:40 a.m. It was like déjà vu – all over again! I was so pumped as I walked to my gobbler, that it was hard not to start shouting. I refrained though for the sake of Gordon and his hunt taking place on the near side of the chop. I had to do something, so I bellowed out a loud "WHHOO, WH-

HHOOOAAAWWW!" mimicking a barred owl. Little did I know that my celebration was about to get a whole lot better.

When I reached the fallen Osceola gobbler, I knelt down in the sand and prayed to my Eternal God in heaven. I thanked him over and over and over, for His blessing to me. How in the world could this have happened? It was providential, to say the least. If our flight hadn't been cancelled, I wouldn't even be hunting here; I would have been where I killed Turkulese. Because we had driven and gotten in so late, I didn't have time to scout. However, if we hadn't been able to purchase the plane tickets, we would have never decided to come to Florida. So in the divine order of things, I needed to buy the tickets, then have them cancelled at the very moment we were planning to leave, then decide to drive to Florida, then miss my opportunity to scout, then agree to help Gordon by parking next to him, then have it rain so I would use my little blind, and then I would have the opportunity to put my hands on my second Osceola gobbler. I am convinced that this is the sort of thing that happens when you put God first and pray about decisions, like Lisa and I had done before buying the plane tickets. It is also the kind of thing that just may happen when you put someone else's desires before your own, like I had done with Gordon's request. I guess what it boils down to is that I am not a very good turkey hunter; I am just a blessed turkey hunter. I was so thankful and pumped about the end result of this hunt, but the best part was still unknown to me at this point.

After praying and giving God the glory for what he had done for me, I triumphantly extracted my gobbler from the logs he was wedged between.

As usual, I was most interested in the bird's battle gear, so I immediately rolled the bird over to inspect his two-year-old spurs. I was not prepared for what I saw. This gobbler was no two-year-old, not by a long shot. The spurs that this bird possessed would be more appropriately referred to as "gaffs." They were incredible! At first glance I knew they were legitimately 1-1/2 inches in length! They were hooked and sharp, just like every Osceola hunter hopes to kill. I just about "freaked-out" when I realized what I had just killed. The bird that I just assumed was a two-year-old because of his behavior at first light and his close association with another longbeard was obviously incorrect. The bird that I shot, because he had an eleven-inch beard and all the primary feathers in his tail fan, turned out to be a monster. I now knew why "Hitman" was the enforcer; he not only had a mean streak, which he displayed for me and my decoy, but he also had the hardware to back it up. After seeing the spurs – that according to my brother when he saw them for the first time were "bigger than the bird's back toe" – I celebrated and prayed all over again! Still not wanting to hurt Gordon's chances during his morning's hunt, it took everything I had not to just start yelling and jumping all over the place.

Spurs not withstanding, I eventually got around to studying everything else about this tremendous gobbler. He had it all. His beard was not only long, but also heavy from its base to the tip. The beard measured just over one-inch in width where it exited the skin at the breast. The beard was very thick, but as a tape measure would later prove, it wouldn't quite make the eleven inches I had assumed. Sadly, it fell one quarter of an inch short, taping out to an even 10-3/4 inches. My next surprise came when I lifted the gobbler off the ground. This bird was heavy, and I knew it the moment he cleared the sand of Ocala's National Forest. He felt to me like he weighed as much, if not more, than the Eastern gobblers I typically kill. The bird's official weight as recorded by the NWTF's Wild Turkey records stands at nineteen pounds, twelve ounces. That makes him one big Osceola gobbler. In fact, when I eventually registered this gobbler with the NWTF, he ranked as the 72nd highest-scoring typical Osceola gobbler ever taken, boasting a net score of 71.25 points. Not only would this turkey be a high scoring Osceola, he remains to date as my highest scoring bird of any gobbler I have ever taken. How about that for a spur of the moment trip to Florida, park next to a buddy, first morning of the year turkey hunt?

Of course, standing there in the wet sand of the Florida clear-cut, I was unaware at the time of how high the bird would eventually score after his official measurements were taken. Even so, I already knew he was special, and I was having trouble calming down. I got myself composed enough to take photos of the gobbler with the little camera I had in my turkey vest. I then used the camera to take pictures of my set-up, the clear-cut, and my decoys lying in the sand, demolished by Hitman. As I looked closer at my poor, valiant turkey imitations, I noticed that they were not only damaged, but they were also spattered with Hitman's blood. The jake had several spatters along his side, and the hen, which was several feet away, had several spots of crimson dotting her side. I made sure I documented the evidence with my camera before picking up my faithful jake decoy. The poor thing was mashed! The metal stake that supported it was bent in two places from Hitman's attack, and I don't mean just a little; I mean it had irreparable damage. In addition to the bent stake, the little metal arms of the umbrella that I put inside the decoy to expand it were poking through the side of my rubber decoy. It was a mess, but it had done its job. I couldn't have done it without him!

It was still early in the day, and even though I couldn't wait to get back to the motel and tell Lisa about my hunt, I knew Gordon was still in his blind because I hadn't heard him shoot. If I left to go back to my 4-Runner, I would have to walk past his set-up to get there, and there was no way I was going to do that and take a chance at messing him up. So instead of leaving, I packed up all my gear and put it neatly in its proper place in my vest. Then I sat down at the tree where I had been hunting, laid my monster gobbler in the sand by my left side, and pulled my Bible out of my hunting vest. Despite all the excitement of my morning's hunt, I hadn't forgotten what day it was. It was Good Friday, the traditional anniversary of my Savior's death on the cross for my sins. I prayed again thanking Jesus for what he did for me there at Calvary, and once again for the blessing of the morning. I then read all four Gospel accounts of the crucifixion. That was a special day for me to sit there in the sand on Good Friday reading my Bible with my left elbow resting on the biggest Osceola I will ever kill. Many who read this story might not get what I'm talking about, but I know a lot of my fellow Christian hunters will. If you don't get it, I hope you will join the latter group I refer to.

After reading my Bible, I had plenty of time to just sit and reflect on my morning's hunt. One neat thing that occurred to me was that the gobbler I had just harvested was most likely hatched the very same spring as Turkulese. My first Osceola gobbler, harvested in 2003, was three years old. Hitman, my second Osceola, was at least five years old, alluding to the fact that he too was hatched in the spring of 2000. I found that very ironic and pretty cool. The other thing that I considered while sitting there watching the sun try to peak through the overcast sky, was that the last two times I had ventured into the swamps of Florida, I had killed a mature gobbler. I mean c'mon, now, who would believe that in my last four hours of spring gobbler hunting on public land in Florida for Osceola gobblers that I had killed two of them? Certainly not me – I have trouble killing one gobbler in forty hours of hunting on my own stomping grounds at home!

Sometime around 11:00 a.m. I just couldn't take it anymore. I had to get outta' there and see Lisa. I rounded up my gun and slung the big swamp turkey over my shoulder. Quietly and carefully I began my walk around the chop following the firebreak back to the road where I had left Gordon at dawn. When I drew near to his blind, Gordon stood and walked over to the road to meet me. He shook my hand and was very gracious in congratulating me. Gordon was impressed with the gobbler and told me I should enter it in the state of Florida's awards program. At the time, that was the last thing on my mind. I just wanted to tell someone about what had happened, and Gordon was my man. The first thing I asked him was if he heard the turkey gobble after I had shot.

He affirmed that he had, stating, "I wondered what the heck you were doing, I thought maybe you had missed him somehow!"

I joked with him saying, "I figure the gobbler stopped after I shot because he imagined that the blast was just another bombing run!"

We laughed together and then Gordon wanted to know what call I had been using because, he said, "That thing lit them birds up all over the place".

I filled Gordon in on the morning's events, while he listened intently just shaking his head. As we talked about the morning, I asked him how close the gobblers had come to his blind. Gordon looked at me like I was nuts and told me that he never saw the two birds. Oh sure, he heard them gobbling below him, but they never came up out of the dip in the chop. That blew my mind. I knew we were about five hundred yards apart, but I had been convinced the birds had traveled all the way past his blind after leaving my decoys and me.

I told Gordon that I kept waiting to hear his gun go off and kept wondering to myself, "Why hasn't he busted one of them yet?"

At this point in our conversation Gordon asked me if I had seen the hen that came to my calls.

"What hen?" I responded with a perplexed expression on my face.

Gordon proceeded to tell me about a hen that he had watched come all the way across the chop heading right to my position. He related that when she started getting near where I was, she just stopped for a few moments before turning around and running all the way back to the woods where she had come from. As we discussed the time that this occurred, it became apparent what had happened. The hen was coming to my blind at about 8:30 a.m. – the time that I had determined to stand up after satisfying the fifteen-minute rule. Though I never saw her, she obviously must have seen me when I stood and turned around to view the prairie behind me. The small dim light that I possess and pass off as a brain came on at this moment during our conversation. I had been cussing myself for standing and getting "caught with my pants down" by the gobblers. Now, however, I conceded that instead of being the blunder of a turkey-hunting lifetime, standing up and unknowingly spooking that hen may have put the "turkey on the table." If I had seen the hen and remained seated, when the gobblers showed up a minute later I would have never been able to get those two longbeards to leave the real hen and come to my decoys. I would have been left hanging again. How amazing to find out my blunder turned into a blessing! If Gordon had not been there to witness what happened, I would have never known the rest of the story!

I shook hands with Gordon thanking him for inviting me to park next to him, before picking up my swamp gobbler and hiking back to the 4-Runner. Once my gear was stowed in the truck, I decided to give Hitman his first ride in my Toyota and pulled the SUV onto the red-sand road leading out of the Ocala National Forest. As I drove the first fifteen minutes through the sand, my excitement began to rise and my mind raced thinking about what I had just accomplished and what this second Osceola could mean to me. I had now taken two Osceolas, of course I had killed two Easterns, I had actually killed two Rios in Oklahoma the previous year albeit one was a jake, and in about three weeks, I was going to Nebraska to hunt Merriam's, and, lo and behold, I had two Nebraska turkey tags! If I filled both tags in Nebraska I would not only accomplish my lifelong dream of a Grand Slam, but I would record two Slams! That was incomprehensible!

"You gotta' be kidding me," I thought!

By the time I reached the hard cap leading to the checking station, I couldn't control my emotions anymore. I'm not sure how to describe what was going on in my truck, but the best attempt I can give is that I was "going off." It became one of the most emotional times of my life as an outdoorsman, just me alone in my SUV driving down the road in rural Florida, probably weaving like a drunk driver. I was yelling, pumping my fists, and throwing my hat.

For some reason I just kept shouting, "I did it! I can't believe it! Yeah, baby! I did it! Yes! Yes! Yes! I did it!"

Over and over again I kept repeating things like that with the only other interjections being, "Thank you Lord!" "Thank you Jesus!" "Thank you!"

When I look back on this hunt, that moment in my truck stands out to me more than even killing the gobbler. It was special for a dumb ol' boy from West Virginia. I hope every turkey hunter reading this has, or will, experience that kind of moment in his or her own hunting career.

After calming down and checking my turkey in at my favorite checking station in the United States, I turned the 4-Runner for town and our motel. I had a forty-minute drive to make, so I got on the cell phone and called Lisa at the room to tell her about my success. After talking to her briefly, I decided to call a good friend of mine, Barry Daniel, at his home in Virginia. I've mentioned Barry before in my stories. He's a brother in Christ, and one of the best turkey hunters I know. Barry is older than I and has probably killed more gobblers than I will ever see. He and I love to talk about turkey hunting with each other. This shared interest of ours has been the cause for both of our wives to be stranded in the car after a church service patiently waiting for us to quit talking. Barry knew I was trying to complete my slam, and he knew I was traveling to Florida. He vowed to pray for me as I traveled and hunted. In fact, he was called on to pray at our church's Wednesday evening service on the eve of our departure for Florida, and Barry prayed for me publicly to have a safe trip. I say all that because I wanted you to know why I felt compelled to call Barry. Barry's wife Brenda answered the phone when I called from my truck traveling back to the motel. She informed me that he was at work and told me to call him there. Brenda, an accomplished turkey hunter in her own right, congratulated me on my bird and provided me with Barry's work phone number. I hesitated to call Barry at work, but then determined that this was an emergency. I was going to bust if I couldn't tell someone about the amazing hunt and the huge gobbler!

Barry answered the phone, and it took him a minute to grasp the fact that it was I calling him, from Florida of all places. I was so excited that I told him the whole story. He was laughing at me over the phone and asking me questions about the hunt and my bird. He then informed me that he wanted to borrow my "golden horseshoe," which he claimed I not only owned, but that I had stuck up my...well, you know...that place where there aint' much sunshine. We were both laughing, and I couldn't really argue with him. Truth is though, I don't really have a golden horseshoe, I just have a loving, Heavenly Father who sits on a golden throne! By the way, that is way better than any horseshoe! Barry and I talked until I pulled into the motel parking lot. He congratulated me one last time as we said good-bye and hung up. I parked the Toyota and headed for our motel room.

Lisa was ecstatic with my success, not so much because I had killed a monster tom, but because I couldn't hunt anymore. Now we could spend the rest of our weekend doing vacation stuff in Orlando. That suited me too, because it meant that I would get a couple of good night's sleep for a change. Lisa and I drove all the way back to the National Forest where I killed my gobbler, and she took photographs of the turkey for me. As we were driving there, I noticed a small breast feather from my gobbler blowing around the inside of the 4-Runner. It finally came to rest on the gearshift, and I drew Lisa's attention to it.

She looked at me funny and said, "What?"

"That's so cool!" I said exuberantly, pointing to the little feather.

Lisa just rolled her eyes at me. Obviously she just doesn't appreciate the effort it takes to get a loose Osceola feather floating around in your vehicle. Anyway, unknown to me at the time of our photograph session, Lisa saw the rouge feather stuck on the backrest of the driver's seat and photographed it to use up the last frame of film on the camera. That picture now has a little more sentimental value to me. At the conclusion of our photo session, I pulled the little feather from the seat and stuck it innocently in the visor of the Toyota as a memento. I still have that little feather. I also have three others similar to it. They are all still stuck in the visor of my 4-Runner. The other three were collected within the next three weeks, each from a longbeard in a different state. To find out about those other three feathers, you'll have to take the time to read about them some other time.

The drive home from our mini-vacation was as pleasant as the drive down. If I shifted my weight just right, the golden horseshoe didn't even bother me! Lisa and I left Florida with fond memories of Disneyland, dinner theaters, fine dining, and Orlando's heavy traffic. I left Florida with the Osceola gobbler of a lifetime, unforgettable memories of a magical hunt, and a new turkey-hunting rule – The Seventeen-Minute Rule!

Osceola (71.25 pts.)

Date: March 25, 2005
Time: 8:40 a.m.
Location: Marion Co., FL
Weight: 19 lbs. 12 oz.
10-¾ inch Beard
1-½ inch Spurs

Gaffs!

Rope!

Clear-cut viewed from my set-up

Decoys after Hitman attacked them

My set-up at edge of chop (Notice gun leaning against tree – that is exactly where it was leaning when birds approached – Also notice swatch cut out of blind at bottom courtesy of my need for a face-mask in Oklahoma!)

Little feather that blew around in truck

Double Beard

–

The Eastern Gobbler

Preface

Being outdoors is something I not only enjoy, but it is something that I need. As I look back on my life, the biggest majority of my time has been spent there. At least the biggest part of the time that I have had any say as to how I spent it, which would preclude going to school or work! As a boy, I spent nearly all of my time outdoors. I'm not sure if this was due entirely to the way that God created me, or if it was influenced by my mother who couldn't stand for me to be inside the house aggravating her all the time.

Although I am forty-two years old as I write this, in my mind's ear I can still hear my poor, exasperated mom yelling at me and saying, "Go outside and play!"

This was one of the few directives issued by my parents that I never had trouble understanding and obeying promptly! All of the organized sports I enjoyed, with the exception of wrestling, were played out of doors – baseball, football, hockey, and running cross-country. Catching fish, lizards, snakes, frogs, turtles and bugs dominated our time in the summer, while ice-fishing, shoveling snow, building snow forts and snowmen got us through the winter. As boys, my friends and I rode our bikes in the woods during the warmer months and went sled riding through the woods in the winter months. As a youngster, I would rather have been in the woods than anywhere else. Some things never change!

My greatest love of the outdoors though was found in hunting, trapping, fishing, and camping – but especially hunting. I was fortunate to be a part of the Boy Scouts of America and to belong to a Boy Scout troop that had for its scoutmasters a group of men that enjoyed the exact same four outdoor activities as I. Our Scout troop went camping every single month of the year, rain or shine, summer or winter. Every camping trip was spent pursuing the current fur, fish, or game that was legally in season.

This was a "win – win" situation for my parents and me. It satisfied my longing for the outdoors, and it gave my mom and dad one weekend of peace each month from their teenage son.

I enjoy nearly all types of hunting; however, my first love of the outdoor sports is bowhunting for whitetailed deer and spring gobbler hunting with a shotgun.

Now I know that you are thinking, "Hey, Dummy, that's two things, not one!"

Although I was born, raised, and schooled in West Virginia, I am capable of counting to two. The reason that I believe my statement to be accurate is that I can't do these two activities at the same time. So if you ask me in the fall, I'm apt to be more enamored with bowhunting, but in the spring it's gobbler hunting, hands-down. I'm just glad I don't have to choose. In reality, neither pursuit is ever set aside or forgotten by me, no matter what time of the year it is. I am constantly scouting for turkeys while deer hunting in the fall, and studying deer sign while running and gunning for gobblers in the spring. Many hunters who read this will understand perfectly what I mean.

As a spring gobbler hunter, I look forward to opening day of the spring season all year. I scout, plan, obtain permission to hunt, practice calling, repair or replace hunting gear, pattern turkey guns, watch videos, and talk with other turkey hunters, preparing throughout the year for the next season's opener. Usually, I am completely stoked by the time I can actually carry my turkey gun and calls to the woods for opening day, anticipating those amazing encounters with America's greatest game bird, the wild turkey. As opening day of Virginia's 2005 spring gobbler season approached, however, my normal anticipation was dampened by fear for what lay ahead. Pre-season scouting and the dismal previous three spring seasons had indicated that this year could be the toughest hunting season I had yet to encounter. And I knew before the season began that I needed to kill a longbeard – I desperately needed to kill a longbeard.

Double Beard

 For me, the start of Virginia's 2005 spring turkey season was preceded by a lot of turkey hunting activity that had nothing to do with hunting in Virginia. In the previous two years, I had harvested three of the four subspecies of wild turkey that I needed to complete my Grand Slam, and for 2005 I had booked a hunt in Nebraska for the fourth and final subspecies, the Merriam's. If all the excitement and nervous anticipation of that event were not enough to consume my thoughts, I had traveled to Florida with my wife, Lisa, on a spur-of-the-moment trip (just two weeks before Virginia's opener), where I managed to kill a monster Osceola tom. The big tom was my second Osceola gobbler, and pending the outcome of my trip to Nebraska, I was now in a position to potentially record two Grand Slams before the spring of 2005 ended. (I had previously killed two Rio Grande gobblers in the spring of 2004.) I was very optimistic that my hunt for a Merriam's would be successful, and since I had purchased two tags on my Nebraska license, I was really going to try hard to get both birds.

 I had taken two consecutive weeks of vacation from my job in order to make my dream a reality. The majority of the first week of my vacation would be spent hunting in Virginia during its opening week of turkey season. The latter part of my first week's vacation and the remainder of my vacation on the second week would be spent driving and hunting for a Merriam's gobbler. While I had high hopes for hunting in Nebraska with my brother, Kevin, during the second week I was off, I was seriously concerned about being able to kill a gobbler at home in the Old Dominion State.

 The reasons for my considerable anxiety regarding Virginia's spring gobbler season were two-fold. Without going into detail once again about the dismal turkey hatches over the course of the last three springs, which were unseasonably wet, my first concern was with the absolute lack of mature gobblers in the areas where I hunted in western Virginia's mountains. The other concern I found myself contemplating was the fact that, although it was never planned by me, I could possibly have the opportunity to accomplish something that I had never even dreamed of – complete a Wild Turkey Grand Slam in a single season. For that to happen, a whole lot of things had to go just right, and a whole lot of cards had to fall in place. One of those cards that would be needed was an Eastern gobbler taken in my home state. As I mulled over the potential importance of killing a gobbler during the first few days of my vacation, I was very worried. I knew that the Eastern piece of the four-gobbler puzzle I wanted to complete would be the hardest to acquire. It would be easier for me to tell you what I didn't do to prepare to hunt Virginia's gobblers than what I did do. I literally did everything I could prior to the season's opener to put myself in a legitimate position to harvest the subspecies of wild turkey that I was most familiar with.

Turkey season in Virginia actually began one week earlier than normal for my brother, Kevin, and I, thanks to the desire of Kevin's son, Caleb, to hunt turkeys on Youth Day. Youth Day is held the Saturday before the regular season opener and is designed to allow young hunters a chance at gobblers that haven't been spooked by hunting pressure yet. Caleb was now nine years old and had demonstrated proficiency with his youth-model Remington 870, both in the duck blind and on the patterning board. Kevin and I had both scouted numerous areas for our outing with Caleb before selecting which area to hunt. Regrettably though, all of our hard work was for naught, as Youth Day opened in western Virginia with severe thunderstorms hammering the county where we live. Not to be deterred, we hunted in the pouring rain anyway. Kevin sat with his son under two camo umbrellas, while I called and videoed from under another behind them. At about 10:00 a.m. Kevin and Caleb were both thoroughly soaked, and I wasn't too far from it. We hadn't heard, or seen, a turkey of any kind all morning. So what do you think Caleb wanted to do, call it a day? Nope, we drove our trucks back to Kevin's house where the two of them changed into dry clothes. The three of us then went to a different area and hunted until the 12:00 p.m. cut-off time. (They hunted in dry clothes while I hunted in wet ones.) That nephew of mine, Caleb, has all the potential signs of a legion member, and he hasn't even killed his first gobbler yet. It must be in the genes. Well that's good news for my mom; she won't have to take all the blame for my love of the outdoors!

With Youth Day a dismal failure, my hopes of locating a mature gobbler during the first few days of the regular season were tempered even further. In order to overcome the negative perception I had derived, I decided to hunt one of my best hunting areas on opening day. However, besides being one of my best areas to hear a gobbler, it was also one of the hardest to get to. To access it, I would have to wade a river, traverse a rattlesnake-den laden series of rock ledges, and then climb a nearly straight-up, rocky mountain ridge. All of this would have to be done, of course, in the dark. There was one other option to access the area, but that option would require my wife, Lisa, to get up at the obscene hour of 4:30 a.m. and drive me to a different location where there was no place to park. I could begin my climb from there, but she would have to return and pick me up at the end of my hunt. I normally would not put my life into my own hands and ask her to get up at 4:30 a.m. to take me hunting, but desperate times call for desperate measures! Lisa lovingly agreed to the pre-dawn task, and when opening day arrived she kicked me out of her car at the drop-off point.

My first morning in the spring woods was beautiful, at least as far as the weather was concerned. I heard two gobblers and one hen during the morning's hunt. The hen came readily to my calls and hung out with me for about twenty minutes, staying approximately thirty yards from my decoys and calling the majority of the time. The gobblers wouldn't so much as give me the time of day. They only gobbled on the roost, and after flying down, they completely shut up. It was April 9th, and both gobblers already had hens. This year was going to be the same as the previous two. I had hoped that the gobblers could be worked during the beginning of the season before they henned-up, but at least in this area of the county, it appeared that I was already too late.

On Monday, I decided to hunt National Forest on the other end of Alleghany County. Tuesday found me hunting on National Forest land in Botetourt County. Wednesday I was back in Alleghany County hunting public land, and Thursday I tried a different area of public land in Botetourt County. Each day I experienced the same results – no gobblers. I couldn't even spell gobblr. During my first five mornings of hunting, I wasn't able to call in a single longbeard and had only seen a total of five hens. It was so disheartening. I could not have been hunting any harder than I already was, and I hadn't even worked a bird yet. To make matters worse, I only had one more morning to hunt before leaving on my trip to Nebraska with Kevin. I knew that even if I left for my Merriam's hunt without an Eastern bird under my belt that I still had some time to hunt in Virginia when I returned. I would be out of vacation though, and my opportunities would be limited. The pressure I felt to kill a gobbler was immense as I pillowed my head on Thursday night. I was nearly sick to my stomach when I thought about the possibility of missing the opportunity for a single season Grand Slam because I couldn't kill a gobbler in my own stomping grounds. I prayed before going to sleep and drew comfort from the fact that, in the overall scope of things, my problems were minor and inconsequential. As true as I knew that was, I still had the potential opportunity of a lifetime (for a spring gobbler hunter) staring me in the face, and I wanted with all my heart to seize hold of it.

I am used to adversity when it comes to hunting. If you have ever seriously hunted for spring gobblers or mature whitetail bucks, then you are too. In spite of that, no matter how poor the rewards are for my efforts in the outdoors, I always keep on trying. I usually find some way to encourage myself to "keep on swinging" and not to give up the fight. After heeding my alarm clock's 4:30 a.m. wake-up call on Friday, April 15, however, I was having trouble doing just that as I dressed for the turkey woods. A positive attitude can make a big difference in life when faced with problems that need to be solved. This applies to all areas of life – at home, on the job, and in the woods. If you're already defeated in your mind at the outset, you are less likely to make choices that lead to victory in the end. You can end up with that "what's the use?" mentality. On the other hand, a positive attitude fosters decision making with a victorious end in view. Even though I am aware of these principles and believe them, I was having trouble fighting that "what's the use?" feeling. I was even trying to convince myself to forget about concentrating so hard on an Eastern gobbler and to start thinking about the Merriam's hunt. At least thinking about my upcoming Grand Slam hunt should perk me up, I thought.

All the negative thoughts I was having, and all of my self-pity, were threatening to suck the life out of my last morning to hunt during Virginia's opening week. Drinking coffee in my truck on the way to my intended hunting spot, I resolved to not allow myself to give up. Getting beat fair and square is one thing, quitting is another. (I don't mean quitting by not going, as that was never even a remote possibility, but I mean quitting mentally. It is possible to just enter the woods and go through the motions of hunting without really working at it and giving it your all. I made up my mind to give this last morning my best effort.) While this decision to not give up mentally was made in my truck, it would become the master link in a chain of events that would unfold in the woods along the ridge tops of Alleghany County, Virginia. And it would take all the mental stamina I could muster to keep this promise to myself.

I began my morning's hunt in very familiar surroundings. Well before daylight, I was in the former stomping grounds of my old friend, "The Bus." I had hunted these ridges too many times to count in previous years, and while not always successful in taking a gobbler, I could usually hear one. My plan for this Friday morning was to aggressively pursue any gobbler that I could hear from the roost – no matter where he might be located, and no matter what I had to do to get to him. To help improve my chances, I secured permission to hunt on a piece of private land that bordered the National Forest I would be hunting, just in case the gobbler I heard was on the posted side of the property line. So when I left my truck and began to hike in the dark, I was cocked and ready to rock. All I needed was a gobbler that was in the same frame of mind.

As another spring morning began to dawn, I was seated at the base of a large oak tree. My decoys were placed in their customary arrangement in front and slightly to the left of my set-up. I had set the fakes out in hopes that a gobbler might be roosted near my location and I could pursue a traditional off-the-roost hunt. I wasn't really expecting that, but was prepared for it nonetheless. I was expecting to hear a gobbler on one of the three different ridges I was situated amongst, and I had every intention of pulling my decoys and getting on him "a.s.a.p." once he sounded from the roost. I prayed before beginning my hunt, as always, and then sat there waiting on daylight and the first birds of the morning to begin singing.

All of the woodland birds greeted the warm, clear morning with their own particular calls. I heard tufted titmice, black-capped chickadees, cardinals, blue jays, and crows. I heard every kind of call you can imagine – every kind of call but what I really wanted to hear – a gobble. With no turkeys greeting the morning on their own, I began calling. I did my best to sound like a family group of hens waking up on the roost and then added further realism to my deception by imitating them flying down to the ground. With no response to my calls from gobblers or hens, I began calling like a group of hens on the ground feeding and fussing at one another. That didn't work either. I couldn't believe it. I had nearly always been able to hear a gobbler somewhere on one of these ridges, even if they were nearly impossible to get to. Today, however, on what could possibly be the most significant Eastern turkey hunt I had ever embarked on, there was absolute silence from the Meleagris-galapavo-silvestris crowd. It was a crushing blow to my confidence and to my plans. During my first five days of hunting, even though I couldn't get a gobbler to answer my calls after flydown, I had heard a total of eight gobblers gobbling from the roost. Without being able to even hear a gobbler on the roost this day, my chances for tracking one down and getting into his comfort zone were seriously crippled. I pulled my decoys at 7:30 a.m. and started running and gunning.

Running and gunning is a method of spring turkey hunting that has become increasingly popular over the last thirty years. While elderly turkey hunting veterans were taught by their fathers, grandfathers, or mentors to sit at one tree and yelp three times each hour on their trusty box-call and then to sit patiently all morning waiting for a tom to come looking for them, my generation of turkey hunters has a tendency to take matters into their own hands, so to speak, by moving and searching for turkeys throughout the entire course of a morning hunt. This involves covering a lot of ground on foot, usually on the top of a ridge or high place, or possibly along an old logging road. This method of hunting requires a hunter to stop every couple hundred yards or so and to make a call at a likely looking spot where sound travels well and where he can listen for a gobbler to respond. The calls a hunter can make are varied, but usually fall into one of three categories: 1) Locator calls, 2) Hen calls, and 3) Gobbler calls. If a hunter gets a response from a gobbler after making a call, he must determine whether to try and move closer to the gobbler before calling again, or set up immediately where he is to try and work the bird. This decision is usually influenced by the nearness of the gobbler and what type of call he has located the gobbler with. Whether a hunter prefers to sit and wait, or run and gun, there is no guarantee that he will encounter a gobbler who is willing to participate in either scenario. Both of these methods of hunting are effective, and both have their respective good and bad points. The old, tried-and-true "sit in the same spot" method has put a lot of notches on double-barreled shotguns and a lot of turkeys on the dinner table. However, if you are somewhat impatient and would rather force a turkey's hand, then running and gunning might be the choice for you. When it is raining, I tend to follow the sit and wait routine, but when the weather is decent, you will almost always find me running and gunning.

With my gun slung over my shoulder and a Woodhaven "Jim Pollard" mouth call in place between my cheek and gum, I began to move out the ridge I had begun the morning on. I would pause and make a series of calls at each strategic location along the ridge top. Strategic locations may be at the head of a hollow, which joins the ridge, or at an area where the ridge top opens up into larger timber, or at a point or bend in the ridge's topography. A strategic location may also be anyplace I just "feel like calling" for whatever reason. Every couple hundred yards I would stop and call before listening intently for a response from a lovesick tom. Actually, I would have welcomed a response from any turkey. Unfortunately for me, I spent the next two hours covering a couple of different ridges, and I got nothing in response to any of my calls. It was nearly 10:00 a.m. now, and I was starting to tire from all the walking, climbing, and calling. I am not referring so much to physical tiring as I am to mental fatigue. If a hunter hasn't even heard a gobbler by this late hour in the morning, his chances of being successful go way down on the probability scale.

It was decision time. The sun was high in the bluebird sky, and it was getting hot. I had one more ridge I could try to hunt. The ridge was high up on the mountain, and it was quite a hump to reach. The thought of another round of climbing and humping in the now extremely warm temperatures wasn't all that appealing to me, especially since the tactic hadn't produced so much as a peep thus far. I began to contemplate the "stay in one spot" method and just spending the rest of the morning hunkered down against a large tree in a good feeding area, blind calling every few minutes. This is when one of the mental battles took place that would prove instrumental in my hunt's outcome. While staying in one spot was a legitimate method for trying to kill a gobbler, deep down I suspected it was just a cop-out. I felt like it was just a half-hearted swing at a curve ball I wasn't able to hit, instead of a swing for the fence. No, despite the heat and my mental and physical fatigue, I wasn't going to sit and call. I was going to hump it to the next ridge, and do my best to cover it before Virginia's twelve-noon hunting deadline arrived.

Having forced myself to maintain that "never give up" attitude, I walked quickly to the base of the next ridge and began my ascent. With my quadriceps burning and lungs straining from packing my shotgun and twenty-eight-pound turkey vest to the top of the ridge, I began the now monotonous task of calling and listening before quickly moving on to the next spot. At each stop I would anticipate the gobble I was so desperate to hear, and at each spot I would be disappointed. After an entire week of these repeated failures, I had actually begun to expect no response. I covered the biggest part of the ridge in record time, taking only twenty minutes to do so. It was now approximately 10:20 a.m. I was a long way from my truck, and despite my weakened condition, I began to wage another mental battle. As I stopped and was trying to decide if I should keep going to the very end of the ridge or sit down and blind call for about an hour, I had another idea. Since I wasn't having any success up high on the mountain, maybe I should try to hunt down low. The only problem with hunting low is that it would require me to hike all the way back to my truck, drive off the mountain, park at the bottom, and then hike into an area I only hoped would be holding mid-morning birds. I estimated that all of this traveling would take me an hour, and that is if I nearly ran back to the truck. Somehow I always manage to dream up some crazy plan that involves me running and climbing, and still going home without a gobbler. I don't know why I can't just fail the easy way. With three options to choose from, I settled for the third one – the hard one. I was still trying to do whatever I thought would provide me with the best opportunity to kill a turkey, no matter what time it was, or how hard it was. This is the mental battle that a turkey hunter has to fight and win if he wants to be successful on a consistent basis.

I turned around and started retracing my steps back along the top of ridge, in order to get back to my pickup truck. Even though I had just been through these woods calling a few minutes before, I continued to pause and call on the way back. My pauses were short and so were my calls. Many times I would hardly even describe it as a pause when I called; I just sort of slowed down, because I had no time to lose. You may be wondering why I would even bother calling and wasting precious time at the same places that I had just been previously without success. The answer to that lies in my experience. Numerous times on past hunts I would call my way out a ridge without a single gobble in response, only to turn around and call my way back off the same ridge and have a gobbler rattle the timber in response to my call the "second time around." Sometimes these answers were only minutes after having been there and sometimes they were hours after the initial trip. I have several theories for why this works, but I won't bore you with them. I have plenty of other material for that.

I had made it about halfway back the ridge, when I came to an unusual place in the terrain. This area had two different and very distinct features. The wooded ridge top came to a spiny, steep drop-off. The wooded area was covered with mature hardwood timber while the spiny ridge was comprised of slate and was covered with yellow pines. Several times in past hunting seasons I had struck turkeys at, or near, this spot and twice had called them in. In every case though, the birds had always been hens.

So when I neared the "dividing line" at the top of the ridge, I stopped to make a call.

"Cluck…Yawp, Yawp, Yawp, Yawp, Yawp,…Cluck, Cluck" said my Woodhaven diaphragm call.

"Garrrobbble!" shot right back to me from the hollow at the bottom of the ridge!

Half in disbelief that I had gotten a response, I muttered, "Finally!" to myself.

I stood there for just a second trying to collect my thoughts and decide what to do. The gobbler was pretty far away, as the ridge I was on was extremely steep and very high. I was on the top, and he was somewhere near the creek in the bottom. I decided to walk about fifteen yards farther along the ridge and to walk slightly over the edge of the ridge on the side the tom had answered me from. I wanted to call again to see if he would answer me a second time, and if he did, try to get a better fix on his exact location. I repeated the exact same series of calls with my mouth diaphragm that had produced the first gobble, and he immediately gobbled again in response. I was sure the bird was in the creek bottom, but I was still unsure if the gobbler could be persuaded to climb the mountain to my location. A lot of times a gobbler will give a hen a "courtesy" gobble even though he has no intention of coming to her, but when he answers her twice and emphatically to boot, chances are good that he is looking for a date. That holds especially true when the gobble comes late in the morning. (I tell inexperienced turkey hunters that if they get a gobbler answering their calls after 10 a.m. that they had better sit down and take the safety off their shotgun because, more times than not, that bird is coming.) I had every reason to believe that this bird was workable; I just needed to find a place to set up and start calling.

As I have mentioned, this wasn't the first time for a turkey to answer me from my calling position at the dividing line high on the ridge top. So one would think that my previous experience at picking a spot to set up and call from would come in handy at about this time. Well, that would be an incorrect assumption to make. You see, every time I had set up in this area previously, the spot that I selected to sit and call from turned out to be a lousy location. Now understand I had set up here on numerous occasions in the past, and every time I had picked a different spot, and every time the new spot sucked as bad, if not worse, than the last one. There were absolutely no trees to sit against on the steep, slate bank, so I retreated approximately twenty yards to the wooded area, which was only about twenty-five feet wide along the ridge top. As I scrambled around looking for just the right tree to sit against, I found myself looking at trees I had tried before, and I knew they were bad news. The problem was the steepness of the ridge and the lack of visibility. Anywhere I found a decent sized tree to sit against, I had no open view of the turkey's approach. In the past, the hens that came were nearly on top of me before I could see them. They popped their heads up over the ridge and looked around for the other hen that had invaded their territory. Usually the turkeys were within fifteen yards of me before I ever saw them. If my gun wasn't already pointing directly at them when they appeared, I had no chance of moving the barrel to get my sights on the birds (of course, assuming they had been gobblers). The hens would stare at me before retreating back the way they came. So on this day, I wanted to make dang sure that same scenario didn't repeat itself with the gobbler that had answered me from the bottom of the mountain. Twice I started to kick out a place to sit and then decided it was no good. I had been goofing around for about a minute playing musical trees, when it occurred to me that I might want to make a call and see if the gobbler would answer me again – so I could determine if by some miracle he had decided to climb the ridge to visit me.

I stopped and turned my body to face the drop-off toward the gobbler's last known location.

"Cluck…..Cutt, Cutt, Cutt,…Cutt,Cu" – that's all I got out before the gobbler cut me off with a booming "stutter" gobble (that's another Brad Day original term).

A stutter gobble is almost like a double gobble with the first of the two gobbles cut short. Kind of like Garrob…Garrrobbble! Anyway if I can't explain it acoustically, I can explain it verbally. It means "Who's your daddy now?" in gobbler lingo. Not only was this tom fired up, but he was coming fast. His "stutter" gobble came from better than halfway up the ridge! The turkey had to be running to cover that much ground so quickly. At this point, he wasn't the only one running. I had to do something quick, even it was wrong. My hopes for picking out the perfect tree, clearing out a big bare spot to sit in, and setting out my decoys vanished before the tom's gobble had stopped reverberating in the timber.

"Sit down! Now!" I told myself, nearly panicked.

Every now and then, a hunter manages to do something unbelievable in his pursuit of big game. These amazing occurrences are extremely rare and might only happen once or twice in an outdoorsman's career. What I did next turned out to be one of the slickest tricks I've ever pulled on an old gobbler. While I would like to be able to tell you that I devised this idea purposefully for the outcome it would produce, I cannot, because to do so would amount to lying. Instead, the maneuver I discovered was happened upon strictly by accident. I had been standing in the same old spot where I normally would have tried to set up on the ridge top when I had made my last call to the gobbler. He had answered me from such a close distance, that I had to make a split decision on where to sit. I knew I couldn't sit down where I was, so I ran about twenty yards back out the ridge behind me (away from the gobbler) and about ten yards over the side of the ridge towards the gobbler. Confused? The ridge I was on ran east – west. As I was walking back towards my truck calling, I had been traveling east. The gobbler that answered me did so from the hollow on the north side of the ridge. I had backed up to the west about twenty yards trying to find a tree to sit against when I called to the bird for the third time. After hearing his stutter gobble halfway up the ridge, I ran further back to the west (about another twenty yards) and then down over the north face toward the gobbler (another ten yards). All of this scrambling and moving away from the gobbler isn't what a turkey hunter normally does, as customarily he works toward the bird. Although I have actually been very successful on past hunts by retreating from a gobbler that was approaching, what I was about to do this time was different. What is most important to note about what I had done is that I had made a call where I normally would have set up, and then I immediately moved back away from that spot.

My twenty-yard dash in retreat left me little choice in where to set up. I saw a large oak tree over the side of the North face and scrambled to its base. Once there, I shucked out of my hunting vest and literally threw it out of my way about six feet to the right of the tree. I sat straight down without clearing the first leaf from the spot, jerked my headnet up into position, put my gun on my knee pointing down toward the hollow the gobbler was in, and popped the gun's scope caps. My heart was racing. This was it, I kept telling myself…a gobbler of a lifetime. Just don't blow it! All this last minute mental wrangling served to benefit me well, because I never made another call. And that is what made this set-up so effective.

I didn't have to wait thirty seconds after sitting down before I heard the familiar cadence of a wild turkey's approach in the dry leaves below me to my left. Another five seconds after that and I saw the white skull cap of a mature gobbler coming straight up the ridge about fifty yards below me and twenty yards to my left. The gobbler got bigger and bigger as his body materialized through the brushy undergrowth. The tom had a long beard, which was easily seen, as he walked briskly up the ridge with his head extended looking for the hen. There was a fallen tree in the path of the gobbler about forty yards down the hill from me. It was a large pine tree and was probably at least eighteen inches off the ground where it intersected the gobbler's path. Upon reaching the downed tree, the gobbler jumped up on top of it and just stood there, looking around. The turkey was in marginal gun range, but I didn't want to take the shot he offered. There were two reasons I wanted to wait. The first was based upon my belief that the gobbler would continue his approach straight up the hill to my left, putting him in my wheelhouse as a right-handed shooter and at a much closer distance. The second was due to my gut feeling that this bird was the "scout" and the real boss gobbler was behind him. I am not sure to this day why I believed there was another gobbler following. I had only heard one turkey gobble each time I had called, but when that first gobbler jumped up on that fallen tree, I thought I could hear another bird coming behind him. So when the scout gobbler jumped down on my side of the tree and proceeded to walk right into good gun range, I didn't shoot. I just sat there, safety off and gun pointed at the log he had jumped on. Now, I could definitely hear another turkey coming, and the first thing I could make out as the bird approached was the tip of a full tail fan. It was a dominant gobbler, and he was strutting up the ridge to my left following in the steps of his predecessor!

Just like gobbler number one, the dominant bird jumped up on the fallen tree when he reached it. The gobbler stood there stretching his neck and turning his head around looking for his woman. After a few seconds, he dropped off the other side and resumed strutting up the ridge to my left. He was in gun range, and I had the gun trained on him as he closed the distance. The first gobbler had stopped straight across from me on the ridge twenty yards to my left. The longbeard was standing in the exact same spot where I had stood and made my final call before moving to my current location. (Gobblers have an uncanny knack for pinpointing a call's exact place of origin, even if there is a great distance between the gobbler and the caller.) This is where my "stumbled upon" set-up unveiled its brilliance. By moving twenty yards to the right of my last calling position and by remaining silent after the move, the gobblers were locked in on my previous calling location. This put me off to the side of their focus zone and put them directly to my left, which is precisely where I want my target, since I am a right-handed shot. I believe the first gobbler was watching me as I followed the boss tom coming up behind him. I wanted

Severe Gobbler Disorder

to shoot so badly, but there was too much trash between me and the bird for a good, clean shot. I had the distinct advantage of being able to watch the first bird's approach, so I already knew when the second bird passed behind a large pine tree, he would be in the open when he exited the other side. As the big gobbler strutted behind the pine tree, I pressed my cheek firmly against the butt stock of my shotgun and glared through the scope, afraid to even blink. The dominant bird came into view on the uphill side of the pine tree, and then he just stopped and put his head up. He had strutted right up to the scout gobbler, which was looking at me. The first gobbler's intense focus in the general direction of my set-up apparently got the dominant bird's attention and caused him to slick up and look my direction too. It was the opportunity I was waiting for, as my trigger finger drew taught.

"KABOOM!" My shotgun shattered the silence of the warm, sunny April morning. It had the same effect on the skull and upper skeletal structure of the dominant gobbler, as he hit the ground in a heap. Conversely, the sub-dominant bird jumped about a foot off the ground, and upon returning to terra firma just stood there looking at his companion for advice about what to do next. Advice was one thing my gobbler was all out of. He beat his wings wildly on the ground and began flopping back down the ridge towards the fallen pine tree they both had used as an observation tower. With a shout of triumph, I stood up to retrieve my bird. I was one happy boy, holding the gun in my left hand and punching the air with my right fist! All this activity on my part was completely unnoticed by the living gobbler who had now become infatuated with my flopping bird. He chased my gobbler down the hill until my bird came to rest behind another large pine tree about thirty yards from where I was standing. The sub-dominant bird now assumed the duties of boss tom as he jumped on my gobbler's back and started strutting, pausing occasionally to peck my bird in the back or neck.

I pumped another round into the chamber of my shotgun as I walked directly up to the strutting gobbler standing on my bird with his back and tail fan towards me. This second bird was paying no attention to me whatsoever. I had shot, yelled, stood up, pumped my gun, and was now walking within fifteen yards of him in the dry, crunchy leaves, and he was too busy to notice. I pulled my headnet down and proceeded to walk closer, contemplating whether or not I would have to shoot this turkey to get him off my bird! At ten yards I raised my gun, and even though his tail fan was blocking his sight, somehow that joker saw me and took off running down the ridge. (I wasn't raising my gun to shoot the gobbler, which would have been illegal; I was raising my gun to try and look at his spurs through my scope. Although if I had seen a large set of hooks on the bird, I don't know how much restraint I could have mustered! I hope you know I'm kidding. The fact is, I had an easy shot at the bird if I wanted to kill him, and I didn't.)

It was actually kind of ironic. I had been trying all week to just find a gobbler, and when I finally did, I ended up having to shoo another mature gobbler away! Talk about feast or famine; this was the epitome of that saying!

I approached my fallen gobbler with more exuberance and satisfaction than I can hope to explain. I had done it! Somehow, I had managed to pull off the impossible at the eleventh hour. Actually, it was at the 10:30 hour to be exact, but who cares! I was leaving in the morning for my trip to Nebraska, and with only ninety minutes left to hunt, I had my big Eastern gobbler on the ground in front of me! Man, if you are a turkey hunter, I hope you can appreciate what that felt like. If you are not a turkey hunter – well I'm sorry, I just can't describe it. I had an Osceola, and now an Eastern in the bag, unarguably the two toughest subspecies to harvest. I had no idea what my trip out west held in store, but I did know that my brother, Kevin, was going to have a much happier traveling companion along the way.

By the time I reached the gobbler, he had quit flopping and beating his wings on the forest floor. All things considered, I was pretty cool, calm, and collected before inspecting the bird. The first thing I did was roll the gobbler over to look at his spurs, which were 7/8-inch long. I was surprised to find that this bird was only two years old, and I have to admit I was a little disappointed. After waiting out the dominant bird, I assumed he would have been older. It really didn't matter; he was a mature bird, and I would have given almost anything to get him when I did. In fact, I was probably just spoiled after killing a monster Osceola with 1-1/2 inch spurs only a few weeks earlier. I dropped to my knees in the deep fallen leaves and thanked my Heavenly Father for allowing me to harvest the gobbler. I can't overstate how important this turkey was to me. Every mature spring gobbler that a hunter kills legally and ethically is special, and this one was no exception. However, this gobbler was an added blessing because he not only kept my dimly lit dream of a single-season Grand Slam alive, but he poured fuel on the fire, igniting it from a remotely slim chance to a blazing possibility. And I knew it.

After praying and thanking the Lord over and over, the numbness that is associated with an event like this started to wear off, and with it, the burden I had been carrying for the last three weeks was lifted from my shoulders. As the reality of what I had accomplished began to sink in, I started going nuts (which isn't too far a trip for me). I threw my camouflage hat up the hill and just started yelling, "Yes!" "Yes!" "Yes!" while I swung my fist in the air. I was elated with a combination of relief, joy, and anticipation. For an entire year I had been dreaming of the spring 2005 turkey season hoping that it would be the year of accomplishing my slam. Now, I felt poised to make the year even more memorable than I had ever even dreamed of. Of all the gobblers I killed in 2005, including my slam birds, this is the one that I was the most worked up about. I was a basket case, half from relief and half from exhilaration. "I did it!"

After calming down just a skoshe, I picked the gobbler up to carry him back to the tree where I had set up. Right away, I knew the bird was heavy. I wasn't sure if he would make the magical twenty-pound mark, but he would be close. As I approached the large oak tree with my bird, I couldn't help but laugh at the scene before me. My hunting vest was slung on the ground about five feet from where I had sat, there was no bare spot kicked out to sit in, and my hat was lying up the hill where I had thrown it. That was probably the first time that I had ever set up without my turkey vest since I had started using one many years ago (with the exception of rainy day hunts). I placed my gobbler gently on the ground at the base of the tree, retrieved my hunting hat, and gathered up my vest. I read a chapter of my Bible, as is my custom, and then tagged the bird. I was about to place the gobbler in the vest's game bag when I decided that I should at least look at the bird's beard, because up to this point I had not. So I placed the bird on his back and pulled the gobbler's beard away from his breast. The beard was decent in length and was fairly thick too. Something about the beard appeared unusual to me, but I couldn't quite place what it was. As I started to drop the beard back onto the gobbler's chest the anomaly revealed itself to me…a second beard fell out of my hand.

"No way!" I cried, "He's a double-bearded gobbler!"

Stop the press and start the party all over again. If I had reserved any emotion from my prior outburst, I expended it now at the discovery of my first gobbler with more than one beard. I threw my hat again, yelled and carried on, swinging my arms and fists like a little boy that had just killed his first turkey. I got down on my knees again and thanked the Lord Jesus in prayer. Then I stood up and just started thanking Him out loud while looking toward heaven. The two beards would make this gobbler score very well despite his 7/8 inch spurs. The main beard measured 9-1/2 inches and the second beard taped 4-3/4 inches. I didn't think things could possibly get any better, but they just had. When I found that second beard, I felt as if I was being rewarded for not killing the second tom when I had every opportunity to do so. Eventually, I managed to regain some sense of composure and resumed the task of packing the bird in my turkey vest. I was almost finished when I heard something walking in the leaves.

I stopped what I was doing and listened carefully. It sounded like a turkey was walking up the ridge to me, and the sound was coming from the exact same spot where the two gobblers had approached earlier. I grabbed my shotgun, which still had one round chambered and one in the magazine. I sat against the tree and put my headnet back on, pointing my gun down the ridge. The turkey was getting really close, and then I realized what I was doing.

"What was I doing?" I asked myself. "You've lost your mind!" I thought, as I pulled my headnet down.

I stood up and shucked both shells out of my Remington, before leaning it against the tree. Even more bizarre, the sound of the approaching turkey continued to get louder! So I just started walking down the ridge toward the sound, looking for the bird. After going about ten yards, I saw him. It was the sub-dominant bird from earlier! He was coming right back to the spot where my gobbler had been shot. The gobbler and I both stopped and stared at each other for about a nanosecond. This time when he decided to exit stage left, he decided to do so through the air. I watched the gobbler take flight and sail all the way across the large, steep hollow to the opposite ridge. I couldn't call in a turkey all week doing my best to sound like a hen, and now I have one show up by yelling, praying, reading my Bible, jumping up and down, and throwing things! If anyone ever figures out the wild turkey, I hope they write about it so I can read it. I guess the living gobbler just felt bad about the way he had treated his fallen comrade, and was returning to attend his funeral and properly pay his last respects!

The sky was blue and the sun was hot as I began the long hike back to my truck. My vest now weighed about forty-eight pounds, causing both my legs and lungs to burn as I climbed and walked. Every time I would get winded, or feel the lactic acid building up in my muscles, I would just smile and think about how fortunate I truly was. I was so glad to have a gobbler on my back that I didn't care how far I had to walk or how steep it got. It hurt so good! In addition, there was an almost greater satisfaction than killing the gobbler, if you can believe it. The other satisfaction lie in the fact that despite all odds and with every excuse to "throw in the towel," that I just wouldn't do it. I had won the mental battles, and in so doing, I had won the day – a day, a hunt, and a moment I will never forget on this side of eternity.

I was soaking wet by the time I reached my truck. After squaring away my gun, vest, and gobbler, I pulled my cell phone from the truck to see if I could get a signal. My truck is sitting off the side of an old logging road near the top of a mountain, and there is usually no cell phone reception anywhere on the mountain. I was so fired up though, I decided to give it a shot anyway. Lo and behold, I had one bar of reception. I called my wife, Lisa, at work. I was so excited that I don't know if she heard half of what I said. Since it was nearly lunchtime for her, we decided to meet in town at Hardees for lunch. I then hung up with her and called my close friend, David. I talked David into meeting Lisa and me for lunch too, so I could tell him all about the double-bearded gobbler. After trying unsuccessfully to get my brother on the phone, I drove my truck out to the hardcap and went straight to a checking station with a certified scale. I wanted to get a certified weight because I knew the bird would score well, and I wanted to register him with the NWTF, especially if I managed to complete a second slam. Second slam? What was I thinking? I hadn't even killed my first one yet.

My double-bearded turkey weighed in officially at twenty pounds and two ounces. I knew that he was one big two-year-old gobbler! By virtue of his weight and double beards, he overcame the small spurs and netted an official score of 66-1/8 points, which is world class for a second-year tom. With an official game check tag in hand, I drove back to town to meet Lisa and David for lunch. On my way I would be driving directly past the paper mill entrance where I work, so I decided to stop in the mill's parking lot and call a couple of my co-workers who are turkey hunters. We joked around in the parking lot during their lunch break, and they congratulated me on my gobbler. I don't know what impressed them the most, the double-bearded turkey, or the fact that I had showed up at the mill while on vacation during spring gobbler season!

Showing up at the mill while on vacation during turkey season wasn't the only abnormal thing I did on this 15th day of April. I showed up at Hardees to eat lunch wearing my hunting clothes. Now I know that this is completely acceptable behavior for many hunters. It is not uncommon for me to see the local Hardees covered in a sea of blaze orange during deer season, or to see an occasional camo clad turkey hunter patronizing the fast food establishment in the spring. However, you just won't see me doing it. I wear my hunting clothes while hunting, and that is it. My deer hunting clothes are protected from any form of human or unusual scent, and my turkey hunting clothes aren't exactly the latest fashion craze, not that I care. I just don't like to be sporting around in public wearing my hunting clothes, like "Hey everybody look at me, I'm a hunter!" I know some guys get off on that; it just doesn't work for me. Be that as it may, I was making an exception on this occasion, as I met Lisa and David for lunch. I told them all the details between bites of my hamburger. It was just a fifteen-dollar lunch for hamburgers and french fries, but the moment spent with my wife and close friend was… yeah, you guessed it…priceless.

After lunch I returned home, where I met Lisa's parents, my brother, and his kids. Once they had a chance to see the two-bearded bird, we took photos of the gobbler and his beards to document them for the NWTF records. I then cleaned the turkey and put him in the refrigerator. It was late in the afternoon by the time I had the gobbler properly cared for, and I had to get busy packing all of my and Kevin's hunting gear into the 4-Runner. We would be leaving for Nebraska at four o'clock the following morning. When all the gear was properly stowed away in the back of the SUV, I still had one smaller item that needed to be put in the truck. I opened the driver's door, and after reaching into my pocket, I produced a small turkey feather that I had picked up from the ground where I killed my double-bearded gobbler. I slid the small breast feather into the driver's side visor, right next to the small feather from my Osceola gobbler killed three weeks earlier. Little did I know that exactly one week later I would park my 4-Runner in this very same spot in my driveway, and there would be four small feathers in the visor.

EASTERN – Double Beard

Date: April 15, 2005
Time: 10:30 a.m.
Location: Alleghany County, VA
Weight: 20 lbs. 2 oz.
Beard No.1: 9-1/2 inches
Beard No.2: 4-3/4 inches
Spurs: 7/8 inch

Double Beards

Beautiful Eastern

Speed Racer
–
The Merriam's Gobbler

Preface

What started as a question to my wife, Lisa, sitting on our living room couch during a cold winter evening in January 2002, has now resulted in the accomplishment of a lifelong dream. When I asked Lisa if she would mind if I went to Florida over the Easter holiday in the spring of 2002 to hunt for an Osceola gobbler, I had no idea that her "No" would put in motion a series of events over the next three years that would lead me to the states of Florida, Oklahoma, Nebraska, and Kansas to hunt wild turkeys. I don't think she had any idea that her answer would result in that either.

With three legs of my Grand Slam quest complete at the conclusion of the 2004 spring season, I began to make plans for a Merriam's hunt almost immediately. This was probably a mistake on my part. With the memories of Oklahoma still fresh in her mind, Lisa informed me that she would not be accompanying me on the final leg of my Grand Slam odyssey. I can't say as I blame her. She only gets two weeks of vacation from her job and spending half her vacation in some forlorn location of a western state twiddling her thumbs while I hunted for turkeys just wouldn't be fun for her. So we agreed that I would travel west for a Merriam's without her.

However, Lisa's loss would be my brother Kevin's gain. I went to see my "bro" in early June to invite him to accompany me on a trip to either South Dakota or Nebraska to hunt for a Merriam's gobbler. I explained to him that he would need to take a week of vacation and would probably have to lay down some cash, as I planned to secure a trespass-fee hunt on private land in whichever state I ended up settling on. Kevin agreed immediately to the deal, and I began to gather intelligence on the Merriam's subspecies of wild turkey and his location in my prospective states of Wyoming, New Mexico, South Dakota, and Nebraska. As I began to review the hunting regulations and permit requirements for the various western states that I was considering for my 2005 spring hunt, I decided to throw out my previous rule that I would only hunt before, or after, my home state of Virginia's hunting season. I wanted this to be a "one-trip" adventure, and I was determined to do whatever it took to put myself in the best position possible to harvest a mature, loud-mouthed Merriam's gobbler.

After considerable thought regarding which state to hunt, I finally decided on the state of Nebraska. I scrapped my original plans to go to South Dakota because I could only purchase one spring gobbler tag with my license there. Nebraska, however, allowed me to purchase two tags and would prove to be a slightly shorter drive. I did my darndest to secure a trespass fee hunt on private land in the Husker State, but I had no success. After much prayer, to make a long story short (the long story follows this preface), I decided to hunt with an outfitter. The outfitter would provide lodging, meals, and a guide, if we wanted one. I had numerous phone conversations with the outfitter, Jason Hamilton, and we agreed that I would hunt on my own on his private property without the use of his guides, but I would still pay the full price for the hunt. After speaking with my brother Kevin and getting his consent, we booked our hunt with Rutting-N-Strutting outfitters for the first week of Nebraska's shotgun spring gobbler season.

I lift weights three times every week. Well, let me rephrase. I used to lift weights three times a week, now I slack three times a week. My weight room is located in my house and is decorated with turkey fans and deer mounts, which tend to get me thinking about the outdoors – like I need any help with that! Each day before I exercise, I pray and thank the Lord Jesus for the health and strength he has blessed me with. After booking the hunt in Nebraska, when I would pray before lifting, I would pray about my trip to hunt for Merriam's gobblers in addition to my prayers for health and strength. I would get nervous in my stomach about whether the hunt would be successful and whether or not I would be healthy enough to go when the time came. This went on for months before the day finally arrived to depart for what I hoped would be the culmination of a nearly lifelong dream – a Grand Slam.

Speed Racer

The states of Virginia, West Virginia, Ohio, Indiana, Illinois, and Iowa lie in our wake as my brother, Kevin, and I arrived at a motel in Council Bluffs, Iowa. We had been driving for nineteen straight hours, and we were both ready for a break and a steak. It was ten o'clock central time on a Saturday night in early April, and we were beat. A Motel 6 took care of the break we needed, and a Golden Corral took care of the steak we wanted, as we spent the first night of our hunting trip on the far western side of the state of Iowa in our quest to harvest Merriam's spring gobblers. My tired physical condition was a culmination of both the long hours behind the wheel, and the fact that I had been turkey hunting every morning during the past week in my home state of Virginia. Hunting spring gobblers in the Virginia mountains the way I do means you get up at 4:30 a.m. and basically climb for the next six or seven hours. This marathon-climbing regimen is repeated each day, unless of course some sort of miracle happens and a spring gobbler actually answers your calls and decides to come in for a look at the new "hen" in his neck of the woods, thereby cutting the morning's aerobic activities short. These little miracles had been few and far between during the last four springs in the western mountains of the Old Dominion State. Nevertheless, I was buoyed by the adrenaline that results from one of these little miracles, courtesy of a beautiful gobbler I had killed the day before we left on our Merriam's hunt, and by the anxiety that plagued me as I endeavored to accomplish the final leg of a spring gobbler Grand Slam. In other words despite being run down physically and mentally from all the hunting and driving, emotionally I was excited and pumped! After a good night's sleep in the Hawkeye State, Kevin and I attended church on Sunday morning at a small Baptist church in Bellvue, Nebraska. We had a wonderful time worshipping our Savior and fellowshipping with the pastor and congregation of Midlands Bible Baptist Church. We hit the road again after the church service and made our way up the Iowa – Nebraska border via I29 to South Dakota. As we made our way along the Lewis & Clark trail in South Dakota, I remarked to Kevin that it was cool to be following the trail on the 200th anniversary of the expedition sanctioned by President Thomas Jefferson in 1803. I also remarked that I had every intention of celebrating the experience of that original expedition by killing and eating a wild turkey along the Lewis and Clark trail just like they had surely done.

The reason we found ourselves in South Dakota when our destination was Nebraska is quite simple: although we would be hunting in Nebraska, we would only be a few miles from the South Dakota state line. The outfitter we would be hunting with operated out of two camps in Nebraska, an east camp and a west camp. Both camps were based out of houses on private farms. From these farms, the outfitter had access to 20,000 acres of private land in north-central Nebraska. The nearest town to this turkey haven is a very small place named Naper. Naper is located in Boyd County and boasts a population of about one hundred and five. My brother and I were booked to hunt out of the west camp for four days during the opening week of Nebraska's 2005 shotgun season. Nebraska has a month-long archery season for spring gobblers beginning in March, with the firearms season opening in mid-April. I had requested the west camp specifically because I wanted to make certain that the birds we would be hunting were true Merriam's birds. Eastern Nebraska has a mixture of Eastern and Hybrid (Eastern/Merriam's) turkeys. Although the outfitter assured me that both camps had true Merriam's birds, I wanted to be extra sure. Our four-day hunt was to begin on Monday, April 18 and conclude on Thursday, April 21. The outfitter had provided us with driving directions to the east camp with the understanding that they would meet us there, and we would follow them to the west camp – but that isn't exactly what happened.

We arrived at the east camp at 4:00 p.m. (right on time) on Sunday afternoon the day before our hunt. There were two trucks at the house, but despite our repeated knocking, no one answered the door. This being my brother, Kevin, and my first experience with an outfitter, we were reluctant to "let ourselves in." So we hung around in the garage checking out the boxes of goose decoys and whitetail deer racks. After fifteen minutes of looking around the garage, the door to the house opened and a camo clad gentlemen about fifty-five years of age named Clifton greeted us.

"I thought I heard someone out here," he exclaimed, as we introduced ourselves, and he invited us into the house.

It turned out that Clifton was a client from Arkansas who was hunting out of the east camp. Kevin and I hung out with Clifton in the very modern and very comfortable home as the Arkansas hunter enthusiastically told us about the triple-bearded gobbler he had killed that morning. In fact, Clifton had just returned from delivering the bird to a taxidermist in South Dakota. As enjoyable as our conversation was though, I was anxious to get on our way to the west camp where our hunt was to take place.

After an hour of chitchat, a young man emerged from the downstairs. He was all of about seventeen years old and was one of the guides. He had been napping in the basement bunkroom. Shortly after we made his acquaintance, he was followed by the outfitter's brother-in-law, Bill, who ran the east camp. I introduced myself and told him we were anxious to get to the west camp. He seemed a little perplexed but phoned the west camp unsuccessfully. Repeated phone calls to the west camp went unanswered, and no answering service responded. I was getting antsy just sitting around looking at trail camera photos, so I suggested that Kevin and I drive to the nearest town to get gas and something to eat before leaving for the west camp. After gassing up the truck and eating at a McDonald's in O'Neill, sixteen miles to the south, we returned to the east camp.

My anxiety turned to frustration when Bill informed us that he still couldn't contact anyone at the west camp. He then suggested that we change our plans and hunt with him out of the east camp. Bill said the other hunters were tagged out after only two days of hunting and the property had plenty of birds we could hunt. I said one of those silent prayers that no one but the Lord himself hears, asking for wisdom of what to do. I then talked to Kevin and suggested that we stick to our original plan. He agreed.

After informing Bill of our desire to hunt as planned from the west camp, he asked me if I thought I could find the camp on my own if he provided us directions.

"I found this place fourteen hundred miles from my home in Virginia," I replied, " I think I can find the west camp forty-five miles away."

So with a "good luck" and a handwritten note of directions in our possession, we said "good-bye" to the east camp and hit the road. "Hitting the road" is both a figurative and literal description of what ensued. The description is literal because after experiencing much of rural Nebraska in our 4x4 SUV earlier in the day, we were accustomed to the driving conditions and left the camp heading due west at the posted speed of 55 mph. The directions indicated that we needed to go straight through two intersections before reaching a "two-track." We drove for quite some time at the 55-mph speed limit looking for Intersection No. 1. When we finally saw the intersection, we were only about fifty yards from it. That was about the same time that I saw the stop sign associated with Intersection No. 1. As my right foot left the accelerator and moved to the brake, I quickly determined that there was absolutely no way I could stop. The one thing that I had in my favor was that Nebraska is pretty flat, and I could see that there was no traffic in any direction. So I put my foot back on the accelerator and resigned myself to run the stop sign at full speed. The one thing that I didn't have in my favor was that for some reason when the hard cap reached the intersection, it ramped up about two feet. When my Toyota 4-Runner hit that ramp at over 50 mph, we went completely airborne – "Oh what a feeling!" We cleared the intersection in Evil Knievel fashion and landed on the other side – hard. So hard in fact, that I had trouble maintaining control of the vehicle. By the good hand of my God upon us, we safely got slowed to a stop and pulled over. I thought for sure we had "tore sumpin' up."

We had landed so hard, I was afraid to get out and look at the SUV. Before beginning our trip, I had made a "hitch-haul" in my welding shop to transport a 150-quart cooler on the back of the Toyota. As we got out to survey the damage, I told Kevin I was sure the hitch haul would be broken. It wasn't. In fact, we couldn't find anything wrong with the truck at all. Most SUVs never see off-road use, but when I bought this truck I knew that it was tough and could handle the off-road stuff. It had proven itself in the swamps of Florida, the mud flats of Oklahoma, and now on the hard cap in Nebraska.

Needless to say, I drove a lot more carefully as we searched for Intersection No. 2, at which I am proud to say that I made a textbook stop. (It helped that Intersection No. 2 had one of those "Stop Ahead" warning signs three hundred feet prior to the stop sign.) After completing my perfect stop at the intersection, we hit the "two-track." The term "two-track" means the pavement ends and there are two dirt tire-tracks through a field. This is the figurative part of hitting the road.

The two-track eventually led to a dirt road, which we began to follow. We drove and drove in the middle of nowhere on this old dirt road. Kevin and I were getting nervous about our whereabouts. We hadn't seen another vehicle since we left the east camp and had been driving for over forty minutes. There were no houses or anything as we traveled the dirt road through Nebraska's farm country. Finally we came to a small concrete bridge crossing a shallow river. Kevin and I collectively breathed a sigh of relief, as our directions indicated that we needed to cross a bridge over the Niobrara River. Crossing that river not only encouraged us that we were indeed on the right road, but it also led us into the turkey paradise we had driven for twenty-six hours to find. We had seen only a few turkeys from the vehicle during our entire trip west, but now we began to see them in good numbers. Seemingly every new pasture we encountered was being visited by wild turkeys – gobblers and hens together. I'm not sure what was more exciting for my brother and me, reaching our destination after two full days of driving or seeing our very first Merriam's gobblers. If I were a betting man though, my money would be on seeing the turkeys. We pulled off the dirt road at one point to photograph a group of mature gobblers that were all strutting side-by-side and gobbling at a group of hens. One frame of film that I shot captured four gobblers with their necks extended gobbling in full strut. If you're a spring gobbler hunter, experiencing that kind of display the evening before you start hunting will really get you pumped up! By the way, I should mention that pulling off the road to take pictures was done strictly as a matter of habit on my part and not as something necessary. There was no need to pull off this road, because there was no traffic of any kind. Kevin and I stopped several more times to photograph and watch birds displaying for hens or chasing one another across a field. We saw fifty-three turkeys while traveling from the east camp to the west camp that evening. Ultimately, we came to another small bridge crossing the Keya Paya River, which was the landmark for us to make a turn to another dirt road leading to our destination. We pulled up to the small, two-story farmhouse and parked the 4-Runner next to a truck with Ohio license plates. As we exited the vehicle and approached the house's side entrance, the sun was beginning to set on a beautiful April evening in northern Nebraska.

The side of the pale, beige house had a sort of "mud" room outside the home's entrance. The mudroom was littered with turkey vests, hip boots, and other hunting paraphernalia strewn about the floor and with shotguns leaning against the wall. I liked the place already. No one answered my knocks on the home's door and the place seemed to be deserted. It was like déjà vu all over again after experiencing the same thing at the east camp.

This time, however, I opened the door and entered the house shouting, "Hello! Is anyone here?"

No response came as I walked through the kitchen and dining area. The déjà vu feeling came only from the lack of someone to meet us. It did not come from the housing arrangements. While the east camp sported wall-to-wall carpet in a very modern home with plush furnishings, modern appliances, and a Home Interiors decorating scheme, the west camp was nothing like it in comparison. The wooden floors sagged and creaked as I made my way through the old, rustic farmhouse looking for our host. There was no coordinated decorating scheme and no plush amenities – just the necessities. Don't misunderstand me; I mean there were decorating touches. There was a skin from a good coyote hanging by the entrance door. (If you're not familiar with the term good coyote…good coyote = dead coyote.) The upstairs bedroom that Kevin and I would eventually sleep in was decorated with a little boy's Mack truck wallpaper probably installed in 1970. (After sleeping in the room for a couple of nights I began considering a career change to driving trucks for some reason.) The décor also sported some turkey fans and beards, some deer horns, and a few framed photos of hunters with whitetail bucks they had killed. The house had no air conditioning and was pretty much what you would expect an old farmhouse to be like.

As I thought about my decision to hunt out of the rough west camp instead of the plush east camp, I concluded, "Man, that was a good decision – the west camp is way better!" Besides, you didn't have to take your boots off before you entered the west camp, which was a major faux pas at the pristine east camp!

Convinced that we were alone at the house, I went outside and got my coffee pot from the SUV. I took it in the house and put on a pot of coffee. Now this wasn't what I had envisioned for my first hunt with an outfitter. I figured they would meet us enthusiastically, and then they would fall all over us trying to get us situated and make us comfortable. Instead, I was making coffee with my own pot while Kevin stood alone on the small front porch!

I decided to take some pictures of the house while the coffee brewed. I had no sooner snapped the first candid photo of Kevin standing on the porch (he was facing away from me unaware of my photo taking) when a gobble boomed from the brushy creek bottom directly behind me. Kevin turned immediately and pointed in the direction of the gobble. If I had waited about one second to snap that photo, I would have caught the expression on his face as he turned and pointed! That gobble brought an abrupt end to my one-picture photo-session, as we both started walking in the direction of the gobbler, which had decided to gobble again, and again. Boy, we were excited! We had traveled fourteen hundred miles to hear a loud-mouthed Merriam's turkey, and there was one gobbling on the roost just before dark no more than two hundred yards from the camp!

Our hunt for the gobbler's location ceased when we spotted a truck driving into the camp. Kevin and I approached the vehicle, and the gentleman in the passenger seat asked, "Can I help you?" in a stern sort of voice.

Kevin replied excitedly, "You sure can. We're here to hunt with Rutting-N-Strutting outfitters!"

Puzzled, the brown haired passenger responded, "Who are you?"

At this point I butted in to their conversation. I was getting aggravated.

"We are Brad and Kevin Day from Clifton Forge, Virginia," I stated sharply.

Now appearing deeply perplexed, and a little agitated himself, the man said, "You aren't supposed to be here until Tuesday."

My aggravation began to give way to anger.

"No," I responded, "I have had this hunt booked since last year, and I spoke to Jason (the owner) just before we left to confirm that everything was still a go. We were scheduled to arrive today and start hunting tomorrow!" I concluded emphatically.

"I'm pretty sure you're not supposed to be here until Tuesday and start hunting Wednesday," he replied, a little less sure of himself.

The man then exited the vehicle along with the driver. I was really mad at this point and was wondering to myself what I had gotten us into.

I had prayed and prayed for the Lord's wisdom and guidance in deciding where to hunt for a Merriam's bird and who to hunt with. Jason Hamilton was a born-again Christian whom I had spoken to on numerous occasions. We had a lot in common, as most turkey hunters do, and had become friends after all the phone calls. I had complete peace in my heart about booking a hunt with Rutting-N-Strutting Outfitters, as did my bother, Kevin. Now though, I wasn't so sure. Since we had arrived at the east camp in the afternoon, Rutting-N-Strutting had let us down. No one met us at the east camp like they were supposed to, no one would answer the phone at the west camp to come and lead us there, no one greeted us at the west camp when we arrived, and now when someone finally shows up at dark they were arguing with us about when we were booked. My first impression with a professional outfitter was that they sucked. I outfit hunters in my home state for ducks, geese, grouse, turkey, and deer – I just don't charge anything. I was qualified to rate this outfit as a dud. However, before you get the wrong idea, let me say right here that our first impression was incorrect. The gentleman I had been conversing with was named Ben. Ben was Jason's uncle and in Jason's absence (Jason's wife was due to deliver their third child) was in charge of the west camp. The driver of the truck was named Chuck, and he was one of Rutting-N-Strutting's turkey guides. Chuck was from Colorado, and Ben made his home in Nebraska, a couple hours away from the camp. Ben and Chuck were returning from guiding a three-hunter party when we met them. By the end of our hunt with Rutting-N-Strutting though, we were all good friends. Things just didn't start off real smooth. It turned out that the west camp had lost phone service; hence, no one could answer the phone when the east camp was trying to contact them. (By the way, there was no cell phone reception at all in this area of Nebraska). To make matters worse for Ben, the answering machine at the west camp had gone belly-up, and he couldn't figure out how to set up the new one Jason had bought. Ben had misread the booking sheet, and after he reviewed the sheet in the house, he apologized. We were indeed booked to hunt as I had explained. I would also learn as our hunt with Ben progressed, that he would get frazzled because he tried so hard to make sure his clients had a good hunt. I believe that was the reason he was so stunned by our arrival. He was concentrating so hard on getting the three hunters that were already in camp their birds, that he couldn't handle the stress of having to satisfy two more at the same time.

Once our itinerary was straightened out, Ben showed Kevin and me to our Mack-truck bedroom, and we unloaded our gear. Chuck had been sleeping in our room, so he had to move out to a couch. I felt bad and offered to sleep on the couch, but Ben and Chuck would have none of it. To make matters worse for our fragile relationship, I had to inform Ben that I was there to hunt without the use of a guide. I carefully told him that I had worked all this out with Jason prior to our hunt. I told Ben that I had my own Double Bull blind, and I didn't want any help harvesting my gobblers. He graciously accepted my request and pulled out some topo maps and aerial photos of the property for us to look at. We decided that he would show me an alfalfa field near the camp in the morning where I could hunt. Chuck would take Kevin to a place along the Keya Paya River called the "Turnip Field" where they already had one of their Double Bull blinds set up. There will be much more to follow about the turnip field, which could just as easily have been called the "Gobbler Field"!

The three other men in camp came to the house shortly after Ben and Chuck had arrived. Two of the men, John and Bob, were buddies from the U.S. Army, and the other gentleman, Ted, was Bob's father. Bob and Ted hailed from California, and John was from Ohio. These three guys were great. They warmly welcomed Kevin and me to camp and were fun to be around. They sat outside the house on fold-up chairs smoking cigars, laughing, and telling stories. All three of them got a kick out of how much gear we had brought along. I told them that we were hoping to hunt in Kansas if our hunt in Nebraska went well. When they heard that I was on the final leg of my quest for a Grand Slam, they were really excited and supportive.

"Don't worry," they said, "You'll get your Merriam's bird here for sure."

Each of the three men had killed one bird already, and both Bob and Ted were now trying to fill their second tag. The gentlemen told us about their hunts and recommended strongly that Kevin and I refrain from using decoys during our hunts, as they had proven detrimental for them. We told turkey stories on the porch until it was time to go to bed. Come to think of it, it was more like I told turkey stories until it was time to go to bed. Chuck and the three hunters were all especially interested in hearing about the swamps of Florida and my hunts for Osceola gobblers – a request that I was more than happy to oblige.

I don't know if I can put on paper a description of my feelings as I pillowed my head after reading my devotions and praying. I was finally here, in Nebraska, on the eve of my first Merriam's spring gobbler hunt. Although untrue, it seemed that I had been waiting for this moment all my life. I was so excited and anxious. I was excited like when I was a small boy on Christmas Eve anticipating the presents under the Christmas tree. I was just one gobbler away from my dream of a Grand Slam, but I was nervous though too. No spring gobbler is ever easy to get, and I would be a fool to think otherwise. What if I failed to kill a turkey? It would be a long, miserable year waiting for another chance. It was hot in the bedroom as I lie there trying to sleep, so I opened the window at the head of my bed. The cool breeze blew across my bed and made me more comfortable, but I still couldn't sleep. Even though I was dead tired from all the previous week's hunting and the two days of driving, sleep just wouldn't come. My inability to doze off was not solely a result of my anxiety for the next day's hunt, but was also encouraged by the snoring which was emanating from the second story of the old farmhouse – mega snoring. There were four other men sleeping upstairs beside myself, and all of them were sawing logs, including my brother in the bed next to mine. I chuckled to myself as I listened to the "bullfrog" serenade. Eventually though, sleep won out, and I drifted off myself, only to be awakened a few hours later by the alarm clock.

It was 5:00 a.m. on April 18, and there was a bustle of activity in that small Nebraska farmhouse. Kevin and I got dressed and readied our hunting gear in the bedroom by the dim yellow light cast from a table lamp on the nightstand between our two small beds. I was feeling nervous, but also confident, as I double-checked the gear in my hunting vest. Kevin and I talked a little but not much – kind of like athletes do before a big game. I had spent nearly a year preparing for this moment, yet I was unsure if I would be able to accomplish my goal. Like any other event in life that is planned and trained for, there comes a time when the training is done, and it is time to "get it on." I felt like I was about to take the mat in the championship match of a wrestling meet. Win or lose though, I was ready to get on with it. We had coffee in the kitchen, and I passed on breakfast. All five hunters wished each other "luck" as we began to depart for our respective hunting areas. I was one of the first to head out, as Ben and I were going to walk to the alfalfa field where I would start my hunt. I shook Kevin's hand and told him to "kill a big one" as Ben and I left the house at 5:15 a.m. That would be the last time I would ever shake my brother's hand short of a Grand Slam.

A ten-minute walk in the dark from the farmhouse put Ben and me at the corner of an alfalfa field. The alfalfa field bordered a cut hayfield to the north and a creek bottom to the west. Ben helped me set up my Double Bull blind on the edge of the creek bottom's tree line, as I questioned him about where he thought the birds would be roosting, and where I was allowed to hunt. The hayfield to my north was owned by Rutting-N-Strutting but was off limits to hunting. It was a protected area to give the birds a haven from hunting pressure. My blind was situated about thirty yards from the hayfield's barbed-wire fence. Ben wished me good hunting as he left me in the pre-dawn darkness to make his way back to camp. I gave considerable thought as to whether I should use my decoys or not, before deciding to follow the advice of my new hunting acquaintances. This hunt would start without my trusty imitations. I got my stool and gear squared away inside the blind before I went to the Lord in prayer prior to beginning my hunt. It was 5:30 a.m.

It was dark inside my blind as I sat alone anticipating the first gobble of the morning. I had decided not to call at all and just listen as the woods came to life. A million thoughts seemed to be racing through my head. Thoughts like: How much should I call? What if I miss? What if I can't call in a longbeard? Finally, I convinced myself that this was just another turkey hunt. This hunt was no different from any other, and it was something that I loved to do.

"Relax and enjoy the experience, no matter what the outcome," I convinced myself.

A sort of calm came over me as my advice sank in, a calm which was shattered at 5:45 a.m. by the booming gobble of a Merriam's longbeard. The gobble came from a wooded area jutting out into the hayfield about two hundred yards to my north. I remained silent and was content to just listen as the gobbler sounded off two or three more times. I'm not sure how many times he actually gobbled because after his second "Hen Tracer" thundered across the open hayfield, another gobbler, then another, and then another, joined him. All of this gobbling apparently succeeded in waking up the hens. Shortly after the gobblers started carrying on, the hens began calling too. The females greeted the graying sky to the east with clucks, tree yelps, and plain yelps, with only an occasional cut by one of the bossy types. The increasing hen chatter only served to encourage the gobblers to continue their own vocal outbursts. It was actually a spectacular stereo experience for a turkey hunter to enjoy. However, once the hens started calling, so did I. There was a big group of turkeys roosting in that block of woods located in the hayfield, and I had to convince them to come my way. There were probably close to a dozen different birds gobbling or yelping about two hundred yards from my blind. I used both a mouth call and a friction call to sound like two roosted hens in the creek bottom. No matter how much or little I called, it seemed to have no affect whatsoever on the roosted birds. They were carrying on with no help from me needed or apparently wanted. The turkeys weren't the only wildlife serenading a new April morning in Boyd County, Nebraska. I heard ducks, squirrels, hawks and crows as well, but at 6:15 a.m. I heard the first turkey fly down into the hayfield.

Normally when turkeys leave the roost in the morning, it is the hens that get the party started. The thing about wild turkeys is, though, they are wild. They may have tendencies that they will typically follow, but there is no script. As one of God's wild creatures they can do whatever they want, and, at least in my experience, they often do. Such was the case on this particular morning, as the first turkey to hit the ground was a gobbler, which immediately began strutting in the middle of the hayfield. He was joined in short order by three other gobblers, which accompanied him in displaying for the still roosting hens. These four longbeards were strutting side-by-side, dead smack in the center of the hayfield about one hundred and fifty yards from my blind. Whatever move one gobbler made, the other three followed suit. They reminded me of a group of male bodybuilders on stage before the judges during the final "pose-off," with each one jockeying for position and trying to "out-strut" the others.

Once the gobblers began strutting, the gobbling activity all but ceased. Every now and then a hen on the roost would say something sexy that would evoke a response, but not often. Needless to say, I was doing my part to persuade the foursome to give up on those sleepy heads in the woods and head my way for a breakfast to remember. (Of course, I tried not to let it out that they were on the menu!) Apparently I didn't hide my intentions very well, because my attempts to lure the bachelors across the hayfield to my position in the alfalfa field were an exercise in futility. However, things were not a total loss. It was a beautiful sight to see those four, full tail fans with their creamy, white tips spinning around in the early morning light as the hens and other gobblers began to fly down and join the strutters in the field – and fly down they did. Turkeys flew down from the roost for the next twenty minutes, sometimes in groups of two, or three, and sometimes intermittently as singles.

By 6:35 a.m. all of the birds were on the ground. I couldn't see all of them, as some worked in and out of the woods, but I know there were at least twenty-five birds. Many of the hens joined the boss gobblers strutting in the center of the field, but some stayed near the wood line with the sub-dominant toms. As daylight began to take control of the new day, the birds along the wood line, which was a good two hundred yards from my set-up, began to work their way away from the strutting longbeards. Unfortunately, they were also working away from me too. I continued my vain calling routine trying to get any of the birds headed in my direction. At one point, the strutting gobbler furthest to my right turned to face me and strutted several paces in my direction, only to do an about face and return to his designated spot in the "chorus line." This served to excite me momentarily and then leave me feeling let down again. That let down feeling would continue for the next hour as I would call in vain and watch the entire group of turkeys exit the hayfield, working away to my right and disappearing over a large hill.

While there was an abundance of excitement at first light, the rest of the morning wore on much more slowly. That is not to say that I didn't see any turkeys, I just didn't see any longbeards. It seemed that all the turkeys were in limbo, still hanging on to their winter flock mentality. This hunt in Nebraska would turn out to be a real puzzler in how to approach a spring gobbler hunt. In fact, this was probably the earliest period of the spring turkey cycle I had ever hunted. Some groups of birds were split up and re-establishing the pecking order, some groups were still in winter flock (hens with hens and gobblers with gobblers), and some of the gobblers were just starting to acquire and assemble their hens. Despite the uncertainty of the turkey cycle, one thing became evident during my first morning in the blind – there was a preponderance of jakes. The spring hatch from the previous year had left the trees heavy with young gobblers.

However difficult it may have been to entice a mature bird into shotgun range, there was no problem getting a jake to respond. Let me rephrase that statement; there was no problem getting jakes to respond. I called in several of the little buggers to within easy gun range of my blind. (In fact, they were within easy bow range – if you are proficient with a stringed weapon out to say ten steps!) From inside my blind, I would sit and watch them displaying and chasing one another in circles. I photographed one jake in full display just ten steps from my Double Bull blind. After they had given up on finding that lonesome hen that had wooed them from afar, the young gobblers picked at the alfalfa as they left my set-up and disappeared into the creek bottom behind me. I also managed to call in a few hens during my first morning, including one that put on a calling seminar for me. In between birds showing up at random intervals, I caught up on some of the sleep I had been losing over the course of the previous ten days.

As noon finally approached, I had to decide whether to stay in the blind for the rest of the day or head back to the camp for lunch and a change of scenery in the afternoon. The corner of the alfalfa field had provided a fair amount of activity during the six and a half hours I had spent there. During my first morning in Nebraska, I had heard twelve gobblers and eight hens, and I had seen four gobblers strutting, seventeen jakes, and ten hens. Since the hunting for toms seemed to be going so slow, I finally decided to head back to camp. My decision called for leaving the Double Bull blind set up where it was, in case I decided to come back to the same spot. Back at camp, I would talk to one of the guides if they were available and see about hunting a different area during the evening. It wouldn't hurt to get a Diet Coke and a sandwich either, I convinced myself. As I was preparing to exit my blind, I heard the faint report of a single shotgun blast. It was 11:45 a.m.

A short walk put me back at the west-camp farmhouse for lunch. I entered the kitchen and hollered a "hello" to anyone who might have been about. The response produced by my boisterous query was much the same as my turkey calls had evoked from the blind – nothing! I was alone at camp, so I made a sandwich and some coffee. After eating, having that Diet Coke, and filling my thermos, with no one else around, I decided to hotfoot it back to my blind and hunt there the rest of the day. I didn't want to be standing around the house waiting on someone to show up when I could be in the field. My only fear was that there would be gobblers in the field near my blind as I walked back from lunch, and I would spook them, as I had to cross a fairly open field. Typically, I could expect one or more gobblers strutting about ten feet from my blind if I pulled a lunch-break stunt like I had just done. Not on this hunt, however. I was both relieved and disappointed as I made my way back to the blind without a turkey to be seen anywhere. The only wildlife encountered during my midday stroll were three whitetail deer. The three does jumped from their beds in some fallen trees in the creek bottom and bounded past me through the alfalfa field. Note to self: Nebraska whitetails are large.

Refueled and refreshed from my lunch break, I re-entered my blind at 1:30 p.m. The next hour or so passed slowly, as I wondered about the shot I had heard around lunchtime.

"Had Kevin gotten a bird?" I pondered.

It was hot in the blind as the midday sun bore down on the fields of northern Nebraska. I unzipped the vent in the top of the blind to help keep cool, and stuck my head out to look around. A large fox squirrel was hanging on a cottonwood tree right next to my blind. He stared curiously at me but went about his business after I pulled my head back inside the blind. Another long hour passed, as I alternated calling on a Primos "Heartbreaker" box call and on a Woodhaven "Jim Pollard" mouth diaphram. I tried cutting, yelping, clucking, and sounding like multiple birds. At about 2:30 p.m., I finally drew a response and heard a turkey gobble in the wooded bottom behind me. He sounded pretty far away, so I called loud and often. The gobbler followed suit and began closing the distance between us. I hammered away at him for a solid fifteen minutes before I caught a glimpse of something black moving through the trees. My heart was beating wildly as I reached for my shotgun and readied it at one of the blind's rear windows. As the gobbler continued his approach, I saw that he was not alone. I also saw that he was not a mature bird. It was yet another jake, being followed by what I took to be his twin brother. Although he had the beard and spurs of a jake, he had the voice of his father. This one-year-old bird could thunder a full gobble with the best of the big boys. (I would find this a common trait with the majority of Merriam's jakes we encountered – full gobbles that were indistinguishable from that of a mature bird.)

The two juvenile birds approached my blind after crossing the creek and were in easy shotgun range when something to the left of the blind caught my eye. Another gobbler had emerged from the woods to the south of me and was coming up the edge of the alfalfa field straight to me. Again my heart began to race as I shifted position to point my shotgun in his direction. This newcomer was not alone either as three more birds followed him out of woods and along the field edge. When I finally got the birds located in my scope, my heart sank again. The four newcomers were jakes as well. All six birds came together about twenty five yards from my set-up, and the race was on. The group of four chased the other two jakes all over the place. After a few minutes, all four of them singled out the jake that had been gobbling and chased him back into the woods behind me. Satisfied that they had put the loud-mouthed yearling in his proper place, the four bullies retreated down the field edge whence they had come. I felt sorry for the lone jake who was walking around in the woods one hundred yards from me like a lost little boy. The poor guy had been picked on by four heathens and deserted by his brother. Eventually he started walking back toward me, when suddenly he stopped and lay down.

I hadn't made a single call after seeing the jake originally. I had purposely remained silent while the bully session took place and had no plans to break the afternoon silence at this point. I had stopped calling because I didn't want to encourage the jakes. Believe it or not, a group of jakes can put even a mature bird on the run if there are enough of them. So I sat quietly in the blind focused intently on the jake lying on the ground facing me. To say I was perplexed would be an understatement. I had never seen a bird do anything like this. My first impression was that he was dusting. Dusting is something all turkeys do routinely during the warmer months to rid themselves of bugs and biting insects. They accomplish this by digging a small depression in the dirt, usually in or near a plowed field or an old road, and then they settle down in the middle of it, throwing loose dirt and dust over themselves with their wings. Once a turkey has created a "dusting bowl" he or she will continue to visit the same spot for debugging purposes as necessary. Other turkeys will also use the site, thus creating a community dusting area. I have seen places that had as many as eleven dusting bowls side by side. In my experience, a turkey only spends a short time dusting – about a minute or two.

As I watched the jake through my eight-power binoculars, he was just lying on the ground like a dog. I'm still not sure to this day what he was actually doing. He did appear to throw dust on his back with his wings, but then he would stretch out his neck and lay his "chin" flat on the ground, lying motionless in the creek bottom. As much as I had trouble believing it, I started to wonder if the four mean jakes had actually hurt him. After several minutes of lying motionless, his head started pecking the ground. He pecked all around from side to side and in front of him. Now I started to wonder if he had lain down on an anthill and was eating the ants, because that is what it looked like. Knowing that I was observing something bizarre, I looked at my watch to see how long he would keep this up. It was now 3:15 p.m., and the bird had already been there for five minutes. Another ten minutes passed before I noticed the jake's companion returning through the woods after having been traumatized himself. He came up behind his brother and stood there gazing at him with the same bewildered look I had. Another five minutes passed before the tired jake finally quit pecking the ground and rose from his siesta. I looked at my watch again and noted that it was exactly 3:35 in the afternoon. The two birds strolled off into the wooded bottom in the direction they had originally come from. Once out of sight, I pressed my Woodhaven diaphragm call to the roof of my mouth and did a yelping series with clucks mixed in. It was the first call I had made in about forty-five minutes.

"Garrroobbble!" boomed in response to my call.

I almost fell off my small stool when I heard it. I turned to my right to look in the direction of the gobble, which had come from the hayfield to my north – the hayfield that all the birds had flown into at first light. And what to my wondering eyes should appear? – a full tail fan, not too far and not too near! A mature bird was in full strut in the center of the hayfield a hundred yards distant. His tail feathers were tipped in white with the sun streaming through them. My senses were on full alert as I eased my shotgun out of the blind's window facing the bird. I began to call aggressively. This bird was alone, strutting, and had answered my first call. I yelped, and cut, and probably made up some turkey vocabulary, as I poured it on the strutting tom. I finally felt like I had a bird that I could work, and my heart rate began to quicken as I realized that this could be it – a spring gobbler Grand Slam. My eyes stayed focused on the gobbler while my tongue stretched the latex in the Woodhaven custom mouth call. The gobbler just wouldn't break and come my way. He continued to spin in small circles, angling his tail in my direction with each turn, and forcing me to view him from every angle. Man, he was a gorgeous gobbler! As mesmerized as I was with the tom, movement managed to catch my eye off to the left.

Another turkey was coming up the fence line, which separated the alfalfa field from the hayfield I couldn't hunt. When I first noticed the turkey, it was seventy-five yards away. The bird was coming fast, pausing only briefly to look straight at my blind. More importantly though, it was a gobbler, and a longbeard at that! This big joker had committed to find the lovesick hen that kept calling from the alfalfa field, and committed he was. I had no doubt that this bird was going to come right to me. The question was – would he cross the fence? There were three other turkeys following the lead gobbler, two hens and another longbeard. They were running along the fence in an apparent race to see who could reach me first – it was amazing! The only problem with all this was that I had to watch them come, and as I watched, boy, did I get shook up! My ragged breaths and pounding heart were familiar precursors to a gobbler's arrival, but on this hunt they were now accompanied by a new biological anomaly; my brain began hammering me with intense waves of pressure not to mess up, as the moment of truth approached.

"This is a Grand Slam bird! This might be your only chance! You've waited all your life for this moment!" These are just a few of the thoughts that raced through my mind, adding to the normal mental chaos that precedes a shot at a spring gobbler.

Also contributing to my sense of impending doom was the fact that I had never actually shot at anything from inside my blind before. I wasn't sure how much gun barrel movement I could get away with. Fortunately for me though, I still had one strand of sanity hanging on with which I reasoned with myself.

"It's not a Grand Slam – it's just another turkey," I told myself.

That simple thought really helped to center me, even if it wasn't true. I convinced myself that I had done this plenty of times before, and I could do it again. My trusty Remington 870 came smoothly to my shoulder, and I slid the safety off, as the longbeard reached the corner of the fence where the alfalfa field and the hayfield met. The gobbler stopped to peer through the strands of barbed-wire, looking for the hen he had heard. He was in gun range at thirty-five yards, but he was on the side of the fence I wasn't supposed to shoot. There was a lot of temptation to take the shot right there, but I wouldn't do it. I purred on the mouth call, and immediately the gobbler ducked under the fence. Once the barbed-wire was cleared, "Speed Racer" wasted no time passing through the six-inch-high alfalfa making a beeline toward the front of my Double Bull. The hens and gobbler that were trailing him also crossed the fence, as I centered the mature gobbler in my shotgun's scope. The bird was in gun range, the safety was off, and I had the cross hairs centered on the tom's waddles, but I still couldn't shoot! He just wouldn't stop! I "putted" to him twice in order to stop him, but "Speed" just kept fast walking on a course past my blind. Two or three times the excitement almost overcame me causing me to take a moving shot. I mean I came really close, with pressure on the trigger, as I began to panic believing he was going to get by me.

"No, No, No!" I told myself. "Do not mess this up! Wait until he stops!"

And then he did. A split second later, the report of my 3-1/2 inch Remington could be heard reverberating over the hills of Boyd County, Nebraska. A split second after that, a sigh of relief and a small prayer of thanksgiving could be heard in my Double Bull blind. My first Merriam's gobbler lay perfectly still in the alfalfa field, twenty-seven yards from my blind. At the sound of my shot he had collapsed instantly and never moved again. Every other turkey in the two fields took immediate flight to parts unknown, but my bird never knew what hit him. "Hit him" would be an understatement. "Mashed him" would be a more accurate description. I did the right thing waiting for the bird to stop, and I have photos taken immediately after the shot to prove it. I killed the gobbler at exactly 3:45 p.m. central time, only ten minutes after the jake left his siesta bed. One more neat thing about the jake – I actually took a picture of him lying in that bed, and the film developed nicely. The photo has special meaning to me, because I know it was taken just before completing my slam. (It also serves as proof about what I saw that day – not that I need it!)

Uncharacteristically of myself, I didn't shout out a loud war whoop after the shot or even take off running to retrieve my bird. I just sat there in my blind, sort of in shock. I had expected to feel some great euphoria of joy when this moment occurred, instead however, I felt almost numb. I guess the influx of different emotions, all at the same time, caused a sensory overload, so to speak. My soul was overwhelmed and didn't quite know how to respond. Certainly I was ecstatic, but I was also relieved, shocked, pleased, satisfied, and proud, all in the same instant. It was, though, a moment and feeling I will never forget. I stayed in the blind, thanking my Savior for His blessing to me, and just sort of savoring the moment. For all the pressure I had put upon myself to succeed in completing a Grand Slam, the old Brad Day was still inside me, like a little boy trying to get out. I wanted to exit that blind and retrieve my bird! This was, after all, just another turkey hunt, and I was the same old turkey hunter. I pocketed the spent shotgun shell as a memento and stretched forth a shaking hand to unzip my blind. The walk to my fallen gobbler was an emotional stroll I can't describe. The twenty-seven paces it took me to reach my first Merriam's bird were special in themselves. Once I was by the gobbler's side, I fell straight to my knees in prayer. I remained in that state for quite some time thanking the Lord with the afternoon sun warming my back. Then it was time to examine my special bird for the first time. Starting now every turkey I would ever examine I would do so as a spring gobbler hunter with a Grand Slam on his resume, and I would have seen at least one representative of every subspecies of Meleagris gallopavo in the United States up close and in person. Not that a Grand Slam made me a better a turkey hunter than anyone else, but it did separate me as different from the average one.

As a side note, I would like to point out that just completing a Grand Slam doesn't mean "squat" in my book. What has meaning to me is how a person completes their Grand Slam. There are plenty of good people out there who have completed slams of their own, but they accomplished it with no particular skill of their own. The only part of their accomplishment that they were responsible for was pulling the trigger and hitting the target after a hunting guide had arranged the set-up, made each critical decision during the hunt, called the gobbler into range, and gave the "take him" signal to the client. While there is nothing morally or ethically wrong with this type of hunt – it just isn't the way a legion member does it. No, a hunter with the same type of severe, outdoor condition that I have wants to make all the decisions and calls by himself. I am not talking about taking advice from a landowner or outfitter with regard to where the birds are roosting or where a good set-up might be found. I am also not talking about taking someone new to the sport hunting with you and helping them kill their first gobbler, or calling in a turkey for a youth hunter or hunting with a friend – I am talking about traveling the country and paying a man to hand-deliver a gobbler twenty-five yards in front of you so you can pull the trigger and then report that you have killed a Grand Slam. I personally have much more respect for any individual (lady, boy, or man) who doesn't even fill a tag during the spring but is out there in the woods trying, than I do for a person who fills all their tags because they paid someone to do the work for them. Folks who read this may disagree with me, but if you are a serious turkey hunter then you know what it is like to get your butt kicked by a spring gobbler and come home empty-handed. (If you don't, get ready 'cause your day is coming!)

"Getting-skunked" is part of the sport of turkey hunting, and that is what makes it so special. It is almost never easy – and that's the way true turkey hunters like it – eventually. It's not necessarily the way we want it, but if you keep at this sport long enough, you learn to accept it and embrace it. Most men that I know, including myself, would rather talk about the gobblers that whipped them than to tell about the ones they have killed. Although, I must confess, none of us will turn down one of those "suicide" gobblers that comes racing in to a turkey call immediately after being struck, should we be so fortunate to encounter one.

Although some might brand me as a hypocrite for stating that I would rather talk about the gobblers that whipped me and then have a book published to the contrary – those who know me best know I'm telling the truth. Meet me in spring gobbler season and ask me about my success and I will most certainly bore you with details about "the one that got away" before I will elaborate on one that I have put on the table. Anyway this story wasn't written to validate my style of turkey hunting or to push some ideological agenda – it was written to remember some special gobblers I have come in contact with. I make the aforementioned comments to help you understand that I don't think any better of myself as a turkey hunter because I completed a Grand Slam. That accomplishment means something to me on a personal level for reasons I fully don't understand. While not at all necessary for fulfillment as a turkey hunter, traveling the country, seeing new terrain, and locking horns with the different subspecies of gobblers that inhabit it is a blessing that I have always had a desire for. On this warm, Nebraska afternoon, that blessing was given.

I took photos of the gobbler before touching him and disturbing him in any way. With the photo session complete, I finally handled the bird that I had been hunting for my entire spring gobbler career. As usual, my attention first turned to his spurs. They were a respectable 7/8-inch long. Typically, Merriam's gobblers have characteristically small spurs, with many birds not having much more than a bump. One theory as to the spur shortages on the western birds is that they break them in the rocky terrain they typically inhabit. One of the advantages I had hoped to gain by hunting for the birds in Nebraska's farmland was that the birds might have better spurs than birds which came from rocky areas. I assumed that my newly acquired bird was a two-year-old gobbler. I would later be informed by the guides at Rutting-N-Strutting that he was actually a three-year-old. Killing a three-year-old Merriam's didn't bother me in the least, as now all four birds that I was turning in to the NWTF's wild turkey records to register my Grand Slam were three years old or older. What an added blessing, to have a slam comprised of not just all four species, but mature birds of all four species, three years of age or older! Also of interest, to me at least, was the fact that all four of my mature "slam" birds were with hens when I killed them. I guess I could claim the completion of a "henned-up" grand slam if I was of a mind to!

Leaving the spurs, I focused on his beard, which was 9 inches in length. While there was nothing spectacular about the beard, it was the heaviest and longest Merriam beard I had ever collected. Okay, obviously it was the only Merriam's beard I had ever collected, but it still was of trophy caliber in my book! The bird appeared to weigh around nineteen pounds as I lifted him from the alfalfa. A scale would later determine the bird's exact weight to be nineteen pounds and three ounces.

The gobbler's wings were worn from strutting, and a couple of his primary feathers were broken from fighting. An even more intriguing feature of the wings was the nearly all-white appearance of the primary feathers. I had read about this genetic characteristic being common in the female Merriam's birds, but I was unaware that gobblers could possess it. The male bird I had just taken though had certainly inherited the unusual trait. As can be seen in one of the photos at the end of this story, the predominantly white wings did possess brown barring, but the larger, white bars dominated it, especially toward the center of each feather. Basically it appeared to me to be the exact opposite of an Osceola gobbler's wing. I really liked the light wings of the Merriam's though. When the birds strutted in the low-light conditions at dawn or dusk, their wings actually looked like they had a light-blue glow; it was awesome! The only thing about the turkey that I would have changed was the color of his tail feathers. Instead of the bleached white tips I was hoping for, this gobbler's tail fan was tipped with a sort of iridescent, light, pinkish-buff color. It was very unique and pretty. It just wasn't the color I had dreamed about for so long. (Pardon me, did I use the word "pretty" to describe my gobbler's tail feathers? How un-macho of me. What I meant to say was his feathers were unique and "cool-looking." Is that better?)

"Color, schmoler," I told myself, "This one's in the bag!"

I tagged the bird by wrapping my first Nebraska license / tag around the bird's left leg and secured it with a rubber band. I then toted him back to the blind, and stuffed him through the opening. Mission accomplished!

In the state of Nebraska, if a hunter possesses two turkey tags, he is legally allowed to harvest both his gobblers on the same day. I had never hunted anywhere before where this was allowed, and I had two tags. So after harvesting my bird, I decided to stay put in my blind for the last few hours of the day and see what happened. It was kind of neat sitting in the blind admiring my gobbler and just thinking about turkey hunting. I was just absorbing the moment. A moment that I knew would be over very soon and that would never happen again. I guess you could say I was hunting, but only in the letter of the law, not in spirit. Sometime around six o'clock, I heard the faint report of a shotgun in the distance to the west. It sounded similar to the lone shot I had heard at lunchtime, and again my thoughts turned to my brother. I hoped he had seen some birds and had taken his first Merriam's bird too. Time would tell I thought as I continued my vigil in the blind. It occurred to me that this was not only my first Merriam's gobbler, but also my first afternoon gobbler, and my first gobbler taken from my Double Bull. Then again, a lot of things occur to you when you hunt alone all day long. I contemplated how far I had come in my turkey-hunting career since those frustrating hunts during my early years as a young teenager in West Virginia. I just never really thought I would be experiencing this moment in my life.

I did make several hen calls which were not answered, but I was mostly thinking and making notes on the back of my Nebraska hunting license: Notes about the day's hunt; Notes that I am referring to as I type this; notes that remind me that on my first day of Merriam's hunting in the Husker State, I saw a total of seven gobblers, twenty-three jakes, and twelve hens. Having made my notes and absorbed all of the moment I could stand, I decided to call it a day and head back to camp a little early. I was excited about seeing my brother and sharing with him the Lord's blessing to me.

I packed up the blind and stool, carefully placed the gobbler in my vest, and grabbed my gun. I had quite a load to haul back to camp. It was shortly before dark when I reached the side entrance of the house. A large cottonwood tree was located just outside the entrance to the house's mudroom. The tree was being used as a gun rack and a turkey depot. Several shotguns were leaning against the trunk and two gobblers were resting in peace at its base. I found an open spot on the tree's trunk to lean my gun against and did so. I slid the Double Bull off my shoulder and shucked my vest off. Before I could do anything else, two human forms appeared in the doorway as the sun set behind me. It was Ben and Kevin. As the two of them approached me they saw the gobbler in my vest. It was "on" then as the saying goes. To be completely honest I'm not sure exactly what all took place as I think back on that moment. It was one happy event though. I do, however, distinctly remember Kevin shaking my hand with a big grin on his face and being the first to congratulate me on completing my slam. I'm not so sure that the large smile on Kevin's face was totally for my sake, as the two gobblers lying at the base of the tree both belonged to him. I congratulated him with a handshake and a hug.

"Man, two gobblers in the same day, that is awesome!" I told him.

I've gone entire seasons without killing two gobblers, and Kevin just up and hammers two on his first day of hunting in Nebraska! I was so happy he had killed both his birds! I wasn't happy just for him but for me. I was worried that if our hunt didn't go well, Kevin would be out the price of the outfitter's fee, and it would have been my fault since I selected the guide service. Nothing to worry about now! Kevin was beaming and rightfully so. He had taken two mature birds, and one had the beautiful white tips on his tail and covert feathers that we both desired. Kevin, Ben, and I stood there talking a mile-a-minute and examining each other's gobblers as daylight faded into dark.

Kevin had killed his first gobbler at 11:45 a.m. with a thirty-yard shot from his old Mossberg Model 500. He had seen four gobblers and two hens during the course of the morning. After killing the tom, which weighed 20-1/4 pounds, had a 9-1/4 inch beard, and 7/8 inch spurs, Kevin had walked from the turnip field where he was hunting to the road to meet the guides. Chuck and Ben were going to stop at the gate near the dirt road around noon to take him back to camp for lunch. At least that is what they were supposed to do. After waiting fifteen minutes for the guides to show up, Kevin decided to just go back to the blind and hunt the rest of the day. It was a good thing they didn't show up! On his way back to the blind, Kevin stopped and put his gobbler in a shady spot across the field from where he was hunting. At 12:45 p.m. he saw the guide's truck from a distance arriving late to pick him up. Kevin just stayed put in the blind and passed on lunch. Finally, at 6:10 p.m. Kevin saw a gobbler in the woods across the turnip field from his blind. The gobbler wasn't alone, as he had an entourage of eight hens and another longbeard following. Instead of coming to Kevin's calls though, the gobbler had his sights set on an object in the woods. Something had attracted his undivided attention. You'll never guess what it was…Kevin's first gobbler! The tom made a beeline for the dead turkey, which Kevin had placed under a small bush. Upon reaching the dead bird, the tom started attacking it! I've heard of kicking a dead horse but not a dead turkey – apparently this bird had! Satisfied with his dominance over the dead bird, the longbeard ventured out into the turnip field, unaware that he was about to join him. When he topped a small rise in the field at thirty-three yards, Kevin's Mossberg barked again, and join him he did. Kevin's second bird was almost identical to his first tom. It too had 7/8 inch spurs, a 9-1/4 inch beard, and tipped the scales at twenty pounds.

With daylight all but gone and the highlights of our day discussed, we decided to cooler our birds and head inside for supper. There wasn't enough daylight left to take any photographs of the gobblers we had harvested. (Did I say harvested? Sorry, I mean killed.) So, we carefully packed our prize possessions in large trash bags and placed them in the 150-quart cooler I had brought for just such an occasion as this. Our plan was to take the birds out the following day, after hunting in the morning, and take a plethora of 35mm pictures to preserve the memory of our first Merriam's gobblers and my first Grand Slam. Once the birds were properly coolered and our hunting gear was stowed in the house, I went upstairs to our bunkroom to change clothes for supper. Now understand that changing out of dirty camouflage in order to eat at the west camp was not required or even encouraged, but I was changing into a pair of jeans and a t-shirt anyway. I was doing so for a reason.

Back in the winter month of January, I received a new mail order catalog from one of my favorite turkey call suppliers. Many of the calls that I like and use cannot be purchased from your regular hunting and fishing catalogs or retail stores, so I have to purchase them from specialty suppliers – suppliers who trade in nothing else but turkey calls and turkey hunting paraphernalia. When I was perusing this latest edition of the referenced catalog and making a list of calls I wanted for the 2005 spring season, I came across a page that had turkey-hunting t-shirts for sale. Ironically enough, the t-shirts were made by Mossy Oak and were called the "Grand Slam Series." They were offering a different shirt for each subspecies of the gobblers found in the United States. Each shirt was a different color, and each shirt had a full color picture of that particular species of gobbler strutting on the back. It was one of those things that "I just had to have." Actually it was three of those things "I just had to have" and one that I was hoping to have. I immediately decided to purchase the white – Osceola, blue – Eastern, and burnt-orange – Rio Grande t-shirts, but I wasn't too sure about whether to buy the gray – Merriam's or not.

Now I am not superstitious, but the Bible says that, "Pride goeth before destruction and a haughty spirit before a fall."

I was afraid that I might "jinx" myself if I bought the Merriam's shirt before actually killing one. After much thought and a prayer asking the Lord to forgive me if I was being presumptuous, I ordered all four t-shirts. I didn't want to have to place two orders and pay shipping twice to get all four, so I convinced myself to get them all at once. However, I did make myself a promise that I was determined not to break. In order to remain humble about my chances of killing a Merriam's gobbler and completing my slam, I vowed to never wear the dark-gray Merriam's shirt until after I had killed one. So when the mail-order package arrived via UPS, I opened it, examined each t-shirt, and then proceeded to wear them regularly...or at least I wore the white, blue, and orange shirts regularly. The gray shirt was folded and placed in a drawer where it remained untouched, until I packed for my trip to Nebraska. Now, on April 18, 2005, as I changed out of my Mossy Oak camouflage, take a wild guess as to what color t-shirt I pulled from my suitcase and donned for dinner? You betcha! It was dark grey and had a strutting Merriam's gobbler printed on the back. You just can't imagine how good it felt to put that brand-new shirt on! However, you probably can imagine how good it felt to join the others in the dining room at 9:15 p.m. for roast chicken and baked potatoes after hunting all day with nothing to eat but a sandwich for lunch. As my wife, Lisa, can attest to, I have a tendency at times to spill food on my shirt when eating. The saying we have (thanks to my nephew, Caleb) when this unfortunate event occurs is, "It's a good thing my shirt was there to keep the food off me!" On this culinary occasion, however, I took great pains to keep the front of my new gray shirt spotless. Which I am proud to say, I managed to do. We had a great meal in the dimly lit dining room that evening; partly because the food was good, and we were all hungry; and partly because of the success Kevin and I had experienced. The fact that my Grand Slam was in the bag, and no longer just a dream, didn't hurt either.

After dinner was over, Ben asked me to look at the camp's new telephone answering service. The phone company had showed up during the day and restored telephone service to the house. Ben couldn't get the new answering machine to operate properly, and knowing my profession as an electrical engineer, he asked me if I would mind helping him out. In short order I programmed the unit as requested and the answering service was up and running. I joked with Ben telling him if he modernized the west camp too much it would start to resemble the east camp. I then told him that if I were running the operation I wouldn't call it the west camp but the "redneck" camp. Ben and I both laughed. (At the end of our hunt, Ben asked if I would serve as a reference for future spring gobbler clients. I told him "sure," but that I was going to recommend that all hunters request the redneck camp!) See, I told you that even though things got off to a rough start, we became good friends during the week.

With the redneck camp's telecommunication problems corrected, I sat down with Ben and reviewed some aerial photos of the properties we were allowed to hunt. After discussing several alternatives, Ben said that he would really like for me to be able to hunt an island in the Keya Paya River. The island was actually a long peninsula, which the river wrapped around after making a 180-degree turn. Ben had watched several gobblers strutting there prior to the season and had observed several turkeys flying to roost on the island earlier in the evening with field glasses. He thought he had a pretty good idea where the birds were roosting. The only problem with hunting the island was he had no way to get us there.

"Can we wade the river?" I asked, not knowing how deep it was.

"Yes," Ben responded hesitantly, "but it is kind of tricky. I would hate to ask you to attempt it."

I almost started laughing and managed to keep from snickering as I said, "Wading the river is no problem for us. We're duck hunters too and wading in the dark is a way of life for us in the winter."

Before he could respond, I continued, "We didn't bring any waders with us. Do you have any extra pairs, or do we need to wade it barefoot?"

Fortunately, Ben said he had two extra pair at the house, but that they were size elevens. I told him that would work for us. (The "us" being Kevin and me. Since he was out of tags, the plan was for Kevin to accompany me on the rest of my hunts and video the proceedings.)

The thing is, I was serious about wading the river barefoot, although Kevin probably had a flashback when I said that. You see many years prior to this turkey hunt when Kevin and I were a lot younger, and also a lot smarter, we found ourselves on another spring gobbler hunt in the mountains of West Virginia. We were tent camping about fifteen miles from the nearest town in pursuit of gobblers along a series of mountains which all had their drainage into a large creek bottom. The large creek, which would be considered a river in many states I've visited, serpentined its way through the wooded bottom at the base of the mountains. I mention the drainage for a reason that will become evident in just a few sentences. To get to our camping and hunting "honey-hole" we had to cross that large creek in a 4x4 truck about seven times as I recall. During the three days we camped and hunted, it did nothing but rain. After three long, wet, gobblerless days without a shower or shave, we had to pack it in for home. The problem with our exit was the size of the raging river that a few days prior was only a creek (pronounced "crick" for those of you non-mountaineers). Each time we reached the edge of the creek on our way out, we had to stop and decide whether it was worth attempting to cross or not. Looking back on it now, I think the only consideration we had as to whether we should attempt to ford the waterway or not, was if the truck was still actually running! Certainly the depth and swiftness of the water didn't play a factor in our decision. Kevin was driving his large Ford Bronco, and, somehow, we actually made it across the first five fordings. Even though the water was over the Bronco's rocker panels, and the swift current would push the vehicle sideways downstream, at each fording we would eventually make it safely across. This would only serve to validate our decision to plow ahead as long as the Bronco was still running.

Unfortunately, at the sixth crossing, things took a turn for the worse, or should I say a "drop" for the worse. Halfway across the raging creek / river, the Bronco's front right tire dropped into a large hole. The hole was in an area you wouldn't normally encounter as you made the fording, but when you cross in the conditions we did, the driver's intentions and destiny are often two different things. Completely stuck in the center of the swollen stream, the water was coming in the Bronco's doors. The plan, you wonder? Kevin would strip down to his under shorts, dive under water, and try to place rocks under the tire for traction. I would then assume driving duties and try to free the vehicle due to my extensive off-road four-wheeling experience. (If you doubt my broad off-roading savvy, contact my parents for details. On second thought, please don't. Their hearts may not be able to handle the stress of reliving the memories.) Now, due to my own aquatic excursions, I personally know how cold the water from mountain streams is in April, but if I had any doubt on this occasion, Kevin's expression when he hit the water in his underpants left no doubt as to the frigidness of this

West Virginia creek. (I told you we were a lot smarter back then!) Much to our chagrin, the plan didn't work – at all. So there we were…stuck. The only option we had was to start hiking out on foot. Kevin felt so bad for getting the Bronco stuck that he volunteered to "piggy back" me across the river to keep me as dry as possible.

As I recall, he felt bad because I kept saying, "Don't do it! Don't do it!" just before he mashed the accelerator pedal and commenced the sixth crossing.

Anyway, I'm just glad no one was around to see him piggy backing me across the muddy river in his underpants during a pouring rainstorm with me holding his clothes above my head. Not many tourists come to West Virginia to experience the breath-taking beauty the wild, wonderful state has to offer. I imagine that is probably because some poor soul has witnessed something like we were doing on a nature hike and was in fear of being entangled in a mess like "Deliverance." Word spreads quickly, you know!

Anyhow, to make a long and humorous story shorter than I should, we hiked a total of fourteen miles in the rain and mud before we found someone with a four-wheel drive truck who would help us. We were a mess after three days of camping and hunting in the rain. Unshaven, unwashed, muddy, soaked to the bone, and dressed in camouflage it is a wonder we got any help at all. Not that I blame the people who hid their children from us, or the poor lady who's trailer door we knocked on asking to use the phone. The terrified woman wouldn't even open the door to talk to us. As we walked away in the rain, she felt sorry for us I guess, and hollered for us to come back. On the porch, she slid a cordless phone through the crack in the door with the safety chain latched. Of course as our luck would have it, no one was home at the number we called. We gave the phone back through the crack in the door, and she offered us a towel, which we refused politely. We thanked her and resumed the hike.

When we finally managed to get the Bronco pulled out, we discovered that the leaf springs were broken at the left rear tire! After all we had been through that day, we just wanted to make the two and a half hour drive home, and not have to find a garage. So I took a hatchet up the hill into the woods and cut a wedge from a white oak tree. I pounded the wedge into the broken springs and then used a heavy-duty three-strand rope to wrap the springs tightly and secure them. We drove all the way home on that temporary fix without a single problem. I may be an Eagle Scout, but all the credit for us getting out of that mess goes to my Lord and Savior, who answered our prayers that day.

Speaking of Boy Scouts, as a Scout I completed two large hikes that retraced the trails taken by General Edward Braddock and General John Forbes as they led their troops in the French and Indian War. Braddock's trail was fifteen miles long, and Forbe's trail covered twenty-seven miles. After completing the hikes and writing an essay on the history of each trail, the Boy Scouts of America commemorated my accomplishment by presenting me with medals and pins. After we got home from that fourteen-mile mud-hike ordeal, I fashioned a medal for Kevin and presented it to him. I waived the essay, but I think I just wrote it for him. Now you know why I said Kevin might have had a flashback when I suggested wading a river barefoot in April, but I digress. I have a habit of doing that – where was I?

Oh yeah, wading the Keya Paya river – in waders – now you probably would have chuckled at Ben's question too, huh? Afraid to wade the river? That was what we decided to do. Ben would go with Kevin and me to help us negotiate the tricky river crossing in the pre-dawn darkness. I would carry the hunting gear and gun, Kevin would carry the tripod and video equipment, and Ben volunteered to carry my Double Bull blind for me. With the next day's hunt planned, we headed to the Mack-truck boodwah (redneck for boudoir) for a much-needed goodnight's sleep. Whether anyone snored that night or not, I wouldn't know. Despite all the adrenaline and excitement of the day's events, all I remember after praying and nightly devotions, is a sweet-smelling breeze blowing through the window at the head of my bed as my head hit the pillow.

Tuesday morning came quick with the alarm clock sounding again at 5:00 a.m. Dressed and one cup of coffee later, Ben, Kevin, and I headed for the river. At the river we swapped out our turkey hunting boots for the hip waders provided by Ben. After securing our hunting boots safely in the back of our vests, the first thing we had to negotiate in the dark was a sheer bank leading to the river. The bank was about six feet straight down – with nothing to hold on to. Once in the river bottom, we followed our guide into the river at a spot only he knew how to find. We hadn't gotten far into the river, when I discovered that I lucked out and got the pair of waders that leaked! The water was nearly over the top of the hip waders, and we had to be extremely careful as we crossed. The Keya Paya was about one hundred and twenty feet wide at the spot where we crossed, and once safely across, we climbed the opposite bank to a stand of pine trees. In the pines we peeled off the waders and put our hunting boots back on. Ben then began to lead us though several thickets and over a barbed-wire fence, before eventually becoming perplexed about our exact location. Undaunted by his uncertainty, we pressed on. Soon afterward Ben stopped again and expressed his confusion as to our whereabouts and intended destination. At this point, I decided to offer some advice.

"We need to turn and go to the right," I suggested.

"No," Ben replied, "We need to keep going straight."

I shrugged my shoulders in submission, and we continued following Ben straight ahead. It wasn't long before I could hear the river gurgling in front of us.

"We've hit the river," I told Ben.

Frustrated, Ben commented, "We're back where we started from!"

"No, we're not," I exclaimed. "I'm not sure where we are, but there is no way we are back where we started."

Ben was convinced otherwise and restated his position.

"Draw me a map of what this area looks like," I asked him.

We dug around in our gear until someone found an ink pen, and Ben then proceeded to draw me a sketch of the peninsula on the palm of his hand, as I held my flashlight for him. Map in hand, literally, I told Ben we had gone clear across the point of land and reached the river on the far side. I again restated that we were "OK" and just needed to go to the right. No matter how hard I tried, I just couldn't convince Ben that my sense of direction was correct. Finally I told him that I would take him down to the river and prove it to him by showing him the direction the river water was flowing. Before that was necessary, Kevin decided to speak up.

He graciously told Ben the following: "I know you don't know my brother very well, but when he says we need to go right then we need to go right. I don't know how he does it, but I have seen him find his way on so many occasions like this in the woods that I have just learned to trust him. There have been times that I was sure he was wrong, and I knew he was taking me in the wrong direction, but in the end he was right. Now, I don't even argue with him, even if I think he's wrong. I just keep my mouth shut and follow him. He always ends up where he needs to be. I vote we follow my brother," Kevin concluded.

I was shocked at Kevin's statement. How could he ever think I was wrong! Ben reluctantly resigned himself to follow me, and I took the lead. After several minutes fighting my way through the brush and trees, I hit the opening on the peninsula we had been looking for. With nothing more than a glance at Ben's palm pilot (that's a funny joke right there…if you don't think that's funny you need to quit reading right now!) I had "guided the guide" to our hunting spot – and not a moment too soon I might add. We had hardly stepped foot into the open area we were searching for, when a gobble boomed from the roost, three hundred yards straight in front of us.

That gobble put all three of us on the run. We hurried toward the gobbler's roost cutting the distance in half, when he gobbled again. I wanted to set-up the blind right there and not chance going any further, but Ben insisted we get closer. The three of us hurried forward another thirty yards, and we all agreed that we shouldn't risk moving any nearer to the roost. I popped up the blind next to a cedar tree, and all three of us piled in. The original plan was for Ben to help us find our set-up spot and then return to camp. Now with daylight coming fast due to getting turned around in his search for the open area we intended to hunt, Ben asked if he could stay in the blind with us instead of risking the birds seeing him leave. I agreed with his suggestion, as I readied my gun and calls for a try at Merriam's number two. Ben lay down on the ground in the back of the blind, and Kevin readied the video equipment. Well, actually he readied the tripod, because he had forgotten the video camera. He thought that I had it in my vest, and I did not. I should point out that while all this activity was taking place in the blind, the gobbler on the roost had intensified the pace of his gobbling activity. He was so fired up that several other gobblers were now gobbling at his calls. These birds were what I call "domino" gobbling. I have also heard it referred to by others as "dynamite" gobbling. What I am referring to is the type of gobbling scenario where one bird gobbles, which causes a second to respond, which in turn stimulates a third bird into gobbling, and so on until all the toms have had their say. It's just like dominos falling right down the line. Sometimes the first gobbler will answer the last one, and they just keep gobbling in succession. That is what was happening on this foggy morning on the Keya Paya River peninsula. Four gobblers were domino gobbling a mere one hundred and twenty yards from our position. It was awesome and, I might add, worth getting wet for too!

I waited a little longer than normal to begin calling to the gobblers. The fog was so heavy it seemed to delay the break of day. Finally, it was time to start working the roosted birds. I began with some soft clucks and tree yelps, which were greeted immediately with a response from several of the gobblers. It always makes you feel good when a gobbler approves of your calling and does so with a hearty gobble. It makes you feel even better when he does so and you have an audience in the blind with you, especially when a member of the audience is a professional turkey-hunting guide. I have to say that even though I have called on stage during many sanctioned turkey-calling contests and now had a Grand Slam under my proverbial belt, I was a little nervous calling with Ben there beside us. However, after the gobblers responded readily, my demeanor went from nervous to cocky. I continued with the soft stuff and then did a flydown cackle. The turkeys would gobble at my calls and then at each other, or at least that is how it sounded to me. As I started to call like a hen already on the ground, the gobblers seemed to cool off somewhat. They weren't the only ones on the peninsula who were becoming unimpressed with my abilities either. As I sat listening for the birds to fly down, I began to hear a strange, yet familiar, sound. It started low and then got louder. It sounded like a man snoring. In fact it was a man snoring. No, let me rephrase; it was two men snoring! You'll never guess who they were! Ben was sound asleep on the ground in the back of my blind, and Kevin was slumped over on his stool. Yep, my calling had impressed the heck out of those two! I returned my focus to listening for the gobblers hoping they would come quickly and allow me to interrupt naptime with a 3-1/2 inch Remington wake-up call!

Eventually, I could tell the gobblers had flown down and were on the ground. My heartbeat began to quicken as I anticipated a possible "off-the-roost" hunt. The gobblers had other plans though, as they walked away from our position, gobbling occasionally. As the old saying goes, "roosted ain't roasted!" We never saw the birds due to the fog and a strip of cedar trees jutting out into the open area to our right. We could only hear their gobbles getting fainter as they moved away – all but one that is. For some reason one of the birds lagged behind his buddies, gobbling at my hen calls. I thought he was going to break and come on several occasions during the next fifteen minutes, but he just wouldn't do it. Try as I might to convince the bird, he began to walk off in the same direction as the other gobblers had gone. He threw out a searching gobble as he left, trying in vain to convince me to join him. I told Kevin that this was the kind of gobbler we might be able to kill later in the morning, if we stayed put. Satisfied that it was now safe to exit the blind and head back to camp, Ben wished me luck and struck out for the river crossing.

Kevin and I waited out the long morning together in the blind. At some point during the early morning, we could hear wings beating behind us, and what sounded like turkeys flying. I suggested to Kevin that the birds were flying across the river to us. That was wishful thinking! We would later determine that the turkeys were indeed flying the river but away from us, instead of toward us. It appeared that the birds were using the island to roost on and then were leaving it in the morning to feed in the agricultural fields just across the river. Even so, around 9:00 a.m. a hen answered my calls from our left and started heading our way. I got ready for a shot, hoping desperately that she had a Merriam's tom tagging along with her. No such luck though, as the hen appeared about thirty yards from the blind – alone – in the still heavy fog. I quit calling to her, and we watched in amazement as the female turkey lay down in the broom-straw grass in front of my blind. Kevin and I whispered to each other chuckling at the hen's behavior. Here we go again I thought, remembering the jake's antics from the day before. I began to wonder if Merriam's birds weren't just plain lazy! What the hen was doing, we may never know. She just lay there like a dog. I mean she couldn't have been too tired; she had only been awake for about two hours. Maybe the fog had something to do with it, but whatever it was, it took her an hour to get over it. We monitored the hen's time-out for sixty minutes on our watches. Then she just got up, shook herself, preened a few feathers, and headed to the river away from us. The next hour passed extremely slowly until 11:00 a.m. when I made a series of yelps with my mouth call. A gobble sounded from the same area where we had last heard the lingering gobbler early in the morning.

"That's him!" I exclaimed to Kevin excitedly. "I'm betting we can work him now," I said confidently.

I wasted no time in finding out either. I immediately cranked up my calling, jumping right in to some aggressive cutting sequences. The gobbler answered regularly, but not as regularly as I would have liked. He would only answer my every third or fourth offering to him, sometimes pausing after I had called for twenty or thirty seconds before gobbling. What his gobbles lacked in regularity though, they made up for in location…they were getting closer all the time! Eventually the gobbler was directly behind us and his gobble was only about fifty yards away. I had my gun positioned for a shot on the left side of the blind, which overlooked a small cut through the cedar trees and brush behind us. The gobbler would have to come through the natural lane I reasoned, and come he did. My heart was pounding as I caught sight of the shining black bird with his white head bobbing up the lane. The fog had burned off, and the sun was now high in a bluebird sky illuminating the gobbler's iridescent feathers as he approached. The only thing that would have been more beautiful to see coming up that lane would have been a longbeard. The bird, which was quickly making his way into gun range, had a man's voice – but only a boy's beard. He was a jake! I pulled my gun back into the confines of the Double Bull and stood to watch the bird come alongside the blind. He was only ten yards from me when I turned my head to look at Kevin. As I motioned to him with my hand that the jake was just outside the blind, the juvenile turkey gobbled…loudly! It scared the daylights out of me! I jumped when he gobbled, and Kevin started laughing at me through clenched teeth, all bent over on his stool. Too bad he forgot the video camera! I composed my embarrassed self, and we watched the young gobbler walk past the blind searching for that sexy hen he had been talking to. The jake was gobbling frequently now because he just knew the hen had to be right there – somewhere.

At such close range, it was amazing to hear this jake's full gobble which was indiscernible from that of a mature gobbler. A jake usually has trouble producing a full, deep gobble. They typically have a higher pitched and broken gobble that is unmistakable as that of a young male. Some jakes I have heard sounded absolutely terrible, while others like this one sound like a longbeard. You just never know, but we found that during our hunt in Nebraska a majority of the jakes we heard gobble had full-throttle vocals like their fathers. The bird we were watching was looking so hard for the hen he had heard, that he failed to see the chuckhole in the ground before him. His right foot found it though, and the jake's whole leg fell into the hole causing him to fall to the ground on his right side. Kevin and I both started laughing at the comical bird again, but he was far from finished entertaining us. After staying in the hole motionless for about ten seconds, the little scutter started trying to get out. This was no small feat for a bird. His struggling eventually paid off, as he managed to pull his leg out and stand back up. I'm not kidding; he shook himself and then started looking around, as if to see if anyone had seen him fall. He then gobbled and looked around again as if to say, "I'm cool!" He looked just like a teenager not wanting to look bad in front of the girl he was trying to impress. Come to think of it, that is exactly what he was doing. We sat there laughing at the bird as he walked away from the blind, gobbling with every other step heading to the river bottom. That jake had made our day.

A short time later we called it a morning. Kevin and I left the blind and scouted the roost area to find where the birds had flown down and strutted in the morning. All the tracks and drag marks left by strutting wings in the gray Keya Paya sand left no doubt as to where we should have positioned the blind. We picked out a better spot to set up in the future, before we returned and packed up our blind and gear. We waded the river and returned to camp for lunch. Back at camp we relaxed and talked with the other guide, Chuck. Chuck was a super nice guy, but he expressed his frustration with the arrangements made by Kevin and me.

"I hate it when I can't be out there hunting," he said. "Sitting around the camp all day is boring."

I could certainly sympathize with him, so I made him an offer.

"If you are bored sitting around camp, maybe you could do me a favor," I offered.

"Sure," Chuck replied, "What do you need?"

I then told him about our morning's hunt and my theory that all the gobblers we heard were jakes. I suggested that they had flown across the river after daylight to feed in the fields bordering the river, but I was just guessing at all this. I asked Chuck if he could find some high ground before evening and watch the peninsula with field glasses.

"What I want to know," I stated, "is if you see any birds fly back across the river to roost in the evening and, if so, are they jakes or longbeards."

I further explained that if he did indeed see birds fly to the peninsula to roost and they were mature gobblers, I had a plan and a better spot to hunt them. If they were jakes, I wouldn't waste my time hunting the island again. Chuck was very enthusiastic about my request.

"Heck yeah," he said, "I'd be glad to do that for you!"

I was starting to like this "hunting guide at your disposal" thing! I could be hunting one spot and have them scouting another!

After a quick lunch, Kevin and I took part in a Nebraska photo-shoot with the gobblers we had killed the day before. We photographed each other and our first Merriam's turkeys on a beautiful, sunny, picture-perfect (pun intended) spring day. With plenty of photos to preserve the memory of our experience and my first Grand Slam, we then undertook the task of dressing the birds and preserving their tail fans, beards, and spurs. It was a relief to have the gobblers photographed, properly cared for, and back on ice in the cooler.

Kevin and I hung out with Chuck at the house until 2:30 in the afternoon. Then we strapped on all the gear and headed out for our afternoon hunt. I decided to take Kevin to the corner of the alfalfa field where I had killed my first bird. I had seen quite a few birds there the day before and hoped we would do as well again. This time Kevin had the video camera with him, and we hoped to film some Merriam's birds. The thought of that big, white-tipped strutter in the middle of the hayfield didn't hurt my decision either. We set up the blind and opted again to hunt without the use of decoys. While the weather was beautiful and the company was good on this Tuesday afternoon, the turkey hunting was slow. We saw a total of four hens the entire evening and not a single gobbler, jake or otherwise. Of course we videoed the Merriam's ladies as they fed in the alfalfa and eventually came right past our blind. Other than that, not much was happening. Kevin and I just spent the afternoon reviewing our previous hunts from the day before and discussing plans for what to do in the morning. We called it a day just before dusk without hearing or seeing any birds go to roost. Kevin and I hustled to pack up the gear and return to camp before dark.

Back at camp we met up with Chuck and asked him about his scouting trip.

"You were right," he said. "Birds did fly the river to roost on the island, but they were all jakes."

That wasn't what I wanted to hear, but it was what I expected. I had a foolproof plan for setting up on those birds across the river after having scouted it after the morning's hunt. Now I needed a new plan for Wednesday morning.

"Jump in the truck with me," Chuck suggested, "and we'll go scout another field I know about, if we can get there before dark."

With no time to lose, Kevin and I piled into Chuck's Suburban. A short, quick ride out the dirt road leading to the camp put us in view of a large field along the river bottom. Immediately we could see turkeys still in the field at the wood line. The birds were two hundred and fifty yards away, and we glassed them from Chuck's truck, which was stopped in the middle of the road.

"There he is!" Chuck stated excitedly.

"There what is?" I questioned, as the only thing I could see was a group of hens and a jake.

"The big gobbler that I was hoping to see," Chuck answered. "He's over to the left where that stand of trees juts out into the field," he continued.

Finally I located the big boss gobbler strutting with another longbeard. I watched them start moving across the field toward the hens. It was starting to get really dark, and I was amazed that these birds were still on the ground. The longbeards then singled out the jake from the pack of hens and began running him around the field edge, past the hens. As the birds started heading into the woods to roost, Chuck turned the truck around and headed back to camp. As we drove, I asked Chuck about the gobbler. Chuck told me that he had been watching the bird for about a month while scouting for the spring season and that the gobbler was a dandy. The tom had been using the field we glassed regularly, until spring gobbler season opened. He had since disappeared, until tonight. In fact, Chuck and Ben had unsuccessfully hunted for this bird with Bob and Ted on opening day. John had taken a stab at him the second day without seeing the tom either. Now it appeared that the gobbler was back. Chuck told me he would be a good one to try for. However, he also said the turnip field was a good spot to try too. Kevin agreed with Chuck, and he also encouraged me to try the turnip field. I have to say that I got pretty excited at the thought of being able to hunt the following morning for the large bird we had just glassed, but I asked Chuck what he would do. (This is something that I do back home when trying to put another hunter on big game: I put them where I would hunt if it were I pulling the trigger or releasing the arrow.) I asked him if he was going to hunt and it was his only morning to go, where would he set up?

"The turnip field," Chuck replied immediately. "That spot has produced more gobblers for us than any other," he furthered. "Last year we killed eighteen birds out of the west camp, and ten of them were taken on the turnip field."

That was pretty impressive coupled with the fact that out of the west camp's early 2005 tally of seven gobblers, five had been taken on the turnip field. Kevin again asserted his opinion favoring the turnip field too. I will admit to being leery about the turnip field because so much shooting had taken place there already that I was afraid the birds were all janked-up. It was going to be a tough decision, but one I had to make. As we turned into the gravel drive leading to the west camp, I had made up my mind. Little did I know then, but a special memory was waiting to be realized because of the choice I had just made. To find out what happened, catch up with me some other time, and I'll share with you the "rest of the story."

Oh, by the way, I almost forgot to mention something that I would like for you to know. I still lift weights (slack) three times each week, and my weight room now has turkey-tail mounts from all four subspecies of America's wild turkeys decorating it. I still pray each day before I exercise, too. But now while I'm on my knees in prayer, I thank my Heavenly Father for allowing me to harvest a Grand Slam. I couldn't have done it without Him!

1st GRAND SLAM

Merriam's

Date: April 18, 2005
Time: 3:45 p.m.
Location: Boyd County, NE
Weight: 19 lbs. 3 oz.
9 inch Beard
7/8 inch Spurs

White Wings

Merriam's Beard

Kevin's Gobblers

Double Bull Blind

Mack Truck Bedroom

Jakes

Puff Daddy

—

The Merriam's Gobbler

Preface

When it was originally scheduled, my hunting trip to Nebraska in the spring of 2005 was all about trying to kill one, mature, Merriam's longbeard. Just one gobbler of the Merriam's subspecies was all that was standing between me and my first Wild Turkey Grand Slam. However, when I was trying to decide where to hunt for a Merriam's gobbler, I wanted to find a state where I would be able to purchase two tags. After all, I thought, if I was going to drive 1400 miles to hunt wild turkeys, it sure would be nice to have a second tag on hand, just in case I was able to kill my Grand Slam gobbler early in the hunt. In my optimistic way of thinking, if I filled my first tag, and thereby completed my slam, with a second tag on hand I could hunt the remainder of the week in a more relaxed fashion. (Of course, in reality, that would be impossible for me to do. I have never hunted spring gobblers with a "relaxed" attitude. In fact, it could be shown that I have a medical condition known as a "Severe Gobbler Disorder," which precludes me from doing anything even remotely related to hunting spring gobblers in a "Ho Hum" manner. If you doubt the veracity of this statement, just ask my wife, Lisa, or anyone else who has known me for more than say, two hours.)

I knew that hunting for my first Merriam's tom was going to involve a huge amount of work, both physically and mentally. Trying to complete my dream of a Grand Slam was going to involve a lot of mental pressure and seriousness. I hoped that if I was successful in filling my first Merriam's tag, that hunting for a second bird would prove to be more recreational and fun, since the "pressure" to succeed would be off. I had always imagined that my quest for a Merriam's gobbler would take me to the Black Hills of South Dakota. I had done a lot of research on where to hunt in the Black Hills and was ready to travel there, until I discovered that I would only be eligible for one turkey tag. Disappointed in the one-tag law in South Dakota, I did research on other states and settled on Nebraska. The Cornhusker State allowed non-resident hunters to purchase two tags for spring turkey hunting in the areas where Merriam's birds were found.

All of this research and decision-making was done in the late summer of 2004, almost nine months prior to Nebraska's opening day of spring gobbler season in 2005. From the very beginning, I had committed my trip out west to hunt turkeys to my heavenly Father in prayer. I can only thank my Lord and Savior, Jesus Christ, for His providential guidance in directing my paths. Little could I have known the series of events that would take place before my trip to Nebraska was to commence. As things would turn out, I would be successful on my first day of hunting in Boyd County, Nebraska, taking my first Merriam's gobbler and completing my coveted Grand Slam. Hunting for my second bird, however, would turn out to be anything but "relaxing," as the opportunity for not only a second Grand Slam would hang in the balance, but for a single-season Grand Slam at that. Choosing a state that offered two tags for Merriam's birds would prove to be a decision with monumental consequences for me.

Puff Daddy

It was Tuesday, April 19, when we pulled into the west-camp's drive, and it was now dark. My brother, Kevin, along with one of the camp's guides, Chuck, and myself exited Chuck's Suburban to enter the old farmhouse that had become our home during the previous three days. We had just returned from a last minute scouting trip, trying to locate an old, elusive gobbler before he went to roost. We had watched the old gobbler strutting from two hundred and fifty yards away through our binoculars as the sun set in the west behind us. This bird had given the guides and previous clients of Rutting-N-Strutting Outfitters the slip during the first few days of the season, and I was considering whether to hunt for him in the morning or to give another area known as "the turnip field" a shot. Both the guide and my brother had advised me to opt for the latter.

On the short drive back to the farmhouse, I had made up my mind where I would hunt. As the three of us entered the camp's mudroom, I divulged my decision to Kevin and Chuck.

"Although I'd really like to hunt that old bird we saw this evening, I'm going to take your advice and hunt the turnip field in the morning," I informed them.

With that settled, Kevin and I put away our hunting gear and then joined the others in the dining room for a spaghetti dinner. Although no turkeys were killed during the day, all seven men present at supper enjoyed the food and fellowship, as the day's events were discussed. Well, almost everyone enjoyed the dining experience. Bob, one of the hunters from California, was a little uncomfortable due to the presence of a bug, which had managed to enter his right ear. This small insect became a conversation point during our meal. Several suggestions were made about how to deal with the problem, including one of my own.

Eight years prior, I had experienced the exact same type of problem while hunting spring gobblers in Virginia. As I was descending a steep mountainside exiting the woods after legal hunting time had expired, a small insect entered my left ear, and I couldn't get it out. I could hear the little bugger (pun intended) buzzing around inside my ear, and I couldn't do anything about it. It was amazing how loud and uncomfortable such a small bug could be when inside your ear canal. The small bug felt like he was the size of a wasp and twice as loud. To extricate the annoying insect, I tried using my finger, pulling on my ear lobe to open the ear canal, massaging the cartilage at the base of my ear, and rubbing my ear – all to no avail. Eventually I resorted to punching, pressing, and beating my ear to kill the thing if it was bound and determined not to leave its newfound home. (I guess the little guy liked his new real estate as it was warm, clean, and, with very little brain matter to interfere with him, he had plenty of room to spread out.) The good news was that I was able to kill the bug – the bad news was that I was able to kill the bug. At least while he was living there was a chance he would free himself. Now that he was dead there was no chance of that happening. With him dead, however, I no longer had to put up with his incessant buzzing that was nearly making me lose my equilibrium. Dead or alive, it was amazing how uncomfortable that bug in my ear had made me. When I finally arrived at home I tried using a cotton swab to remove the intruder, and all that I was able to get was a couple of legs. In spite of my attempts to extricate the dead insect, I was still having trouble with my sense of balance. Not knowing what else to do and concerned about a possible infection, I went to the local hospital. The nurses used a bottle of saline to irrigate my ear, and after about a minute, "Whah-Lah," out came Mr. Bug. It was embarrassing to see the pitiful little critter that had caused me so much discomfort. I guess I just wasn't used to having anything between my ears!

So after hearing about Bob's unfortunate predicament, I related to him my experience and suggested irrigating his ear with water. Bob's dad suggested using peroxide instead of water, and after dinner, relief was soon found for Bob as he lay on the couch and Ted applied the stream of peroxide. With Bob's ear empty and all of our bellies full, we all felt better. I took a shower and contemplated my plans for hunting the turnip field in the morning.

The turnip field was actually a relatively small food plot, which was planted annually for whitetailed deer. The turnip plot was roughly the size of a football field in both length and width, and while not directly on the Keya Paya River, it was very near the waterway. Planted with turnips during the summer, the field provided an ideal source of forage for the deer after a hard frost in the winter. The deer would use the food source heavily once a good frost had converted the starch in the leafy greens to sugar. The whitetails would eat every inch of the turnips' sweet, green leaves and stalks – right down to the bare ground. This left only the tops of the turnip bulbs exposed, which for some reason the deer refused to dig up and eat. So in mid-April, this once flourishing food plot was now nothing more than a big, bare dirt field. The beauty of this barren field, however, lay in its appeal to gobblers of the strutting type. As attested to by its previous history of dead gobblers being hauled from it, the turnip field was a great place to set up and call to a longbeard. So good, in fact, that the guides at Rutting-N-Strutting had permanently set up their newest Double Bull blind at a strategic location on the edge of the field. The blind was located in some cedar trees on the river-side of the field, about one-third of the way along its length. Because it was such a good spot from year to year, the guides had even taken the time to "brush-up" the blind with cut cedar branches, making it even more effective in concealing a hunter from the wary eyes of a wild turkey. My brother, Kevin, had already put the new Double Bull blind to the test, killing two mature gobblers from it the previous day.

Before going to sleep that night in the old farmhouse's upstairs bedroom, Kevin and I lay awake for a short time discussing our plans to hunt and video together in the morning. As we conversed in hushed voices between our two small beds, Kevin was confident that I was making the right choice in hunting the turnip field. I was optimistic about our chances, but not quite as confident as my brother. One cause for my concern was the amount of hunting pressure already applied to gobblers in the area around the turnip field, and the other reason for my doubts was the weather – the rain was pouring outside our bedroom window as we turned out the light and wished each other goodnight.

Kevin and I were both awake and up before the alarm clock sounded at 5:00 a.m. It had rained all night, and was showing no signs of letting up as we dressed in our Mossy Oak camouflage. We readied our hunting gear and video equipment, and we donned our rain gear, ready to embrace the Nebraska rain in search of our fourth Merriam's gobbler. We skipped breakfast and just filled a thermos and our cups with coffee. By now the outfitters had grown accustomed to our morning routine of declining to eat and heading straight for the field. Kevin and I loaded our gear into Ben's truck, and he drove us to an old cattle gate, which led to the turnip field. As we exited the vehicle, the rain could be seen steadily falling through the truck's headlights. Ben gave Kevin a two-way radio for us to contact him if we needed anything and then wished us luck before driving away. Kevin now became my hunting guide, as he led the way through a field bordering a fairly large stand of timber on our way to the blind. The rain began to slack off as we walked in the dark, encouraging both of us about our chances to hear and see a big Merriam's tom.

We entered the blind well before daylight and got ourselves squared away inside. Kevin set up the video camera and tripod, while I loaded my trusty Remington 870 Super Magnum with 1-7/8 ounce rounds of No. 6 Hevishot. After all the preliminaries of setting up were completed, I asked Kevin to explain the window system on the blind. This new style blind allowed a hunter to view three hundred and sixty degrees around its perimeter. It accomplished this through the use of see-through netting and a series of buckle straps, which could be adjusted at various locations to open or close the continuous window. Although manufactured by the same company, this blind was much different from mine with respect to the windows. (The windows on my blind are either "open" or "closed.") In order to shoot from this new blind, I had to lift the camo netting and slide my gun barrel underneath it. It was a little awkward, but I practiced it a couple of times in the dark before shooting light. Kevin and I discussed the three hundred and sixty degree viewing options, with Kevin informing me what had worked during his hunts from the same blind. I opted to play it safe and keep the viewing window open only in the front. One of the biggest mistakes a hunter can make when hunting from a portable ground blind is to have windows on opposing sides open at the same time allowing game to spot movement in the blind. We endeavored to keep the sides and back closed to prevent this from happening.

As daylight began to break in the East, the rain continued to slacken; before long it was only drizzling outside our dry, cozy blind. I placed a Woodhaven "Jim Pollard" diaphragm call in my mouth, contemplating when and how I should use it. The heavy rain clouds did their best to prevent daylight from appearing, but only managed to delay and dim its arrival. The morning had a sort of somber mood to it. It was dark, dreary, and wet. My method for calling in any given situation is based on two things: my gut feeling and my experience. On this particular morning, both of my barometers were sending me the same signal. In order to sound as realistic as possible, I needed to just keep silent. As the rain dripped from the cedar branches outside our blind, not a single bird was calling to welcome the melancholy morning. I didn't want to be the first one to break the silence. Besides, I knew the turkeys would hang in the roost a little longer than normal on a day like this. So Kevin and I just sat in the blind half dozing and waiting on the avian inhabitants of northern Nebraska to make their presence known.

Eventually we heard a few crows and a red-tailed hawk, as the morning grew brighter. There was no sense in trying to imitate a hen still on the roost, so I began calling on my Jim Pollard mouth call with clucks and plain yelps. I wasn't surprised when my calls went unanswered, and I kept up my calling regimen, trying to sound like a lonely hen in the turnip field. Knowing that turkeys like to position themselves in a field or open area after a rain storm to dry off and avoid the constant dripping from a woodland canopy, I felt confident about our location at the edge of this wide, open field, even though we hadn't heard so much as a peep from a turkey. My persistence finally paid off though when a faint gobble sounded at the conclusion to one of my calling sequences.

The gobble had sounded from behind and slightly off to the right of our calling position. It was one of those distant gobbles that you think you heard, but you're not quite sure. It was nice to have my brother along at a time like this to confer with, and Kevin affirmed that he had heard the gobble too. I began calling to the tom with both my mouth call and with a peg and slate style call made from cherry with a crystal striking surface. The gobbler didn't answer me again until he had closed the distance between us considerably. When he did decide to let his next gobble fly, he was within two hundred yards of the turnip field and coming from our right. The atmosphere inside the blind began to get a little more excited, as Kevin and I readied ourselves for what we hoped would be a close encounter with a big, wet Merriam's gobbler.

Waiting for the gobbler to reveal himself at the edge of the turnip field, I cautioned my brother about the use of the video camera. The last thing I wanted was to mess up this hunt because we were trying to videotape it. Kevin and I have both had plenty of experience ruining a perfectly good turkey kill with camera equipment.

"Don't take any chances," I reminded Kevin. "I don't care if we get the kill on video or not, I just want to make sure I get my gobbler," I concluded.

Kevin nodded in agreement and assured me that he understood.

When the gobbler finally appeared, he was about fifty yards to our right, and he wasn't alone. He wasn't a gobbler either, in the strictest sense of the word. He was a jake. He was a fat, beautiful Merriam's jake with a six-inch beard, and he had two other jakes with him. The three young gobblers entered the turnip field cautiously at first and then began to make their way across the entire field, passing through the center of it.

They shook the water from their feathers, beat their wings in the air, and preened themselves, pausing occasionally to peer at their surroundings for the hens they had been planning a date with.

Once I had seen that the birds were jakes, I quit calling to them. There was no sense in encouraging them to stick around. So Kevin and I just sat in the blind admiring the young birds and chuckling at their adolescent antics. Methodically the birds made their way to the far end of the field about eighty yards away from us. Satisfied that they had made a diligent search for the lonely sounding hens they had heard earlier, the jakes turned around and seemed somewhat puzzled. Although Kevin was concerned about calling to the jakes and having them stick around all morning, I decided to call to them. Nothing else was happening, and we could get some video footage of them if they decided to come back.

It took about three notes produced from my Woodhaven mouth call to convince the juvenile gobblers to come back toward our blind. The two sub-dominant jakes led the way with the six-inch bearded bird following. I called sparingly to the jakes just to keep them interested and acting up for the video camera. The dominant jake strutted and gobbled straight at our blind from about ten yards away. It was really fun to watch the gobbler spreading his beautiful, bleach-white-tipped tail feathers against the dark cedar tree background. Kevin captured all of the jake's actions on tape, including his close range gobble, which couldn't be distinguished from that of a mature tom. Once we were satisfied with the footage we had laid down, we sat silently and waited for the jakes to exit the field.

The jakes left the turnip field at approximately 7:00 a.m., and I refrained from calling for the next ten minutes to make sure I didn't call them back again. Satisfied that I had waited long enough, I resumed calling with the mouth yelper. I limited my calls to clucks and yelps and abstained from cutting. Fifteen minutes had passed without a response, when Kevin decided to slip open the blind's back window and take a peek into the wooden bottom behind us. Both Kevin's intuition and timing were perfect, as he spied some hens working their way through the woods toward us.

I remained seated, while Kevin peered through the one-inch slit he had made in the back of the blind giving me a virtual play by play of the turkey's approach.

"I can see at least five turkeys," he said. "Three of them are hens, but I'm not sure about the other two," Kevin continued.

Eventually he could see six turkeys, and as they drew nearer, he informed me that the last three were jakes.

I just sat there asking him dumb questions like, "Can you see any longbeards?"

In case you have believed the lie that there is no such thing as a stupid question, let me re-educate you and enlighten you to the truth. Stupid questions not only exist, but they tend to actually thrive in some areas – amazingly enough, I may be privileged to live at the epicenter of the dumb question universe. In fact, my place of employment is one of the hotbeds for such brainless inquiries. So much so, that at one point in my career I actually kept in my wallet a "top ten" list of stupid questions that I had been asked. I eventually got rid of the list because seemingly every week someone would come up with one better, and I would have to rewrite the list. For fear of offending one of my fellow employees who might read this account, I will not divulge my professional material – although being asked, "Would you like to have Friday off?" comes to mind. To illustrate my assertion I will, however, share a couple of anecdotes from my personal life. Indulge me, if you will, and suffer me to elaborate on a few examples – I am confident that I can convince you of the existence of stupid questions. However, in order to grasp the level of stupidity achieved by the inquiry, I must provide you with a little background to "set up" the question.

For starters, travel with me – if you dare – to a large mountain lake. My brother, Kevin, and I have just completed a successful Canadian goose hunt and are returning to the lake's boat launch in my War Eagle duck boat. The boat is completely camouflaged and is full of decoy bags, shotguns, and layout blinds. My chocolate lab, Hammer, (who believes he is in charge of the entire affair) is in the front of the boat keeping watch over nine dead geese, which are stacked on the bow. As we pull up to the boat dock, a small boy and his mother are standing there.

"Hey, mister," the little boy asks as I exit the boat, "are those real geese?"

Smiling at the inquisitive youth, I replied, "Yes, they sure are. They are called Canadian geese, and we have been hunting for them today."

Now, so far so good, as the query posed by the eight-year-old boy was both valid and appropriate. However, the young lad's mother seemed compelled to show her son the proper way to ask a stupid question.

"Why are they dead?" she asked me.

Now, I ask you – how do you respond to a question like that? I could have explained the physics associated with double BB steel shot traveling at 1200 feet per second and the torque required and imparted to compromise the skeletal structure of a mature goose, but I just didn't feel compelled to respond in that manner. Or, I could have borrowed a line from a blue-collar comedian and said "Here's your sign." Instead, I gave her the only answer that I could think of that would satisfy her inquiring mind…

"Because," I said, as seriously as possible, "that's the only way I can get them to ride in my boat."

While the little boy just stared at his mother while petting my dog, Kevin busted out laughing. He laughed so hard that it was embarrassing. He laughed so hard that he made me start laughing. I walked up the boat ramp to get my pickup truck just shaking my head.

Speaking of goose hunts and stupid questions, Kevin and I were hunting during the September early goose season on a large farm, which bordered a river. We were hunting with one of my wife's cousins who worked at the farm, and who had secured our permission to hunt. The three of us and my Labrador retriever, Hammer, were concealed by layout blinds, which were situated among three dozen decoys in a field near the river's edge. Just as we were about to call it a morning, a frantic woman in a sport utility vehicle interrupted our hunt. The distraught lady left the gravel road and drove her vehicle straight into the farmer's field amongst my decoys. We stood and approached the vehicle to find out what her problem was. Little did we know that she had a stupid question that she needed to unload.

"Just what gives you the right to be out here hunting these geese?" she ranted at us. "Are you members of that Wild Turkey Federation or something?"

I was a little more angry than humored at this passer-by's stunt, but we answered her politely, explaining that the owner of the farm wanted the geese killed and that goose season was in. Eventually she calmed down and quietly drove off. Kevin, who for some reason had a firm grasp on my arm, and John, my wife's cousin, laughed as I told them what I really wanted to say to the dear, sweet woman.

"No, actually we're members of Ducks Unlimited and that is what gives us the "right" to kill these geese, but since you mentioned it, we also belong to the National Wild Turkey Federation, and we love to bust turkeys in the head too!"

In most instances, we try our very best to be good ambassadors for the hunting sports we enjoy. While we will never apologize for exercising our God-given right to hunt and eat the animals He has created, we do our best not to intentionally offend others who elect not to hunt and who are content to let someone else kill their meat for them. However, there are times when a man's (or my case a boy's) patience wears thin and he just has to be blunt.

By the way, members of the fairer sex do not have the corner on the stupid question market. Oh no, men are quite accomplished at asking absurd questions too.

Take for example the fine gentleman who politely questioned me after I had returned from a successful waterfowl hunt. My duck boat had already been trailered, and in the boat-launch parking lot my brother was helping me load decoys, guns, and dead waterfowl from the boat into the bed of my truck. Kevin and I were both dressed in camouflage from head to toe, and Hammer was in his dog box, which is plastered with duck-hunting stickers, in the back of the truck. In an apparent attempt to impress his pretty girlfriend, the middle-aged man stopped his brand new BMW next to me and with the push of a button, put the passenger-seat window all the way down. Leaning across his "beamer's" center console, he slid his designer sunglasses down his nose to peer at me from above them. Nearly in his girlfriend's lap, the gentleman looked up at me.

"Catching anything?" he asked.

Glancing over at my brother, I could see him wincing as he prepared himself for my response. Silently, I reached into the bed of my Ford F250 and grasped the neck of a large and, by the way, dead Canadian goose. I brought the goose's lifeless head up to bed rail of the truck and pointed it, like a puppet, at the shocked driver. The goose's mouth was open and it kind of resembled the "AFLAC" duck from TV – except the AFLAC duck isn't usually that bloody.

"We're not fishing," I said stoically.

Appalled, the man jerked back into the driver's seat, put the window up, and hit the gas.

"How rude was that?" I remarked to Kevin. "He didn't even congratulate us on our successful hunt!"

These three examples of dumb questions were all associated with waterfowl hunting, but believe me, I get asked them about turkey hunting too. Why seemingly every year in the middle of spring gobbler season someone will ask me if I have been turkey hunting yet.

A deep breath and a quick check of my pulse is all that is required to answer, "Why yes, yes I have."

Thank you for your patience. Now, let me get back to the story... where were we?

Oh yeah, Kevin was watching six turkeys behind the blind, and I was asking him if any of them were longbeards.

Anyway, asking my brother, eyeballs bugging out of his head as he strains to identify the gender of the turkeys behind us, if he can see any longbeards would meet the criteria for a stupid question. As if he would actually see a big gobbler coming though the wooded river bottom and just fail to mention it to me – but hey, I've been trained by the best, and I just had to ask.

The thing about stupid questions is that sometimes, if you keep asking them, you get the stupid answer you've been waiting to hear. Like kids who keep asking their parents for candy before dinner, sometimes if they keep on asking the "no" finally gives way to a "yes." Such was my hap on the turnip field this dreary April day in Nebraska. I kept on asking and finally Kevin's "no" turned into an "I think so." Kevin related to me that he could see two large turkeys following the hens and jakes, and they appeared to be gobblers. I turned around to look at the birds myself, but they were still too far away to be sure. I returned to my seat and called on the mouth call, while Kevin continued to update me on the bird's progress.

In short order, I got the answer I wanted to hear as Kevin stated, "Yep, they look like two longbeards!"

Whether or not the turkeys were coming to the field because of my calls, or in spite of them, I'll never know. I would like to think that all my effort on the mouth call is what drew them, but there is just no way to know for sure. One thing I do know, when a hunter has hens and jakes responding to calls, he should keep up the good work of calling, because in the spring of the year there is probably a big gobbler not too far away. This appeared to be the situation in our case, as Kevin was pretty well convinced that the two birds lagging behind were in fact mature gobblers.

The wooded bottom that the birds were coming from was directly behind and below us. The turnip field we were situated on was elevated from the river bottom by about twenty-five feet. As the birds approached in the bottom, they were going to be forced to climb the steep embankment behind us to reach the open field. All of the turkeys were coming at a fairly crisp pace and were doing so in single-file manner. The three hens were in the front, followed closely by the three jakes. The two gobblers in the rear were lagging about forty yards behind the jakes. All of that changed, however, when the turkeys reached the steep bank behind us.

As the hens and jakes began their ascent up the hill to the field, they slowed down somewhat and appeared to become much more cautious. The gobblers, on the other hand, picked up their pace and closed the gap that existed between themselves and the other birds. The gobbler's change in tempo had a ripple effect on the two hunters from Virginia inside the Double Bull blind on the edge of the turnip field. Kevin and I had to switch places so I could position my gun for a shot out of the left side of the blind. It appeared that all of the turkeys were going to enter the turnip field less than twenty yards from our position, just to the left of the blind. During the transition inside the blind, it was hard for either one of us to keep an eye on the birds. Once we got situated properly, the gobblers had caught up with the other turkeys and they all approached the field in one large group.

I had done my best to single out the dominant mature gobbler as they approached and climbed the hill, but now I was in a pickle. The hens and jakes all came to a complete stop at the edge of the turnip field, and the mature gobblers walked up into the midst of them. All of the turkeys were standing still and just looking around, either for the hen that had been calling or for any signs of danger, before proceeding out into the barren field. The birds were all in easy shotgun range, and I had my 3-1/2 inch twelve-gauge trained on them – safety off and finger on the trigger. The bird I had singled out as the one I wanted to shoot, however, was being screened by the three young jakes. All five of the male turkeys' heads were red in color and lacked the traditional red, white, and blue markings of a mature spring gobbler, so I couldn't be positive that the birds farthest away from me were adult toms. I couldn't see the beards on the two gobblers being screened, and I was afraid to shoot at the bird that I thought was the dominant gobbler because of the uncertainty. With my scope's crosshairs settled at the base of the back gobbler's head twenty yards away, I asked Kevin if the bird in the back was a gobbler. Kevin used his binoculars to try and verify that the bird was indeed a longbeard, but he couldn't be absolutely sure.

In short order, the small flock of turkeys proceeded into the field as a unit, with the two gobblers that we suspected were mature birds staying behind the screen provided by the bodies of the three jakes. Upon entering the field, all of the birds proceeded to walk directly away from us and traveled to the far end of the turnip field. I lowered my shotgun and turned to Kevin just shaking my head.

"I might have just made a huge mistake, but I couldn't take a chance at shooting a jake," I said disgustedly.

Kevin nodded in agreement commenting that he couldn't have lived with himself if he had given me the go-ahead to shoot, and the bird turned out to be a juvenile. Little did I know that my frustration was about to get worse.

When the eight turkeys reached the far end of the field, the gobbler that I had singled out previously and had passed a shot at, decided to reveal his true identity. He dropped the red-headed, all slicked up jake look, and opted for the full-blown, spread-out and buzzin', "Puff Daddy" appearance. He was one big, beautiful Merriam's gobbler and so was his running buddy. The two toms began strutting side by side to impress the ladies about one hundred yards from us. When I saw the big, full, white-tipped tail fan, I was almost sick. I had my gun on that bird at less than twenty yards and let him walk because I couldn't see his beard! The bird I had been focusing on was easy to distinguish from the other mature gobbler. The gobbler I had intended to shoot was bigger than the other tom and was missing one primary tail feather in the middle of his fan. It was easy to determine that he was the dominant gobbler as he strutted for the hens with his tail spread full-out, angling it towards the ladies. He strutted around and in front of the other mature bird, which just stood in one spot with his tail fan only spread about three-quarters of the way. While the sub-dominant bird had all his primary tail feathers, and both of these birds would make a beautiful Merriam's mount, I made up my mind to take the dominant bird – if by some stretch of a miracle I was able to get him back into gun range.

Kevin and I sat there in the blind agonizing over the fact that we had blown our chance to take a perfect specimen of a Merriam's longbeard at chip-shot distance. I made a few calls with my mouth call trying to encourage the hens to return to my end of the field, while Kevin powered up the video camera. Kevin videotaped the two gobblers strutting, and I just sat there with my gun pointed in their general direction. Several long minutes passed as we watched the turkeys doing what turkeys do in the spring of the year. The hens scratched around at the edge of the turnip field with the jakes right in amongst them. Puff Daddy strutted a circle around the other tom and took any opportunity he could to intimidate a jake that wandered too close to his personal space. The big Merriam's tom's skull cap was bleach white, and his deep red waddles looked huge even from our distant vantage point at the other end of the turnip field.

My calling appeared to have no effect on the hens, or gobblers for that matter, as they continued to feed and strut. Kevin whispered to me that the birds might come back towards us, as that is what a lot of the turkeys he had watched from the blind previously had done.

As Kevin was videoing the gobblers, I noticed first one, and then each of the other hens, starting to make their way back toward us along the far edge of the field. The hens began their retreat by just easing along, and then their pace became quicker. Of course when the hens started to move, so did the jakes, the gobblers, and the hunters. Both the gobblers' and the hunters' movements were captured on videotape by my brother who had the camera rolling. Well, actually the video footage shows the camera shift from the gobblers to pointing straight up toward the sky while hushed voices say things like, "We need to switch places and get the gun pointed out of the other window."

The hens were coming so quickly that we had to hurry to get into position. Kevin killed the video camera at my request, and helped me get the window netting up far enough for me to get my shotgun barrel out of the blind after I had switched to a different shooting position. The hens were now coming through the center of the turnip field just behind a small rise in the field about thirty yards from our blind. They would be in gun range when they reached the rise and revealed themselves from behind it. The hens came to the rise on a string, and I knew it was just a matter of time before big boy followed suit. I had my shotgun shouldered with the safety off and my cheek buried in the buttstock. Through my scope, I watched the hens top out on the rise and asked Kevin to help me make sure I was on the dominant gobbler, as the two toms appeared behind the hens.

"He's the one in front, isn't he?" I asked Kevin excitedly, as I centered my scope's crosshairs on the first gobbler's waddles.

"Yes, that's him," Kevin stated firmly with no doubt about his assertion.

"He's in range, right?" I asked, just to be sure, as the big tom topped-out on the rise.

"Yes, he's about thirty yards," Kevin assured me.

The next line in this dialogue is supposed to be mine, but instead of saying anything, I let my old 870 Super Mag do the talking.

"KABOOM!" thundered across the wet, muddy turnip field, as Merriam's hens, jakes, and one gobbler took flight and scattered in every direction. The other gobbler never moved – besides a short drop with a sudden stop. He was laid to rest in what I believe was one of his favorite places – the turnip field. The turnip field had already become one of Kevin's favorite places and at that moment it became one of mine. I had done it. I had completed a second grand slam. Kevin congratulated me, and we exited the blind to retrieve my second Merriam's gobbler in three days of hunting.

Kevin brought the video camera with him as we approached the fallen gobbler. He videoed the bird lying in the mud amongst the turnip tops and amongst the large puddle of blood that surrounded his head. I don't write this to be gross or morbid, but I write it to point out that a properly matched firearm, choke tube, shotshell, and sighting system can, and should, be devastating when patterned properly and used within its ballistic limits. There wasn't a single feather missing from this gobbler. All of the shot struck him in the head and neck, just like all moral and ethical shotgun hunters strive for. The camera's battery died about fifteen seconds into Kevin's video, but I'm thankful for the short amount of footage he was able to get of the fallen bird.

Kevin and I hugged and shook hands, standing in the middle of the turnip field alongside our fourth Merriam's gobbler. He congratulated me on my second Grand Slam, and we were both so thankful and relieved that we had accomplished our hunting goals in Nebraska. I unloaded my shotgun before admiring the beautiful, mature gobbler that the Lord had just blessed me with. The big tom was a quintessential Merriam's. His beard was characteristically thin but was 9-1/4 inches in length, and in true Merriam's fashion, his spurs were each only 7/8 inches long. What the bird lacked in spurs, he made up for in body weight, tipping the scale at 21 pounds and 12 ounces. The gobbler had an exceptionally large head, which complemented his big body. His wings were worn from strutting in a perfectly even fashion that looked fake, like someone had intentionally trimmed his primary wing feathers with a pair of scissors. But for all the gobbler's noteworthy attributes, the one that I liked the most was his tail feathers. The primary, secondary, and covert feathers were all tipped in the classic white of a Merriam's turkey. They were exactly what I had been dreaming of for the majority of the past year, and now I had my hands on them. I couldn't have been any happier with any other turkey at that moment.

Kevin and I prayed together, kneeling in the mud, and I thanked my heavenly Father for His blessings. After reading from my Bible, we took numerous photos of the gobbler with my small camera that I keep in my hunting vest. The dreary, overcast sky dulled the natural light available for the photos, but it couldn't dull the smile on my face. I tagged the bird, and we were officially "tagged-out" in Nebraska. I plucked a small feather from the neck of my gobbler and gently placed it in my pocket – I had a special place for this feather back in the cab of my 4-Runner. After packing up the camera equipment and my trophy Merriam's, Kevin and I said good-bye to the turnip field and headed back to the main road where we had been dropped off.

Kevin used the two-way radio to contact Ben and advise him of our success. The rain returned and drizzle began to fall off and on. While we stood at the cattle gate waiting for our ride to show up, I pulled a thermos of coffee out of my vest and shared it with Kevin. A cool, overcast morning, a hot cup of black coffee, time spent with your brother, and a big, dead gobbler in your vest – these are a few of my favorite things. It was one of those moments in life that as you're experiencing it you're impatient and hoping the truck will hurry-up and get there so you can get back to camp. However, after it is over and you're back home in Virginia, you wish you could go there again and relive the satisfaction and simple pleasure of that special moment in time.

My impatience, however, wasn't so much with the weather as it was with our itinerary.

Now that Kevin and I were tagged out in Nebraska, we had the rest of the week available to just rest in camp and take our time traveling home, or we could try to squeeze in another turkey hunt in a different state. I'll let you be the judge of which option I was plotting. In my mind I formulated a game plan for getting photos of my gobbler, cleaning and prepping him for the taxidermist, packing our gear, and hitting the road – all before 1:00 p.m. Shortly thereafter, Ben showed up in his pickup to give us a ride back to camp. He was so happy that I had killed my second Merriam's, and that the bird was such a beautiful representative of the subspecies.

Actually, I think Ben was just as much relieved as he was happy. Due to the proprietor of Rutting-N-Strutting being absent from camp for the birth of his child, all the responsibility for the west camp fell on Ben, who normally only handled managing the camp, not guiding the hunters. During our hunt, he was saddled with all the responsibility, and not for just two or three hunters but for five. Fortunately for Ben, Kevin and I are pretty easy going when it comes to food and accommodations, and neither one of us required a guide for our hunts. So hopefully that eased some of his burden. When he picked us up, I could see the stress leave his expression after he knew that my final bird was in the bag a day before our hunt was scheduled to end. Even more comforting for our host was that the trio of hunters from California and Ohio had taken their final bird on this same morning – killing the gobbler within hours of having to leave camp to catch their flight home. So everybody was happy, as we drove in the rain back to camp.

Back at camp, Ben offered to fix us breakfast, as Kevin and I prepared to take pictures of my tom during a lull in the rain showers. Kevin and I hadn't eaten breakfast once during our stay at Rutting-N-Strutting because we were too focused on hunting. We hesitated to accept Ben's offer because we knew that he had just cooked breakfast for everyone else at the camp and had then cleaned up all the dishes. Ben insisted that it wasn't a problem, and once convinced, we agreed to his invitation. Ben went right to work frying bacon and eggs and fixing toast – dirtying up all the dishes once again. That just goes to show you what kind of hard-working man Ben is and how concerned he was about his clients. The smell of bacon frying helped to "speed-up" our photo session and made me think of home.

Back home in Virginia, my family has a saying in spring gobbler season. The saying is more like a prefabricated conversation, which had its inception over a decade ago. The saying starts off with a question (asked by a turkey hunter who has been successful in killing a spring gobbler) and is answered by the person it has been posed to with always the same answer. It goes like this:

Question: "What's for breakfast?"

Answer: "Must be turkey!"

Now this little question / answer game has been going on in my family for quite some time. The point is, if your phone rings at 9:30 a.m. in mid-April, and when you answer it you hear me ask, "What's for breakfast?" You have just been informed that I have killed a gobbler and are thereby obligated to give the standard answer – "Turkey." In other words my question "What's for breakfast" is in reality a statement and not a question. (If you have any doubts as to my mental instability at this point, we might be somehow related. Don't bother asking me how this stuff gets started;

it just does!) The thing is, something strange happened one spring that caused our little saying to take on even more tradition.

It was early one morning in April. I had just killed a big, mountain longbeard and couldn't wait to call my in-laws and tell them about it. When I phoned Lisa's parents, Earl and Nancy, it was about 8:00 a.m. as I recall. Nancy was still asleep when her phone rang.

"What's for breakfast?" I asked ritualistically.

"Uhhh…Huh?" Nancy said, still half asleep.

"What's for breakfast?" I asked again.

"Umm…I don't know," she replied, "Whatever you want, I guess."

I started laughing, as I realized that Nancy didn't know the "What's for breakfast" code game. I apologized for waking her, and tried to explain that I didn't want her to fix me breakfast, but that I had killed a turkey. She was a little confused at first. (Who wouldn't be!)

After explaining the question / answer scenario to her a couple of times as she was waking up, Nancy finally understood my little game and answered, "Turkey!" after I had asked her for the third time, "What's for breakfast?"

Then she did some explaining to me. She told me in no certain terms that she was fixing me breakfast, that she wasn't taking "no" for an answer, and that I was bringing the gobbler to her house for her and Earl to see. After waking her up out of a deep sleep, I was obliged to comply with her request and did so. My in-laws are great country folk and great Christians too. When Lisa's mom cooks, she cooks for an army. She fixed a breakfast spread so big that Earl and I couldn't eat it all. The breakfast was so good that Earl remarked to me that I was going to have to kill a turkey more often so he could get fed like that again. From that simple beginning, a new tradition was started. Now, anytime I kill a gobbler when hunting in Virginia, I call Nancy and ask the standard question and she gives the standard answer, and then she fixes a huge breakfast for all of us. In fact, if my season is going slow, Earl will sometimes pull me aside and let me know that I had better get to killin' somethin' because he hasn't had bacon in a while!

A big breakfast after a successful spring gobbler hunt is hard to beat, and a big breakfast after killing a huge, mature Merriam's that completes a second Grand Slam is even better. That breakfast that Ben fixed was probably my favorite meal of the trip, and I sure am glad he offered to prepare it.

After breakfast, Kevin and I put ourselves in high gear. We cleaned and prepped my gobbler for the taxidermist before gently packing him into the 150-quart cooler on the back of my 4-Runner. That cooler now had four mature gobblers in it and was starting to get cramped! With the bird cared for, we began packing all of our gear into the SUV. After hot showers and a change of clothes, it was time for us to depart from the west camp and say good-bye to our new friends, Ben and Chuck. We took some group photos and exchanged contact information before shaking hands to part ways.

It had been raining all night and most of the morning, making the back roads to and from the west camp extremely muddy and slick. Ben suggested that I follow his truck, and he would lead me to the nearest paved road – taking a different route than Kevin and I had traveled when arriving to camp. Ben and I both had to put our trucks in four-wheel drive to negotiate the nasty, greasy back roads of rural northern Nebraska. It took us forty minutes to reach a paved road, and at an intersection in a small town, we parted ways, acknowledging one another with our horns.

As Ben's truck disappeared in my rearview mirror, I turned my Toyota and headed south. The 4-Runner was covered with gray Nebraska mud. The cooler was full of Merriam's gobblers. Our thermoses were full of hot, black coffee. It was only Wednesday of our vacation week, and Kevin and I were all smiles. The visor above my head in the cab of the 4-Runner now had three small turkey feathers in it – the latest compliments of Nebraska Merriam's killed in an old turnip field. Three subspecies of spring gobbler killed in three weeks of hunting, and now my truck was headed straight for Kansas – western Kansas that is – home of the Rio Grande subspecies of wild turkey. If we hustled, we could possibly hunt for two mornings in the Sunflower State before starting the long drive home to Virginia. When it comes to spring gobbler hunting, Hustle is my middle name!

Merriam's

Date: April 20, 2005
Time: 8:30 a.m.
Location: Boyd County, NE
Weight: 21 lbs. 12 oz.
9-1/4 inch Beard
7/8 inch Spurs

Merriam's Beard

Merriam's Spurs

4-Runner in Nebraska

Double Trouble
–
The Rio Grande Gobblers

Preface

In the summer of 2004, I began making plans to hunt for a Merriam's gobbler. One Merriam's gobbler was all I needed to complete a Wild Turkey Grand Slam. My brother, Kevin, had agreed to join me on the Merriam's hunt, and after much prayer and many phone calls, I booked our hunt with an outfitter in Nebraska.

The hunt that I booked allowed for both of us to kill two gobblers each. As I pondered our chances for success, I decided that it might be a good idea to have a back-up plan – a back-up plan to hunt gobblers in a different mid-western state, just in case we were fortunate enough to tag out early on our Merriam's hunt.

As the summer of 2004 turned to fall, I told my brother that I was going to do some research on hunts in other states. While Eastern gobblers of the mountain variety are my normal turkey hunting quarry, I have always wanted to have an opportunity to hunt the really big gobblers of the Midwest. Although a true twenty-pound tom is big for the mountains of Virginia and West Virginia, Eastern gobblers in the Midwest are known to reach weights in excess of twenty-five pounds.

As I considered our options for a back-up hunt, Missouri quickly came to the head of my list. The Show-Me State offered turkey tags and hunting licenses over the counter, it had the highest turkey kill statistics in the nation, and it was home to the giant Eastern gobblers that I wanted to pursue. Iowa, Illinois, and Indiana were also on my list of great places to hunt Easterns, but all three of these states required a hunter to draw a turkey tag in a lottery. This requirement seriously impacted my decision to hunt these states, as both Kevin and I would have to be successful in the draw for things to work out. I made up my mind that "Plan B" would have to take place in a state where we could buy our hunting licenses over the counter, given the fact that the opportunity to hunt in another state would be totally dependent on the success of our Nebraska hunt.

Kevin has never traveled to hunt other subspecies of spring gobblers. Our Merriam's hunt would be his first opportunity to kill a gobbler other than an Eastern. As I thought about this and tried to plan a back up hunt, I decided that instead of big Easterns, maybe I should consider hunting for Rios once again. We would already be in the Midwest, and although I had no need to harvest one, a successful Rio Grande hunt for my brother would provide him with three of the four turkeys needed for a Grand Slam of his own.

Like a good big brother should, I put my desire to hunt big Easterns on the back burner and began pursuing options for a place to hunt Rio Grandes. To make a long story short, after much research on game laws and public hunting access in states which are inhabited by the Rio Grande subspecies of wild turkey, I ended up on the phone with an outfitter from Kansas. Sometimes in life, you meet someone new that you instantly have a rapport with – that happened for me when Jack Tindall returned my phone call.

Jack runs Smoky Hill Adventures, an outfitting business in Kansas. He works as an outfitter because of his love of the shooting sports. In his other life, Jack is a full-time police officer in one of our nation's largest cities. He spends all of his vacation time in Kansas providing private-land hunting opportunities in the spring and fall for turkeys and whitetail deer.

I told Jack about my scheduled hunt for Merriam's gobblers, and that I hoped, if possible, to put my brother on a Rio if things worked out well for us during our Nebraska hunt. When Jack heard about my situation, he offered to help me out more like a friend than a business man. He informed me not to worry that he would hold a spot open for us to hunt in Kansas with no obligations on my part. I thank the Lord for directing my path to meet Jack.

Jack and I spoke by phone numerous times before the opening of spring gobbler season. The two of us had a lot in common – we both have demanding full-time jobs, but we both spend the majority of our free time hunting whitetail deer with a bow in the fall and hunting gobblers in the spring. A friendship developed between us before we ever met face to face. That is one of the benefits of traveling our great nation to hunt – meeting other people with similar likes and interests. It helps me realize that I am not the only one with a severe gobbler disorder.

In the hunting account that follows, Jack will be instrumental in the outcome and will become a special friend to both Kevin and me. Everything Jack did for us, he did for the price of a trespass-fee hunt – with no obligations on our part.

The Bible says in Psalms 37:4-5, "Delight thyself also in the Lord; and he shall give thee the desires of thine heart. Commit thy way unto the LORD; trust also in him; and he shall bring it to pass."

The truth of this scripture was played out for me in the spring of 2004. Seeking God's will and bathing my decisions in prayer would bring down His blessings upon me. What I had planned to be a blessing for my brother would, in fact, turn out to become a huge blessing for myself. These plans to potentially hunt in Kansas were made well before my impromptu hunt in Florida where helping a friend had put me on the Osceola of a lifetime – an Osceola that was followed by a double-bearded Eastern, and then two Merriam's. Could my brother's hunt for a Rio in Kansas now put me in a position to do something that I had never even imagined when planning for the hunt? With only taking two weeks of vacation and driving to all of my hunting destinations, could it be that I could harvest a single season Grand Slam?

Double Trouble

Our trip began on a rainy spring day after a successful hunt for Merriam's gobblers in northern Nebraska. It was Wednesday, April 20, 2005, and my brother, Kevin, and I had the whole state of Nebraska before us as we headed south toward our next destination – Kansas. It was already early afternoon, and we had a long way to go to get to the area we planned to hunt the following morning.

After a short stop for fuel at a small gas station, I used Kevin's cell phone to reach our hunting contact in Kansas, Jack Tindall. I got in touch with Jack just in time.

"Jack, this is Brad Day from Virginia," I began.

"Hey Brad, how is your hunt going in Nebraska?" Jack asked.

"It went great," I replied. "We're tagged out and headed for Kansas. Do you still have a spot open for us to hunt?"

"Yeah, no problem. In fact, all of my hunters are tagged out and gone," Jack informed me. "I was just about to leave and drive home to Indiana to visit my girlfriend, but now that I know you are coming, I'll change my plans and stick around for you."

That portion of our conversation should give you an idea of the kind of person that Jack is. However, Jack's helpfulness didn't stop there. As I drove the mud-caked 4-Runner south on U.S. Route 281, we continued our conversation. I tried to give Jack my best guess for our estimated time of arrival, and our intended travel route. It appeared to me that we wouldn't reach the nearest town to where we planned hunt until somewhere around midnight. Jack asked if we had made arrangements for a place to stay, and I informed him that we hadn't. Jack told me not to worry about it.

"I'll reserve you a room at a Best Western and put it on my credit card, since the office will be closed when you arrive so late," Jack offered.

"That's really kind of you," I replied, as I accepted his gracious offer.

We agreed to hang up for the time being, so he could try and secure a motel room for us. We made plans to contact each other by cell phone a few hours later to confirm our plans.

Kevin and I had a very enjoyable trip through rural Nebraska, as we continued our southbound journey. The sky was overcast, but the rain held off, and the traffic was light. We stopped in Grand Island, Nebraska for gas and a bite to eat and managed to stretch our legs at the Wal-Mart there too. Before leaving Grand Island, we called Jack on the cell phone, and he gave us the good news that he had a room reserved for us in Ellsworth, Kansas. We talked for several more minutes as he gave us directions on where we could buy our hunting licenses and where the Best Western was located. We also made arrangements for where to meet the following morning, with my brother making notes of all the details on a piece of scrap paper. Satisfied we had all our bases covered, we ended our conversation politely. I was not only excited about the chance to hunt Rios in the Sunflower State, but I was also looking forward to meeting Jack in person.

Kevin and I resumed our road trip to Kansas with high spirits. We now had a place to spend the night, a game plan for our next morning's hunt, and our bellies were full. The only hurdle we had left to cross was getting our hunting licenses. Our plan was to stop in Hayes, Kansas and purchase our licenses and tags there. We knew there was a Wal-Mart in Hayes, but we weren't sure if it was open twenty-four hours or not, and we were going to be getting there late. I prayed to the Lord and asked Him to guide us and help us get our licenses.

Despite the need to buy hunting licenses in Kansas, our travel route took us too close to the Cabela's store in Kearney, Nebraska for us not to stop and spend a few minutes there. While visiting the store, Kevin and I each bought a Primos turkey-hunting ball cap in Mossy Oak camouflage. There were only two of the hats in the whole store, and we bought them both. We picked up a few other things before getting back in the Toyota and heading for Hayes. I felt like my whole spring had been spent in the turkey woods or behind the wheel of that truck – I know, how lucky can a fella get!

Darkness fell shortly after we left Kearney and hit Route 183 South. Driving in the dark, we could see lightning flashing in the distance – especially off to the east. I'm not used to the wide-open spaces of the Midwest, so I couldn't determine how far away we were from the storm. However far we were from it though, it looked to be pretty violent. We didn't pay much attention to it at first. It was really neat to be able to see the streaks of lightning so clearly and to watch the entire eastern horizon light up in orange and blue. (I would later learn, while watching a documentary on tornados, that Hayes, Kansas is nicknamed "the doorway to tornado alley" – it is probably a good thing that I didn't know it at this particular point in time!) No, at this point my biggest concern was getting to Hayes, finding the Wal-Mart, hoping it was open, and securing our hunting licenses. Kevin and I had both brought our Hunter's Safety cards with us because we knew Kansas law required possession of one to obtain a license. You just never know what kind of problem you might run in to though. I would feel a whole lot better once we had those licenses. I didn't want to lose a morning of hunting because we couldn't get our tags at night.

We arrived in Hayes, Kansas at 10:00 p.m., and the first business we saw was the Super Wal-Mart. Its lights lit up the Kansas sky and called to us like a beacon. I thanked the Lord for His good hand upon us, as I pulled the 4-Runner into the parking lot. The wind was howling as we made our way across the parking lot and entered the biggest Super Wal-Mart I have ever seen – so much for worrying that it might not be open twenty-four hours!

Kevin and I went straight to the sporting goods department and secured assistance from a kind, elderly gentleman who reviewed our Hunter's Safety cards and provided us our hunting licenses and spring gobbler tags. It was 10:20 p.m. by the time we had secured our licenses. We bought a few groceries to take with us to the motel in Ellsworth – not knowing how many days we would be staying.

We returned to the Toyota, and the Kansas wind was whipping as we resumed our road trip toward Ellsworth. Traveling eastbound on Interstate 70, the electrical storm was directly in front of us. We tuned the radio in to a local station, which was constantly updating listeners with Tornado warnings. Every couple of minutes the broadcast would be interrupted with:

"The National Weather Service in Topeka, Kansas has issued a tornado warning for the following counties…" The broadcast would then proceed to list numerous counties.

I hadn't studied up on the county geography before our trip, and therefore, I didn't know one county in Kansas from another – so we just kept driving toward the storm. We were somewhat concerned, but what else were we going to do? Finally, sometime after 12:30 a.m., we arrived at the Best Western in Ellsworth, Kansas. The office was closed, but I saw a night phone near the main entrance. As I exited the 4-Runner, the wind tried to carry me away. I picked up the phone, and it began to ring on the other end. After about the third ring, a sleepy female voice answered. I explained who I was, and the kind lady told me that she had left a key to Room 110 in the night box for me. She told me to have a good night, and we would settle up the paperwork the next day.

After locating the key, we parked the truck outside Room 110 and prepared to unload our luggage and gear. The weather was wild as Kevin and I pulled the gear from the 4-Runner and carried it to the room. Lightning was flashing and thunder was booming. The wind was blowing so hard that it had ripped portions of the motel's soffit off. Other types of debris and large pieces of metal flashing – from who knows what – were blowing wildly across the parking lot. We got the SUV unloaded as quickly as possible and made our way inside. I remember looking up at the sky as I locked the doors to the 4-Runner and seeing the motel's guttering being torn at by the wind and thinking, "We will be lucky if we get to hunt at all tomorrow!"

Inside the room, Kevin and I unpacked our hunting gear and readied it for the morning's hunt – if there was one. (As pumped up as we were after our Nebraska hunt, it was going to take a tornado to keep us out of the woods!) After making sure our turkey-hunting gear was squared away, we both decided to wear our new Primos ball caps, which we had bought at the Cabela's store, on the next day's hunt, and we set them out with our camo clothing. We watched a little TV in the room and ate a sandwich before reading our nightly devotions and turning in for the night. It was 1:30 a.m., and it had been a long day. It was going to be a short night though, as I set the alarm for 4:30 a.m.

With a full three hours of sleep under our belts, Kevin and I awoke at the sounding of our alarm clock. I started the coffee before having my morning devotions, and with a glazed-over look in our eyes Kevin and I dressed for the woods. I grabbed a cup of coffee and told Kevin I was going to step outside and check on the weather. I was unprepared for what greeted me when I stepped from Room 110.

As I exited the motel room's doorway, I was greeted by nothing – no wind, no rain, and no cold. The air was completely still and the temperature was strangely warm. I looked up into the pre-dawn sky, and what had been a nasty, cloudy, lightning-streaked heaven just three hours earlier, was now crystal clear with every star visible. I said a little "Thank You" prayer right there on the spot and then re-entered the room to share the good news with Kevin.

"It's gonna be a good day for a turkey hunt!" I exclaimed, as I burst through the door smiling.

The glazed-over look in my eyes was gone, and my "game face" was starting to show. Kevin was excited about the change in weather too. We stepped into a higher gear, as we loaded our guns and vests into the 4-Runner.

We left the motel at 5:15 a.m. in order to keep our rendezvous with Jack at a small convenience store about fifteen miles from the motel. Jack was there waiting on us, even though we arrived about ten minutes early. After all the phone conversations, I finally got to meet Jack in person and put a face with the name. We shook hands, and I introduced Kevin to him. We didn't chat long because morning waits for no man, and we had another fifteen-minute drive to reach our hunting destination.

Smoky Hill adventures leases the hunting rights to approximately 25,000 acres of Kansas farmland. I had agreed to pay Jack a trespass fee in order to hunt the private land that he had leased. The trespass fee would allow us to hunt for three days and kill one bird each. To begin our Kansas Rio hunt though, Kevin and I wouldn't be hunting the leased property that Jack controls. Instead, Jack was taking us to his own piece of hunting heaven – his own private farm. Even more exciting than getting to hunt Jack's private land – Jack was going to take us to a special hunting spot; a hunting spot that he affectionately called "Money." When Jack told me the name of the spot, I wasn't sure how to take it, but it sounded like a good thing.

Kevin and I followed Jack's truck as he led the way through rural Kansas toward our hunting destination. Along the way, my brother and I had an important conversation in the 4-Runner. I had told Kevin previously that this was his hunt. The main focus of our time spent in Kansas was to get him his first Rio Grande gobbler. If we were fortunate enough for that to happen, then I would try to harvest another Rio myself and thereby complete a single season Grand Slam of all four subspecies. (The guides at Rutting-N-Strutting, Jack Tindall, and Kevin all thought I was a little bit crazy for not trying to get my single season slam first, but that was just non-negotiable to me. I love my brother and this Kansas hunt was originally planned for his benefit. I wanted him to get his bird and then hopefully mine would come.) So as we drove, I reminded my brother of the intent of this hunt – if we called in a gobbler, he was to kill it. With that settled, I brought up another topic.

"Now, if we happen to call in two longbeards," I said, "you kill the one on your side, and I will kill the one on my side."

I then began to overstate the obvious, giving examples like: "If you're on the left and I'm on the right, then you kill the bird on the left, and I'll kill the bird on the right." For a little humor I threw in a joke from an old T.K. & Mike video – "Unless the one on the right doesn't feel right to me!" Kevin chuckled at my remark. In all seriousness this "Left / Right" business was nothing new to Kevin and me. We have shared too many duck blinds, goose layouts, and upland bird hunts to not know which bird to take when presented with multiple targets. However, this turkey hunt was too important to leave anything to chance. I wanted to make absolutely sure we were on the same page, should the improbable happen, and more than one gobbler come to our set-up.

Satisfied that we had the "which-bird-to-shoot" issue settled, I began to explain to my bro' how we would time our shots.

"Once we have our guns on the birds, I will ask you if you are ready," I stated. "When you tell me you're ready, I'm going to count – one, two, BOOM."

"One, two, boom?" Kevin asked. "Are you going to short-shoot me?"

"No, I'm just not going to say three." I answered him. "I've seen too many guys mess up after the 'three" is said – they pull the trigger at different times. I want you to pull the trigger when I would normally say 'three", that way we're much more likely to pull the trigger at the exact same time, " I explained.

"I'll ask if you are ready and when you say "yes", I'll count one, two, BOOM," I repeated.

Kevin understood what I meant, and we went over the "one…two…boom" deal several times just to be sure. I remember thinking to myself at the time that we had probably just wasted several minutes of conversation time going over this two-bird scenario, which was so unlikely to happen anyway. Better safe than sorry though, right?

We arrived at Jack's farm shortly before 6:00 a.m. We pulled off the hardcap and parked in front of an oil well, just behind Jack's truck. When we exited our vehicles, the warm, spring air had a strange odor permeating it.

"Do you smell that?" Jack asked us.

"Yeah, I sure do," I replied.

"Doesn't it smell good?" Jack questioned me enthusiastically.

"Not really," I said hesitantly.

"That is oil that you smell," Jack informed us, "and it smells like money to me."

With the price of gasoline what it was, I'm sure it did smell like money to him. Owning a piece of farmland in Kansas where you could hunt whitetailed deer and Rio Grande gobblers plus make money from an oil well was a win-win situation as far as I was concerned. I was just hoping that the smell of oil wasn't the reason for the name of the area we were going to hunt. I was hoping "money" was short for something like "money in the bank" when it came to killing a gobbler. Speaking of money, Jack wanted to take us to our hunting location before we had even paid him the trespass fee for our hunt. I insisted that he take the payment up front, and so by the dim glow of his truck's dome light, Kevin and I both counted out our agreed upon fee and paid Jack in cash.

Jack informed me that he had his personal hunting blind already set up in a good location where he had been bowhunting for gobblers earlier in the week. He offered to let us use it so we wouldn't have to carry my Double Bull blind all the way in. Kevin and I agreed to Jack's offer as daylight was coming fast, and we needed to get moving. After uncasing our shotguns and donning our hunting vests, we followed Jack on foot as he led us to a cattle gate near our parking spot. As Jack opened the gate, he explained to us that the spot where he wanted us to begin our hunt was only good if the cattle weren't feeding there. He commented that we should be in good shape since the cattle were all gathered near the fence where we had parked. I was feeling pretty good about our chances as I talked to Jack while we walked. I was feeling good until the cattle that had been gathered at the fence began to follow us through the pasture – mooing and bellowing as they came. I prayed as we walked and asked the Lord to stop the cattle from ruining our hunt, if it was His will. The cattle followed us for about one hundred and fifty yards before finally realizing we weren't going to feed them. One by one they began to stop, until eventually we put some distance between us, and the cattle turned and started back the way they had came.

"Thank you, Lord," I prayed under my breath.

Jack's blind was a pop-up style like mine but made by Cabela's. It was situated near a creek bottom at the edge of the large pasture we had walked in on. Directly behind the blind was a barbed-wire fence separating Jack's pasture from an adjoining one. We had no sooner arrived at the blind, when a gobble rang out. As if we had been trained together, all three of us turned and pointed in the direction of the gobbler who had made his presence known. The gobble had come from a stand of cottonwood trees that lined the creek bottom we were situated at, but had originated from a spot three to four hundred yards away on the property that adjoined Jack's.

Once that turkey gobbled, we dispensed of the leisurely approach to getting set up and went into a scramble. The sky was just starting to gray up in the east, as Kevin and I entered the blind and readied our gear. Jack offered to place a couple of decoys off to the right of his blind as we got ready, and we accepted his offer. While all of this was happening, gobbles had started streaming from the wooded creek bottom four hundred yards away. We could hear at least five or six turkeys "dynamite" gobbling from their location on the adjoining property behind us. Regrettably though, there were no turkeys anywhere close to our location that were sounding-off to welcome the arrival of another mid-April Kansas morning.

"Can we cross the fence and hunt the ranch behind us?" I asked Jack when he returned from setting out the decoys.

"No, I am afraid not," Jack replied with frustration in his voice. "I have been talking to the owner and trying to lease that property for hunting, but I haven't been successful in getting them to agree to it yet."

"Well," I said, "then we'll just have to try and call them across the fence to us."

Jack wished us luck and told us to call him on his cell phone if we needed anything. Then, as he was walking away, Jack stopped, turned around, and took a few steps back toward the blind.

"Oh yeah," he whispered, "don't be afraid to call to these birds. These gobblers love to be called to."

I gave him a "thumbs-up" to acknowledge that I heard his advice, before leaning over to whisper to my brother.

"That's about the nicest thing anyone has ever said to me," I joked, while placing a well-worn and trusty H.S. Strut "Cutt'n 2.5" diaphragm call into my mouth.

Kevin laughed in agreement, but with a serious tone – he was already in "war mode" and had his "game face" on. Kevin pulled out a friction call and placed a Primos "True Double" stacked-frame call in his mouth. I wasn't the only one who was excited about Jack's recommendation to let the calling hang out. Kevin was looking forward to it as well. The gobbling intensity continued to increase behind us, and I readied both a Woodhaven friction call and a Primos "Heartbreaker" box call. We now had two shotguns and five turkey calls "locked and loaded" inside the Cabela's "Lightning Set" hunting blind.

Jack's blind had large, triangular-shaped windows in it that could be zipped open or shut. When Kevin and I entered the blind all of the windows were open. We decided to close all of the windows – except for the ones in front of us, which faced out into Jack's ranch. We left one of the windows in the rear of the blind just barely open so we could watch the un-huntable property behind us where all the turkeys were roosted.

As daylight continued to increase, hens also began to call from the vicinity of the roosted gobblers in the trees behind our set-up. Finally, at about 6:15 a.m., I decided to officially start our Kansas Rio hunt and make our presence known to the wildlife that inhabited the surrounding creek bottom. I used my Cutt'n 2.5 mouth call to make some soft tree clucks and then some tree yelps. (I prefer a mouth call with fewer reeds in it to do my tree calling, as fewer reeds generally means less volume – and tree calls are usually low-volume affairs.) The roosted gobblers behind us were gobbling so frequently now that there was no way to discern if they were responding to my calls. Despite a wild turkey's exceptional hearing, I was calling so softly that I don't think my tree calls were even audible to the loud-mouthed Kansas toms behind us. However, my calls at this point were not necessarily intended for those birds anyway. I was still hopeful that there might be roosted gobblers on Jack's side of the fence – gobblers that hadn't made their roosting location known yet. Although any gobbler that may have been roosted near us would have had to be basically deaf and dumb to not be awake and responding to the ruckus going on up the creek. Heck, I felt like gobbling myself! Instead of gobbling though, I pulled a turkey wing from my vest and used it in conjunction with the Cutt'n 2.5 mouth call to sound like a turkey cackling as she was flying down to the ground. After repeating the fly-down scenario a couple more times to give the impression that several birds had left the roost at our location along the creek, I sat back to wait for a few minutes before making another call.

It was so enjoyable to be in the turkey woods once again. With a successful hunting season already in the bag, including my dream of a Grand Slam accomplished, sitting there in that blind beside my brother, hearing turkeys yelping and gobbling, and anticipating events of the morning yet to unfold, I experienced a satisfaction that few people probably ever get to enjoy. The money we spent for the trespass fee to hunt in Kansas was worth the price just for the blessing of this moment in my life – in the words of a credit card commercial – priceless.

Poets, philosophers, and psychologists may have taken that moment to reflect on their life and analyze in retrospect the events that had led them to their euphoria. Me – I said a prayer to thank my heavenly Father for what He had done for me, and then I switched mouth calls. Hey, I'm a legion member and there were turkeys out there that needed a good killin'.

I switched mouth calls to one that in the previous two years had quickly become one of my favorites – a bat-wing cut "Jim Pollard" diaphragm manufactured by Woodhaven Custom Calls. I loved the volume and raspiness that I could produce with this call, as well as the subtle flock-talk that the call would realistically produce when birds had worked in close. I had used this call so much that when it was in my mouth it felt like it belonged there. I switched to it at this point because I felt it was time to start "cranking things up" a bit.

Using mouth calls and friction calls, Kevin and I both began to call loudly, giving the illusion that there were now multiple hens congregating on the ground at the edge of Jack's pasture. The turkeys roosted behind us definitely heard our calls and answered them aggressively with booming gobbles that seemed to just roll on forever through the flat farmland of central Kansas. The gobblers weren't the only avian creatures that found it necessary to answer my hen calls though. Kevin laughed at me because nearly every time I made a series of yelps, I got a response from a male, ring-neck pheasant.

If you have never heard a cock, ring-necked pheasant's call, it is hard to explain, but the best way I know to describe it is that it closely resembles the sound of an automobile's starter being cranked. They make this raucous call by starting it with a loud, crowing "caw-cawk" and follow it with a resonant beating of their wings – sounding like your neighbor trying to start his old truck that just won't run. On this morning in Kansas, cock pheasants were calling all around us, sounding like the commencement of a NASCAR race – with no fuel in the vehicles – when the "Gentlemen, start you engines" command is given! Even more bizarre than the pheasants answering my turkey calls was the fact that they were closing in on us as they answered. I'm not kidding. I don't know what was going on, but those birds were coming to us – if only the turkeys would do the same!

Kevin was helping me call, but every few minutes he would lay aside his friction call and turn to look through the crack we had in the rear window of the blind. Much like the previous morning in a blind on a turnip field in Nebraska, Kevin was scanning the expanse behind the blind for any sign of a turkey, while I continued calling. It was 6:40 a.m. when

Kevin finally saw a turkey in the large pasture behind us. He grabbed his binoculars from his vest and resumed his vigil, peering out the peephole in the rear of the blind.

"I can see three hens and one gobbler," he informed me, "but I can't tell if he's a longbeard or not."

"Now where had I heard that before?" I wondered to myself.

It was like déjà vu, all over again, sitting in a blind next to my brother, while I called and he looked out the rear of the blind telling me about hens and jakes. This time though I didn't ask him any stupid questions – at least not yet. Instead, I turned around and observed the turkeys with my own binoculars. I could see three hens and a lone jake about two hundred yards behind us in the open pasture. The birds were out in the field about fifty yards from the wooded creek bottom and had arranged themselves in a most unique pattern – they looked like they had lined up for a game of football. The three hens were all standing side-by-side about three feet apart and were facing us like an offensive line. The jake was playing the position of quarterback, standing directly behind the hen in the center position of the line. As I watched the birds, I decided to call to them with my mouth call and observe their reaction with the binoculars.

"Cluck…yelp, yelp, yelp…Cluck, cluck…yelp, yelp, yelp, yelp, yelp, yelp," I hollered to the opposing team.

Each of the turkeys raised their heads to its highest position when I made my call. Gobblers that were still on the roost hammered back at me with booming gobbles, but none of the turkeys in the pasture made a peep. They just stood their ground looking in our direction, apparently awaiting a play to be called from the sideline. I started yelping, cutting, clucking, and generally just making a ton of turkey racket. Eventually, four more turkeys entered the pasture from the wood line, almost directly across from the "K-State practice squad." At 6:50 a.m., much to my delight, the jake must have called "Hike," because the hens started to run straight toward us with the jake right behind them. I mean it really looked like a football team with three down-linemen! The hens were running at full speed in a side-by-side line, and the jake was still directly behind the one in the center!

As the football-foursome came charging toward us, the newcomers to the pasture decided to follow suit. We now had eight turkeys closing the distance between us. The two groups of four birds had started their approach with about fifty yards of separation between them. After closing the gap to within one hundred yards of us, the foursome from the wood line joined the original birds, and the two groups of birds began to merge, forming a sort of "running-V." It soon became apparent that the second foursome was gobbler-poor like the first group. The second bunch was comprised of two hens and two jakes. As exciting as it was to see our calling efforts pay off, Kevin and I both knew that there wasn't a longbeard in the bunch. This didn't bother me though. If we could get those hens and jakes to come to our side of the fence, our chances for enticing a mature gobbler to do the same would go way up. I turned around and resumed my normal hunting position, and Kevin kept an eye on the approaching turkeys.

According to Kevin, when the birds were about fifty yards behind us, they started to slow their advance and began to break ranks from their "V" formation, merging into a single-file approach. The line of approaching turkeys spotted the two decoys to the right of our blind before they reached the barbed-wire fence, and they adjusted their course to intercept the fakes. All eight turkeys crossed the fence just ten yards to the right of our blind, and made a beeline for the decoys. It was 7:00 a.m., and we had three jakes and five hens just outside our blind, rubbing wings with our decoys. All the gobbling activity from the neighboring farm had ceased now, indicating that the big boys were flying down themselves. If only we could convince one to come to us like we had the hens and jakes!

I cut back on the turkey calling with so many birds in close proximity to us. Even though the hunting blind concealed us, I was afraid to move any more than was absolutely necessary – just habit I guess. So we sat there watching the hens preen and feed as the jakes jostled with each other for position and at times started to display. At 7:05 a.m., Kevin whispered to me that he could see two more turkeys in the pasture, two hundred yards behind us. Just the tone of his whisper was encouraging, as he informed me that the birds looked huge compared to the ones we had watched emerge earlier from the same spot. Hoping that we now had two of the loud-mouthed gobblers from the creek bottom behind us, I started yelping and cutting loudly, in spite of the birds less than thirty feet from our blind. The response from the two birds behind our position wasn't immediate, but after ten minutes of my best calling persuasion, they finally started coming. They were coming straight to us, and they were coming quickly!

Adrenaline began to surge through my veins, and my heart rate quickened – two big birds were coming on a string, and most likely they were gobblers! With the birds traveling at such a fast pace toward us, we didn't have to wait long to find out how long their beards were.

"They are both longbeards!" Kevin finally exclaimed to me in as hushed a voice as he could, given the circumstances.

"Maybe that conversation in the 4-Runner about one-two-boom wasn't a bad idea after all!" I thought to myself, as Kevin and I both reached for our shotguns.

The two longbeards didn't take the same route to our position as the previous birds had done. Instead, despite the fact that eight live birds were just below the blind on our right, the mature gobblers veered above the blind – up to our left. They covered the two hundred yards across the open pasture in a matter of minutes and did so without any gobbling and without the first sign of strutting. I guess they didn't want to waste any time getting to that barbed-wire line-fence, because as soon as they crossed it, twenty yards to our left, both gobblers commenced doing both – gobbling first and then dropping into full strut! It was unbelievable! We had turkeys on both sides of us, and we were smack-dab in the middle of them!

The two longbeards started to strut in an arc from where they crossed the fence on our left to a point directly in front of the blind. The mature, Rio Grande toms were in easy shotgun range the whole time, but we were having trouble getting our shotguns into position with ten turkeys surrounding us. Kevin managed to get his shotgun up and shouldered first. I was being extra cautious because I was on Kevin's right, and the hens and jakes were just outside the window on my side of the blind. While I was doing my best trying to get my gun shouldered, the two longbeards became nervous and slicked-up (quit strutting). I managed to get my shotgun barrel out the window on my side of the blind, but I was in an awkward position and couldn't get my gun trained on "the one on the right". The gobblers had started moving off – directly away from us. I started to panic. Frustrated, I stopped trying to get my gun on a bird, and I glanced over at Kevin.

"Are you on your gobbler?" I asked.

"Yes, but I'm not in the best position," Kevin replied.

Wanting to remain true to my promise, I resigned myself to the fact that the smartest thing to do at this point was just let Kevin take his bird. I wasn't about to take a marginal shot and possibly cripple my gobbler, and I wasn't about to let Kevin miss his opportunity.

"Go ahead and take him if you have the shot," I said. "I can't get on mine without spooking these other birds."

"No," Kevin replied, "I'll reposition, and you try to get on yours."

"OK," I said gratefully, as I made a bold move to reposition myself and get my gun trained on the right-hand gobbler.

Kevin adjusted his position too, and finally we both had our respective gobblers in our sights. When we pushed our safeties "off", the gobblers were almost out of shotgun range and were going straight away from us. The gobbler on my side was farther away than the one on Kevin's side, which was fortunate for us since my gun was a 3-1/2 inch model, and Kevin's was only a 3-inch gun.

"Are you on him?" I asked.

"Yes," Kevin said confidently.

"Are you ready?" I questioned him as planned.

"Yes," he said again.

"One…Two…BOOBOOM!" sounded from within the blind.

The two guns sounded almost as one, with my shot coming just slightly before my brother's. In front of the blind, lying in the open Kansas pasture, were two Rio Grande gobblers – one lying forty yards from the blind and the other three yards farther out. The sky and pasture to the right of the blind were filled with running and flying turkeys, which were scrambling for safety. The area within the blind was filled with two hunters scrambling to get out of it! I exited the blind first and took about ten steps toward our gobblers before stopping in my tracks. I took a deep breath and looked heavenward into the Kansas sky.

"Thank you, Jesus. Thank you, Lord." I said, stunned by what had just taken place.

Kevin had just killed his first Rio Grande turkey, and I had completed a single season Grand Slam – all in the same instant in time! In all our years of turkey hunting together, Kevin and I had never doubled on spring gobblers – I couldn't think of a better time for it to have happened!

My pause outside the blind gave Kevin time to catch up with me. We high-fived each other before putting our arms around each other and shaking hands.

"Congratulations on your second Slam!" Kevin said to me beaming.

"Congratulations on your first Rio!" I replied, still grasping his hand in a handshake.

We unloaded our shotguns, and I took a photograph of the gobblers lying in the field where they had been shot before we went to examine our Rios. It was 7:20 a.m. – forty minutes since the first turkeys had flown down from the roost. I reached my gobbler and inspected him for all the particulars. He was a three-year-old gobbler with one-inch spurs, an eight-inch beard, and as scales would later reveal, he had a body weight of nineteen pounds – even. I found a small feather lying in the pasture near my fallen bird, which I picked up and held between my thumb and forefinger. I just knelt there smiling and admiring that little feather before placing it in my pocket. That little feather meant almost as much to me as the rest of the turkey, as I paused and reflected what a little Osceola feather floating around in the 4-Runner three weeks earlier had grown into. My little moment of admiration and reflection was interrupted, however, when I heard Kevin start whooping and hollering. His whooping and hollering coincided exactly with his first glance at the hooks on his Rio Grande gobbler.

Kevin's bird had 1-1/4 inch spurs, a 9-3/4 inch beard, and a live-weight of 19-1/2 pounds. Kevin was ecstatic with his gobbler, and I was so happy for him. We admired each other's birds for a few moments, and then we knelt down together to pray and read passages from our Bibles. We took numerous photos of each other and our Rio Grande gobblers. I even took a photo of the sunrise that broke the eastern sky behind the wooded creek where the gobblers had roosted. After we packed up our gear, we called Jack via cell phone to advise him of our success.

Jack was extremely happy for us and told us that he wanted to come by and see the birds before we left. Jack also asked if we would allow him to have his picture taken with us holding our gobblers for use on his website, to which we agreed. It was really painful having to sit there in a Kansas cattle field next to our Rio Grande gobblers, drinking coffee from a thermos, and watching the sun come up while waiting for Jack to arrive – yep, it was real painful! (Forget about the beer commercial filmed on a beach – this was my idea of "miles away from ordinary!") As we waited for Jack, it occurred to me that Kevin and I had both been wearing our new Primos hunting hats for the first time. I liked the hats when I saw them in the store, but I really liked them now! Those hats were just a little thing, but they added to the uniqueness of the hunt. (I retired mine after we returned home from Kansas – it was undefeated and I planned to keep it that way, unless of course I should find myself in dire need of killing a turkey someday – then I might just have to bring it out of retirement!)

When Jack arrived he congratulated us and thoroughly inspected our gobblers. He laughed audibly as he told us about his morning. He was checking on another piece of property he had leased, when he thought he heard one of us shoot. He told us he couldn't believe we had gotten a shot so early. When he learned about us doubling, he was even more impressed with the single-shotgun report he heard. I informed him about my little "one-two-boom" plan and the conversation I had with Kevin as we followed him to the farm. Jack was almost apologetic as he told me he was sorry our hunt was over so fast, because he knew we were planning to hunt for two full days if necessary. I reassured him that I couldn't have asked for a better hunt – a hunt where you call nearly a dozen turkeys off the neighbor's posted-property, and then proceed to double with your brother for the very first time – no apology was needed. After all the niceties, Jack graciously used my camera to take photos of Kevin and me together with our birds. Then we used the timer function on my camera to take pictures of all three of us displaying the toms.

With the final photo session complete, Jack decided to pack up his blind, while Kevin and I placed the gobblers in our vests. We hiked back to our vehicles, and I saw the cattle, still hanging out near the fence. I thanked the Lord once again for his kindness to us on this day.

At the 4-Runner, Kevin and I asked Jack to verify that our field tagging of the birds was correct. With Jack's approval that the gobblers were properly tagged, we loaded the Rios into the back of my SUV. The three of us just hung out at the vehicles for several minutes talking about turkey hunting and hunting gear – imagine that! The sun was now plainly visible in the cloudless, blue sky, and it was starting to get really warm. The weather had done a "Jeckle and Hyde" turnaround from the previous day, turning into a picture-perfect mid-western morning. Traveling to the Midwest in the early part of spring, a hunter always faces the possibility of bad weather. However, on this trip for my brother and me, we couldn't have asked for a better week. (The week after we returned home, the Midwest was struck by a cold front that dropped up to twelve inches of snow in some areas and caused temperatures to plummet twenty-five degrees – I cut the newspaper article describing the storm out of our local paper and put it in my turkey hunting file just as a reminder of how good the Lord had been to us on our trip.)

Remembering our big breakfast from the previous morning after my successful Merriam's hunt, I asked Jack if we could buy him breakfast before we parted ways. Jack accepted my invitation, and we followed him to a small country store and restaurant. The proprietors of the small establishment were very kind and gracious as they took our order of eggs, bacon, hash browns, toast, and coffee. We sat and talked and enjoyed the food while downing several cups of coffee. We spent an hour in that small store talking to each other and to several elderly folks who were enjoying breakfast there as well. Even though we were dressed in camouflage and snake boots, the local folks were extremely nice to us, and they seemed to be genuinely interested in the two boys from Virginia who would travel so far to hunt wild turkeys. Well, I must be a redneck, because my favorite restaurant in Kansas has a gas pump in the front of it!

We paid for breakfast and said good-bye to Jack, who was going to get to travel home and see his girlfriend after all. Kevin and I drove back to the motel and decided to do our best to get showered and packed by check out time – we would start the long drive home as soon as we checked out.

While Kevin showered at the room, I went to the motel's desk to request a late check out. The lady behind the counter was very gracious in granting my request but was somewhat puzzled that we were checking out so soon. When Jack had reserved the room for us, he had done so for three days expecting that we would possibly be hunting that long. I explained to the clerk that my brother and I had killed our turkeys at the same time, nearly at daybreak, on the first morning, and since we couldn't hunt any more, we were checking out.

Before returning to the room to shower myself, I decided to take the 4-Runner to a high-pressure car wash. My poor green vehicle was absolutely covered in hard gray mud still present from our exodus from Nebraska. Five dollars in quarters and thirty minutes later, I had the Toyota looking pretty clean. (I chose the word "clean" purposely for that sentence – I refrained from using the phrase "looking pretty good" because to be honest, I think the mud coating really made the 4-Runner look cool. However, the mud was covering my license plates and NWTF stickers, and that wasn't cool.) With my Nebraska-mud deposit made to the state of Kansas, I gassed up the SUV and returned to the motel. After parking in front of our room, when I exited the vehicle a camo-clad gentleman approached me from across the motel parking lot.

"Hey, how you doin'?" the man asked. "You guys have any luck hunting this morning?"

"Yeah, we sure did," I replied as I walked toward my room.

The man followed me to the doorway and commented, "I saw your truck had NWTF stickers on it, and when I saw the Virginia license plates, I figured you were probably serious turkey hunters…traveling so far to hunt."

"We got in last night from hunting in Nebraska, and today was our first morning to hunt in Kansas," I responded.

I entered the motel room and invited the man in for coffee.

Before pouring us each a cup of coffee, I introduced myself and learned that the gentleman's name was Mike. Mike was from Arkansas and was hunting spring gobblers in Kansas too. I introduced Kevin to Mike, and we continued our conversation. Mike was vacationing with his wife and children, and this trip to Kansas had become a yearly tradition for them. Mike had killed a gobbler during his morning's hunt, but he knew where another bird was roosting on public land. That was the reason he had approached me. Mike was going to offer to take us to the spot where the gobbler was and "share" him with us.

Now for those of you who read this and do not hunt spring gobblers, you may not be able to comprehend the value of Mike's offer. Sharing a gobbler with another hunter in the spring is one of the greatest gifts one hunter can give to another. I was very impressed with Mike's genuine kindness as he explained to me how he hoped he could help us on our hunt. I thanked him for being so thoughtful toward two total strangers. I told him that we had actually doubled on two mature birds and were tagged-out after less than an hour of hunting, so we couldn't accept his offer. When I thanked him, Mike explained that, "We turkey hunters have got to stick together," to which I agreed. As we were finishing our coffee, I went to my duffle bag and retrieved a small Bible. I told Mike that I was a born-again Christian, and that I wanted to share something better than a roosted gobbler with him. I gave Mike the Bible while explaining to him that I carried the same kind of Bible with me when I hunted, so I always had something to read. (The Bible that I gave to Mike has God's plan of salvation printed in the back cover which explains how a person can receive Jesus Christ personally and have their sins forgiven – oh, by the way, Jesus is the greatest gift one hunter can share with another!) It turned out that Mike was a Christian too, and he really appreciated the Bible.

I apologized to Mike for rushing around the room as we talked, but I was trying to get packed so we could meet the late check out time extended to us by the motel. He told me that he understood, as we shook hands and said good-bye. After packing, I jumped in the shower and changed into clean clothes. Before leaving Room 110, Kevin and I bowed our heads and prayed, thanking our Father for all His many blessings to us during the week and asking for his protection as we began the long drive home. After praying, we stepped out of the dim motel room into the bright Kansas afternoon. As we walked to the 4-Runner, Mike came rushing through the parking lot to speak to us before we left.

Mike had changed into shorts and a t-shirt, and upon intercepting me at my truck's door, he grabbed my hand and shook it. He thanked me again for the Bible and handed me a folded McDonald's napkin. Written on the napkin was a note that said:

"If you are ever in Arkansas, and you want to hunt ducks, deer, or turkey…call me. God bless you."

The note was signed by Mike and listed his home phone number.

I thanked him for the offer and told him to look me up if he was ever in Virginia. We talked for a few minutes before finally saying good-bye once again.

As Kevin and I left the Best Western in Ellsworth, I thought about all the really nice people we had crossed paths with while hunting. There were several we had become friends with like Ben, Jack, and Mike, and there were some who we just waved to – like the young man who pulled his pickup truck alongside my 4-Runner while traveling west on I80 in Iowa. The young man had seen the NWTF stickers plastered on my truck and 150 quart cooler on the hitch-haul – so while traveling 70 mph side-by-side on the interstate, he held up a Primos mouth call so I could see it, and I gave him a "thumbs-up" in response! Yep, there are good ol' boys, legion members, and rednecks all over this great nation of ours, and it always a pleasure to meet them.

Shortly after starting the drive home, I asked Kevin to use his cell phone to call our dad back in West Virginia. After being informed that we were on our way home, my dad asked how the Kansas hunt went.

I told Kevin to tell him: "We spent more time eating breakfast in Kansas than we did hunting!"

That's exactly what Kevin told him, and all three of us laughed.

Our trip home was interrupted by a stop at Bass Pro Shops in Columbia, Missouri (where we saw a huge Missouri tom strutting in a creek bottom three hundred yards from the store) and an overnight stay at a motel in Mt. Vernon, Illinois. Our arrival in Illinois was late at night, during a driving thunderstorm. Kevin and I scrambled to unload overnight bags and our gobblers from the Toyota. If it hadn't been raining so hard, I would have taken a picture of the cargo area in the rear of the 4-Runner. It was packed nearly full with hunting gear and topped off with two big gobblers that needed to be field dressed. The gear and gobblers were stacked nearly to the roof – it looked awesome! We cleaned our Rio Grande gobblers in the motel at 11:30 p.m. that night and placed the meat in the cooler – that thing was jam-packed! We finally got to bed around 1:00 a.m. and slept for about seven hours. It was the first decent night's sleep I had in two weeks. After breakfast, we departed Mt. Vernon and drove straight through to Virginia. We arrived at my house at 7:15 p.m.

I greeted my wife, helped Kevin unpack his luggage and put it in his truck, and then he helped me unload all my gear. We sorted out our turkeys and discussed our trip with Lisa and her parents, who had come by to see us. In the midst of all this commotion, however, I slipped away from my family and walked out to the 4-Runner. I had just completed a 2928 mile round trip, but I got back in the driver's seat. I just sat there for a minute looking at the four little feathers stuck in the visor above my head – four little feathers from four different subspecies of wild turkey. I looked away from the feathers and stared at my driveway, remembering how I had sat in the exact same spot four weeks earlier before departing for Florida. Who could have known what that drive to Florida would lead to? – Four little feathers in four weeks. I had no idea then, but my Father in Heaven had it all planned. Four little feathers – by themselves insignificant and worthless, but together in my visor they were precious. Together they were a symbol of blessing and success and the fulfillment of a dream that I dared to dream. Thank you, Lord Jesus.

I mentioned that a traveling turkey hunter is privileged to meet some very fine people while pursuing his passion for spring gobbler hunting. However, people aren't the only blessing that a hunter encounters while traveling, for a spring turkey hunter also has the privilege of meeting gobblers. What a grand lot they are: some are loud, some are quiet – some are bold, some are shy – some are quick, some are slow – some are loners, some travel in groups – some are pristine, some are rode hard and put up wet – some strut, some sneak – some you wish to forget, and some you never will. They all have one thing in common though – their mystique. In the spring of the year a normally quiet and reclusive bird becomes boisterous and visible, gobbling and strutting for all to hear and see. While they are always wary, the spring gobbler is even more on edge during the mating season, in constant touch with his surroundings. To hunt them is a privilege, and to kill one is an honor. If you are a turkey hunter, I hope you'll join me in thanking and praising God for creating such a good bird and for giving us the opportunity to pursue them. If you are not a turkey hunter, all you need is a hunting license, a shotgun, and the desire to try it for yourself. Won't you come and join us?

Rio Grande

Date: April 21, 2005
Time: 7:20 a.m.
Location: Hollyrood, Kansas
Weight: 19 lbs. 0 oz.
8 inch Beard
1 inch Spurs

One, Two, Boom

Rio Spurs

Kevin, Jack, and Brad

Kevin and Brad

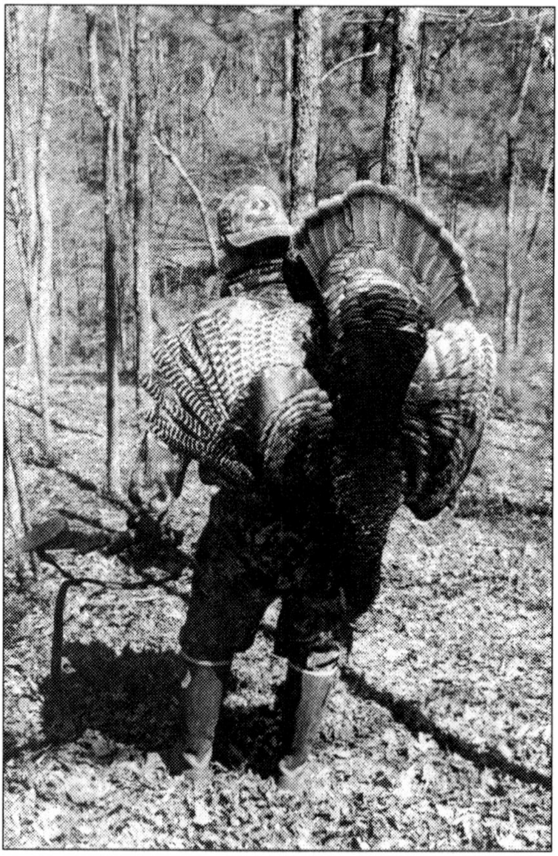

Final Thoughts

The Bible says in Ecclesiastes 12:12 that in the "making of many books there is no end." Severe Gobbler Disorder is just another book – one of many. If you have taken the time to read my stories, then let me thank you and at the same time offer my condolences! One of the great things about being an author is being approached by someone who tells you that they have read your book. For me, it is a humbling and gratifying comment that I truly appreciate – knowing that someone would spend their valuable time reading something that I wrote. However, no matter how much anyone enjoys my book, it won't last. Severe Gobbler Disorder will fade into time and eternity with many other books. There is one Book though that will never fade, the Bible. God's word is forever settled in the heavens, and while heaven and earth may pass away, God's word will never pass away (Mark 13:31). Jesus said that not even one jot or tittle of the Bible will fail, but that every word would be fulfilled (Matthew 5:18). I wonder how many Christians will stand before their heavenly Father one day and will be able to say to Him, "I read your Book!" Sadly, I am afraid there will be very few who have read the Bible from Genesis to The Revelation.

While my book is about turkey hunting, I have encouraged the reader throughout the collection of short stories to consider more important things – spiritual things.

If something you have read has sparked your desire to find out more about the God of the Bible and His only begotten Son, Jesus Christ, then maybe this book is a little different than the myriads of others written about hunting. My greatest hope and prayer for anyone who has read this book is that they will be saved. God's plan of salvation is simple, free, and offered to whoever wants it. But don't take my word for it; take His. God's word is the only thing that can miraculously change a person's heart and life. It has certainly changed mine. In fact, the Bible is what sets true Christianity apart from all other religions of the world. No other book has changed the lives of so many people like the Bible has. No other Book has been so persecuted, and yet no other book has endured like the Holy Bible. It is the best selling book worldwide every year.

If you are interested in reading what the Bible says about how to be saved (forgiven of all of your sins and promised a home in Heaven when you die), then I have included several Bible verses at the end of this chapter for you to consider.

They are true whether you choose to accept them or not, and they offer to man God's precious gift of love in the Person of His Son. Dear reader if you are not sure that when you die you will go to heaven, please take a moment to read the Bible verses about salvation. Don't make the fatal mistake of trusting in anything other than the Lord Jesus Christ for your forgiveness and eternal salvation. Jesus told his disciples, "I am the way, the truth, and the life: no man cometh unto the Father, but by Me." (John 14:6) Jesus also said in Isaiah 45:22, "Look unto me, and be ye saved, all the ends of the earth: for I am God and there is none else."

Quite a bit has happened since I wrote the stories that comprise this book. I traveled to Florida again to hunt the public-land swamps of the Sunshine state, and you won't believe what happened this time! Let me just say that Slam's Number Three and Four have had their way paved! My nephew, Caleb, killed his first spring gobbler, and consequently another Legion member has been born. My poor Virginia seasons have stopped, and I matched wits with an old longbeard for four straight weeks, filling my third tag by killing him on the last day of the season – with hens. But those are other stories for another time. I wish you the very best in the turkey woods, and may God bless you and your family.

Brad

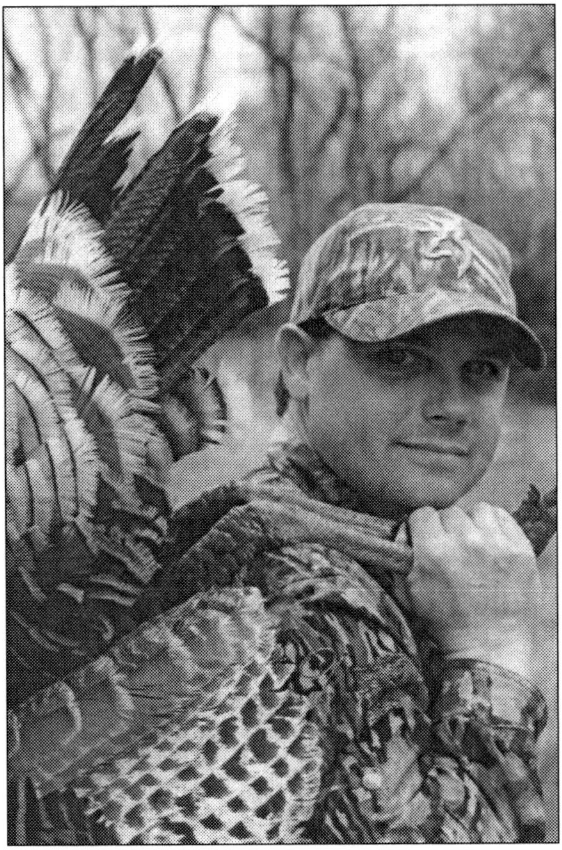

God's Plan of Salvation

In the Bible, God tells us how to be saved from our sins. Being saved doesn't require a church, a priest, or baptism. Being saved only requires a sinner to believe in their heart that Jesus Christ died on the cross for their sins, was buried, and on the third day rose again from the dead. A person who repents of their sin and believes in the death, burial, and resurrection of the Lord Jesus Christ only has to call on Him in prayer and ask for salvation to be saved. Please note the following verses quoted from the King James version of the Bible:

All are sinners:

> "For all have sinned, and come short of the glory of God." (Romans 3:23)

All sinners are condemned to hell when they die, eternally separated from God because of their sin:

> "For the wages of sin is death;" (Romans 6:23a)

Even though you are a sinner, God loves you so much that he gave His Son, Jesus Christ, to die for your sins:

> "But the gift of God is eternal life through Jesus Christ our Lord." (Romans 6:23b)

> "But God commendeth His love toward us, in that, while we were yet sinners, Christ died for us." (Romans 5:8)

To be saved one must simply believe on Jesus as the one who bore their sin, died, was buried, and rose again:

> "That if thou shalt confess with thy mouth the Lord Jesus, and shalt believe in thine heart that God hath raised Him from the dead, thou shalt be saved. For with the heart man believeth unto righteousness; and with the mouth confession is made unto salvation." (Romans 10:9-10)

> "For whosoever shall call upon the name of the Lord shall be saved." (Romans 10:13)

That "whosoever" includes you dear friend. Call upon Jesus in prayer and you "shall be saved" – not might be saved, or may be saved, but shall be saved.

Just take God at His word - it is impossible for Him to lie. Go to Him in prayer right now, confessing your sin and claiming Jesus' salvation by faith. It will be the greatest decision you will ever make, and one you will never regret!

Notes

1. Tom Kelly, Tenth Legion
   (New York, NY: The Lyons Press, 1973, 1998)

About the Author

Brad Day was born and raised in West Virginia and has been an avid outdoorsman for more than 35 years. Contrary to what his friends say, Brad doesn't have the ability to turn any conversation into a turkey-hunting story; it just seems like he does.

A born-again Christian whose faith is evident in the stories he writes, Day has a unique way of transporting his readers into the hunts he details. Brad currently resides in Virginia with his wife, Lisa, and their three dogs.